Contents

Instant Pot Ginataang Salmon (Filipino Salmon in Coconut Milk) 10

Instant Pot Strawberry Iced Tea 11

Instant Pot Beet Hummus 12

Instant Pot Salmon Piccata 13

Instant Pot Vegan Borscht 13

Instant Pot Chicken Pot Pie Risotto 14

Instant Pot Chicken and Mushrooms with Gravy 15

Instant Pot Chocolate Cherry Cheesecake 16

Instant Pot Clam Chowder 17

Instant Pot Low Country Boil 18

Instant Pot Chicken Soup 19

Instant Pot Brown Butter 20

Instant Pot Buckwheat Minestra 20

Instant Pot Korean BBQ Tacos 21

Instant Pot Spinach and Mushroom Orzo 22

Quick Instant Pot Baked Beans 23

Instant Pot Pickled Jalapeno Rings 23

Instant Pot Chicken and Wild Rice Bowls 24

Instant Pot Guinness Corned Beef 25

Instant Pot Sweet and Spicy Chicken Thighs 26

Instant Pot Galbi (Korean-Style Short Ribs) 27

Instant Pot Red Beans and Rice with Sausage 28

Instant Pot Chicken Congee 28

Instant Pot Red Beans and Rice with Sausage 29

Instant Pot Caldillo 30

Instant Pot Tomato Soup 31

Instant Pot Chicken Marsala 32

Instant Pot Lebanese Lentil Soup (Shorbat Adas) 33

Instant Pot Chicken and Rice Stracciatella 34

Instant Pot Roasted Melting Sweet Potatoes 34

Instant Pot Risotto 35

Instant Pot Classic Hummus 36

Instant Pot Pork Stew 36

Instant Pot Chicken Drumsticks 37

Instant Pot Vanilla Extract 38

Instant Pot Farro 39

Instant Pot Vegetable Soup 39

Instant Pot Beef Burritos 40

Instant Pot Chili 41

Instant Pot Moroccan Chicken Tagine 42

Easy Instant Pot Baby Back Ribs 43

Instant Pot Corn Chowder 44

Instant Pot Southern-Style Green Beans from a Can 45

Instant Pot Cheesy Broccoli Rice 46

Instant Pot Refried Beans 46

Instant Pot Tomato and Beef Sauce 47

Instant Pot Turkey Stock 48

Instant Pot Chicken Pot Pie Stew 49

Instant Pot Protein-Packed Vegetarian Chili 50

Instant Pot Split Pea Soup 50

Instant Pot Cabbage and Beef Soup 51

Instant Pot Piccata Israeli Couscous 52

Instant Pot Pilau Rice 53

Instant Pot Mexican Quinoa 53

Instant Pot Beef Stew with Frozen Meat 54

Instant Pot Venison Chili 55

Instant Pot Cream of Asparagus Soup 56

Instant Pot Sweet Baby Back Ribs 57

Instant Pot Celery Soup 58

Instant Pot Orange Chicken 58

Instant Pot Creamy Vanilla Rice Pudding 59

Instant Pot Gyros 60

Instant Pot Bang Bang Shrimp Pasta 61

Instant Pot Chocolate Cheesecake 61

Instant Pot Dark Chocolate Brownies 63

Instant Pot Curried Chicken Thighs 64

Instant Pot Asparagus Risotto 65

Instant Pot Chilorio 66

Instant Pot Sweet Potato Chipotle Soup 67

Instant Pot Salsa Verde 68

Instant Pot Colorado Chile Verde 68

Instant Pot Beef Panang Curry 69

Instant Pot Orange Chicken 70

Instant Pot Coconut-Orange Rice Pudding 71

Instant Pot Asparagus Risotto 72

Instant Pot Roasted Garlic 73

Instant Pot Sweet Baby Back Ribs 73

Instant Pot Tomato-Spinach Risotto 74

Instant Pot Shepherd's Pie with Potatoes and Yams 75

Instant Pot Beef and Vegetable Soup 77

Instant Pot Midwest Goulash 77

Instant Pot Egg Bites 78

Instant Pot Pork Loin in Cranberry-Dijon Sauce 79

Instant Pot Chicken Tinga 80

Instant Pot Pineapple Chicken (Frozen Chicken Method) 81

Instant Pot Vegan Steel-Cut Oats with Apple and Cinnamon 82

Instant Pot Mexican Lentil Soup 82

Instant Pot Butternut Squash and Pear Soup 83

Instant Pot Cajun Jambalaya 84

Instant Pot Butter Chicken from Frozen 85

Instant Pot Wheat Berries 85

Instant Pot Bahn Flan (Vietnamese Flan) 86

Instant Pot Chicken Paprikash with Egg Noodles 87

Instant Pot Shrimp Broth..88

Instant Pot Beef Pho...89

Instant Pot Chicken Breasts 90

Instant Pot Chicken and Farro Soup 91

Instant Pot Mongolian Chicken..91

Instant Pot Keto Thai Chicken Soup (Tom Kha Gai) 92

Instant Pot Ground Chicken Chili 93

Instant Pot Coconut Chicken Curry with Sweet Potato 94

Instant Pot Kalua Pig (Quick Hawaiian Pulled Pork)..95

Instant Pot Quinoa..95

Instant Pot Salt and Vinegar Boiled Peanuts 96

Instant Pot Live Crawfish Boil for Four 97

Instant Pot Cheddar Cheese Sauce...98

Instant Pot Asparagus Risotto 98

Instant Pot Chilorio 99

Instant Pot Egg Bites...100

Instant Pot Pork Loin in Cranberry-Dijon Sauce 101

Instant Pot Chicken Noodle Soup..102

Instant Pot Pineapple Chicken (Frozen Chicken Method)....................................103

Instant Pot Lemon-Garlic Chicken Thighs with Rice..104

Instant Pot Midwest Goulash 105

Instant Pot Mongolian Chicken..106

Instant Pot Colorado Chile Verde 106

Instant Pot Chicken and Farro Soup 107

Instant Pot Vegan Steel-Cut Oats with Apple and Cinnamon 108

Instant Pot Butter Chicken from Frozen 109

Instant Pot Vegan Chili 109

Instant Pot Bahn Flan (Vietnamese Flan) 110

Instant Pot Mexican Lentil Soup..111

Instant Pot Live Crawfish Boil for Four 112

Instant Pot Wheat Berries 113

Instant Pot Beef Pho 114

Instant Pot Keto Thai Chicken Soup (Tom Kha Gai) 115

Instant Pot Coconut Chicken Curry with Sweet Potato 116

Instant Pot Beef and Vegetable Soup 116

Instant Pot Kung Pao Broccoli 117

Instant Pot Cheesy Mexican Lentils and Rice 118

Instant Pot Potato and Bacon Soup 119

Instant Pot Spicy Macaroni Salad 120

Instant Pot Lentil Chicken Noodle Soup 121

Instant Pot Spicy Orange Chicken 121

Instant Pot Beef Paprika 122

Instant Pot Savory Sriracha Oatmeal 123

Instant Pot Egg Roll in a Bowl 124

Instant Pot Ham and Bean Soup 125

Instant Pot Make-Ahead Breakfast Burritos 126

Instant Pot Strawberries and Cream Oatmeal 127

Instant Pot Spanish Rice with Ground Beef 127

Instant Pot Jamaican Chicken Curry 128

Instant Pot Chicken in Milk 129

Instant Pot Green Bean Casserole 130

Instant Pot Sausage Dressing 131

Instant Pot Taco Bowls 132

Instant Pot Vegan Lentil Soup 132

Instant Pot Sausage Queso 133

Instant Pot Pudina Pulao (Mint Rice) 134

Instant Pot Goulash 135

Instant Pot Eggs and Soldiers 136

Instant Pot Sweet Acorn Squash 137

Instant Pot Swiss Steak 137

Instant Pot Au Gratin Potatoes 138

Instant Pot Pulled Pork 139

Instant Pot Apple Pie Steel Cut Oats 140

Instant Pot Hard-Boiled Eggs 141

Instant Pot Chicken Tortilla Soup 142

Instant Pot Collard Greens 143

Instant Pot Mississippi Roast 143

Instant Pot Keto Chicken Thighs in Lemon-Garlic Cream Sauce 144

Instant Pot Double Bean and Ham Soup 145

Instant Pot General Tso's Chicken 146

Instant Pot Pepper Chicken 147

Instant Pot Pork Adobo 148

Instant Pot Kielbasa, Sauerkraut, and Potato 149

Instant Pot Red Beans and Rice 150

Instant Pot Canned Tomato Salsa 150

Instant Pot Chicken Fried Rice 151

Instant Pot Indian Chicken Curry 152

Instant Pot White Beans 153

Instant Pot Peel-and-Eat Shrimp 154

Instant Pot Pork Tenderloin 155

Instant Pot Frozen Turkey Breast 155

Instant Pot Teriyaki Chicken Thighs 157

Instant Pot Borracho Cranberry Beans 157

Instant Pot Rice Pudding 158

Instant Pot Spicy Beef Curry Stew 159

Instant Pot Spicy Butternut Squash Soup 160

Instant Pot Steamed Artichokes 161

Instant Pot Taco Soup 162

Instant Pot Vegan Korma 162

Instant Pot Chicken Biryani 164

Instant Pot Chickpeas 165

Instant Pot Fresh Corn Risotto 165

Instant Pot Chicken Taco Soup 166

Instant Pot Mac and Cheese 167

Instant Pot Sauerkraut 168

Instant Pot Vegan Rice Pudding 169

Instant Pot Lentil and Ham Soup 169

Instant Pot Yardbird Chili with White Beans 170

Instant Pot Creamy Chicken and Leek Alfredo 171

Instant Pot German Red Cabbage 172

Instant Pot Vegan 15-Bean Soup 173

Instant Pot Lentil Soup 174

Instant Pot No-Stress Buffalo Chicken Dip 175

Instant Pot Puerto Rican Arroz con Pollo 175

Instant Pot Keto Chicken and Kale Stew 176

Instant Pot Pickled Jalapeno Rings 177

Instant Pot Chicken and Wild Rice Bowls 178

Instant Pot Guinness Corned Beef 179

Instant Pot Sweet and Spicy Chicken Thighs 180

Instant Pot Galbi (Korean-Style Short Ribs) 181

Instant Pot Red Beans and Rice with Sausage 182

Instant Pot Chicken Congee 183

Instant Pot Caldillo 184

Instant Pot Tomato Soup 184

Instant Pot Chicken Marsala 185

Instant Pot Lebanese Lentil Soup (Shorbat Adas) 186

Easy Instant Pot Cranberry Sauce 187

Instant Pot Chicken and Rice Stracciatella 188

Instant Pot Roasted Melting Sweet Potatoes 189

Instant Pot Tortellini Soup 189

Instant Pot Barbacoa 190

Instant Pot Risotto 191

Instant Pot Classic Hummus 192

Instant Pot Cabbage and Beef Soup 193

Instant Pot Khichdi 194

Instant Pot Piccata Israeli Couscous 195

Instant Pot Pilau Rice 195

Instant Pot Mexican Quinoa 196

Instant Pot Beef Stew with Frozen Meat 197

Instant Pot Venison Chili 198

Instant Pot Cream of Asparagus Soup 199

Instant Pot Celery Soup 200

Instant Pot Sweet Baby Back Ribs 200

Instant Pot Orange Chicken 201

Instant Pot Creamy Vanilla Rice Pudding 202

Instant Pot Chocolate Cheesecake 203

Instant Pot Curried Chicken Thighs 204

Instant Pot Gyros 205

Instant Pot Bang Bang Shrimp Pasta 206

Instant Pot Chicken Congee 207

Instant Pot Caldillo 208

Instant Pot Tomato Soup 209

Instant Pot Chicken Marsala 210

Instant Pot Lebanese Lentil Soup (Shorbat Adas) 210

Easy Instant Pot Cranberry Sauce 212

Instant Pot Chicken and Rice Stracciatella 212

Instant Pot Roasted Melting Sweet Potatoes 213

Instant Pot Tortellini Soup 214

Instant Pot Barbacoa 214

Instant Pot Risotto 215

Instant Pot Classic Hummus 216

Instant Pot Cabbage and Beef Soup 217

Instant Pot Khichdi 218

Instant Pot Piccata Israeli Couscous 218

Instant Pot Pilau Rice 219

Instant Pot Mexican Quinoa 220

Instant Pot Beef Stew with Frozen Meat 221

Instant Pot Venison Chili 222

Instant Pot Cream of Asparagus Soup 222

Instant Pot Celery Soup 223

Instant Pot Sweet Baby Back Ribs 224

Instant Pot Orange Chicken 225

Instant Pot Creamy Vanilla Rice Pudding 226

Instant Pot Gyros 227

Instant Pot Bang Bang Shrimp Pasta 227

Instant Pot Chocolate Cheesecake 228

Instant Pot Curried Chicken Thighs 229

Instant Pot Dark Chocolate Brownies 230

Instant Pot Curried Chicken Thighs 232

Instant Pot Turkey Chili 234

Instant Pot Sweet and Sour Pork 235

Instant Pot Green Chili Chicken and Rice 236

Instant Pot Crispy Chicken Carnitas 236

Instant Pot Loaded Baked Potato Soup 238

Instant Pot Yankee Pot Roast 239

Instant Pot Pinto Beans (No Soaking) 240

Instant Pot Vegan Cabbage Detox Soup 241

Instant Pot Mexican Rice 241

Instant Pot Best Beef Stew 242

Instant Pot Honey-Garlic Chicken 243

Instant Pot Corned Beef 243

Instant Pot Ground Beef Stroganoff 244

Instant Pot Mushroom Risotto 245

Instant Pot Salisbury Steak with Onion and Mushroom Gravy 246

Instant Pot Chicken and Gravy 247

Instant Pot Salsa Chicken...248

Instant Pot Lasagna 249

Instant Pot Coconut Curry Chicken 250

Instant Pot Pork Chops and Gravy..251

Instant Pot Meatloaf 252

Instant Pot Quick and Easy Spaghetti Sauce 252

Instant Pot Simple Steamed Crab Legs...253

Instant Pot Pot Roast with Potatoes and Carrots...254

Instant Pot Pasta with Italian Sausage...255

Instant Pot Haluski with Kielbasa...256

Instant Pot Pot Roast 256

Instant Pot Popcorn 257

Instant Pot Roasted Brussels Sprouts..258

Instant Pot Red Thai Curry Chicken 259

Instant Pot Bacon-Ranch Chicken Thighs 260

Instant Pot Beef-Stuffed Peppers 261

Instant Pot Charro (Refried Beans)..261

Instant Pot Coconut Cream Chicken Noodle Soup..262

Instant Pot Creamy Mushroom Soup...263

Instant Pot Ginataang Salmon (Filipino Salmon in Coconut Milk)

Prep: 10 mins Cook: 25 mins Additional: 15 mins Total: 50 mins

Servings: 2

Ingredients

- 1 tablespoon vegetable oil

- 3 drops sesame oil, or to taste

- ¼ cup diced onion
- 2 eaches diced green onions, white and green parts
- 1 teaspoon garlic powder
- ½ cup diced fresh tomato
- 2 tablespoons fish sauce
- 1 cup vegetable broth
- 1 (11 ounce) salmon side, bones removed with pliers
- 1 cup coconut milk
- 1 ½ cups broccoli florets
- 1 cup chopped kale
- ½ teaspoon salt
- ¼ teaspoon ground black pepper

Directions
- **Step 1**

Turn on a multi-functional pressure cooker (such as Instant Pot) and select Saute function. Warm vegetable oil in pot, and add sesame oil. Add onion and green onions and saute for 1 minute. Add garlic powder; cook for 1 minute. Mix in diced tomato and pour in fish sauce; cook until heated through, about 2 minutes.
- **Step 2**

Add vegetable broth to the pot and place salmon on top of the liquid and vegetables. Select Cancel to turn off Saute mode, and close and lock the lid. Select high pressure according to manufacturer's instructions; set timer for 5 minutes. Allow 10 to 15 minutes for pressure to build.
- **Step 3**

Release pressure using the natural-release method according to manufacturer's instructions, 10 to 20 minutes. Remove lid. Pour in coconut milk, then add broccoli and kale. Mix vegetables gently around the side of salmon, but be careful not to break up the cooked salmon. Sprinkle salt and pepper over top. Replace lid and set vent to "Sealing."
- **Step 4**

Select the Steam function and steam for 2 minutes. Release pressure by turning the seal to "Venting." Remove lid.

Cook's Notes:
Use a side of salmon weighing between 10 and 12 ounces. If you are using frozen salmon, set the timer during the High pressure cooking phase to 7 minutes.
You can use coconut milk or coconut cream, depending on your preference.

Nutrition Facts
Per Serving:
651.2 calories; protein 37.6g 75% DV; carbohydrates 16.7g 5% DV; fat 50g 77% DV; cholesterol 92mg 31% DV; sodium 2041.1mg 82% DV

Instant Pot Strawberry Iced Tea

Prep: 5 mins Cook: 30 mins Additional: 5 mins Total: 40 mins

Servings: 10

Ingredients

- 8 cups water
- ⅓ cup white sugar
- 3 family size teabags family-size tea bags
- 1 pound strawberries, sliced
- 10 cups ice cubes

Directions
- **Step 1**

Combine water, sugar, and tea bags in a multi-functional pressure cooker (such as Instant Pot). Close and lock the lid. Select high pressure according to manufacturer's instructions; set timer for 4 minutes. Allow 25 minutes for pressure to build.
- **Step 2**

Release pressure carefully using the quick-release method according to manufacturer's instructions, about 5 minutes. Unlock and remove the lid. Remove tea bags using a slotted spoon.
- **Step 3**

Add strawberries to a blender and puree until smooth.
- **Step 4**

Allow tea to cool completely. Stir strawberry puree into the cooled tea and serve over ice.

Cook's Note:

Reduce sugar to 1/4 cup if you are using very ripe strawberries.

Nutrition Facts

Per Serving:

40.3 calories; protein 0.3g 1% DV; carbohydrates 10.2g 3% DV; fat 0.1g; cholesterolmg; sodium 12.7mg 1% DV

Instant Pot Beet Hummus

Prep: 10 mins Cook: 45 mins Additional: 5 mins Total: 1 hr

Servings: 10

Ingredients

- 3 cups vegetable broth
- 1 cup dry garbanzo beans
- 2 medium beets, peeled and cut into large pieces
- ⅓ cup lemon juice
- 3 tablespoons tahini
- 2 tablespoons olive oil
- 2 cloves garlic, chopped
- 1 teaspoon ground cumin
- ½ teaspoon salt

Directions
- **Step 1**

Combine vegetable broth, garbanzo beans, and beets in a multi-functional pressure cooker (such as Instant Pot). Close and lock the lid. Select high pressure according to manufacturer's instructions; set timer for 35 minutes. Allow 10 to 15 minutes for pressure to build.
- **Step 2**

Release pressure carefully using the quick-release method according to manufacturer's instructions, about 5 minutes. Unlock and remove lid.
- **Step 3**

Strain garbanzo beans and beets, saving 1/3 cup liquid. Place garbanzo beans and beets in the bowl of a food processor; add lemon juice, tahini, olive oil, and garlic. Blend until smooth and creamy, about 3 minutes. Scrape bowl and add 1/3 cup reserved liquid, cumin, and salt; blend for 1 minute more.

Nutrition Facts
Per Serving:
143.2 calories; protein 5.3g 11% DV; carbohydrates 17.1g 6% DV; fat 6.6g 10% DV; cholesterolmg; sodium 277.6mg 11% DV.

Instant Pot Salmon Piccata

Prep: 10 mins Cook: 15 mins Additional: 10 mins Total: 35 mins

Servings: 2

Ingredients

- 2 (5 ounce) salmon fillets
- 1 pinch salt and freshly ground black pepper to taste
- ½ cup water
- 1 tablespoon butter
- 1 tablespoon minced garlic
- 1 cup chicken broth, divided
- 1 ½ teaspoons cornstarch
- ¼ cup heavy cream
- 2 tablespoons lemon juice
- 1 teaspoon onion-herb seasoning (such as Savory Spice Capitol Hill)
- 2 tablespoons capers

Directions
- **Step 1**

Place salmon on a steamer rack; season with salt and pepper. Place rack inside a multi-functional electric pressure cooker (such as Instant Pot). Fill liner with water. Close and lock the lid. Select Steam setting; cook for 15 minutes.
- **Step 2**

Combine butter and garlic in a skillet over medium heat. Saute until garlic is golden and fragrant, 2 to 3 minutes. Pour in chicken broth; reserve 2 tablespoons. Mix cornstarch with the reserved broth and stir into the skillet. Add heavy cream, lemon juice, and onion-herb seasoning. Stir sauce to combine.
- **Step 3**

Release pressure using the natural-release method according to manufacturer's instructions, 10 to 20 minutes. Place each salmon fillet on a dinner plate. Spoon sauce on top and sprinkle with capers.

Nutrition Facts
Per Serving:
383.1 calories; protein 32g 64% DV; carbohydrates 5.5g 2% DV; fat 25.5g 39% DV; cholesterol 122mg 41% DV; sodium 1102.7mg 44% DV.

Instant Pot Vegan Borscht

Prep: 25 mins Cook: 55 mins Additional: 5 mins Total: 1 hr 25 mins

Servings: 12

Ingredients

- 1 tablespoon canola oil, or as needed
- ½ large onion, diced
- 8 cups water, divided
- ½ medium head cabbage, finely shredded
- ¾ pound beets, grated
- ½ pound potatoes, cut into small cubes
- 2 eaches carrots, grated
- 1 green bell pepper, chopped
- 3 leaf (blank)s bay leaves
- 1 pinch salt and ground black pepper to tast

Directions

- **Step 1**

Turn on a multi-functional pressure cooker (such as Instant Pot) and select Saute function. Add oil and onion. Cook, stirring often, until translucent, 3 to 5 minutes. Add a splash of water to stop cooking.

- **Step 2**

Add 8 cups water, cabbage, beets, potatoes, carrots, bell pepper, bay leaves, salt, and pepper to the pot. Close and lock the lid. Select high pressure according to manufacturer's instructions; set timer for 40 minutes. Allow 10 to 15 minutes for pressure to build.

- **Step 3**

Release pressure carefully using the quick-release method according to manufacturer's instructions, about 5 minutes. Unlock and remove the lid.

Cook's Note:

To serve, add maybe a tablespoon of vegan sour cream (I like Tofutti(R) in the white package). It's to be stirred before eating. It's optional though, and I often eat this borscht without it. Add some green onions or dill weed (optional). Another idea is to add some croutons. Eat borscht with bread; rye is authentic. Alternatively, I often toast some tortillas.

Nutrition Facts

Per Serving:
56.1 calories; protein 1.6g 3% DV; carbohydrates 10.4g 3% DV; fat 1.3g 2% DV; cholesterolmg; sodium 51.8mg 2% DV.

Instant Pot Chicken Pot Pie Risotto

Prep: 10 mins Cook: 45 mins Additional: 25 mins Total: 1 hr 20 mins

Servings: 4

Ingredients

- 1 tablespoon olive oil
- 1 tablespoon butter
- 2 (5 ounce) boneless skinless chicken breasts, diced
- ⅓ cup diced onion
- ¼ cup Chardonnay wine
- 1 ¾ cups chicken broth, divided
- 1 cup Arborio rice
- 1 tablespoon Chardonnay wine
- ¾ cup corn
- ¾ cup peas
- ¾ cup heavy whipping cream
- ⅓ cup freshly shaved Parmesan cheese
- ¼ teaspoon garlic powder
- ¼ teaspoon dried oregano
- ¼ teaspoon dried thyme

- ¼ teaspoon dried marjoram
- ⅛ teaspoon salt

- ⅛ teaspoon ground black pepper

Directions
- **Step 1**

Turn on a multi-functional pressure cooker (such as Instant Pot) and select Saute function. Add oil and butter. Add chicken and onion once the butter melts. Saute until chicken is browned and onion is soft and translucent, 5 to 6 minutes. Cancel Saute mode.
- **Step 2**

Pour 1/4 cup Chardonnay and 1/4 cup chicken broth into the Instant Pot . Insert an elevated trivet into the pot.
- **Step 3**

Combine 1 1/4 cups chicken broth and Arborio rice in a medium silicone bowl, stir together, and set on top of the trivet. Seal and lock the lid into place. Select Rice function and cook for the preset time of 12 minutes. Allow 10 to 15 minutes for pressure to build.
- **Step 4**

Release pressure using the natural-release method according to manufacturer's instructions, about 15 minutes. Release remaining pressure carefully using the quick-release method, about 5 minutes. Unlock and remove the lid.
- **Step 5**

Remove rice and trivet. Pour remaining 1/4 cup chicken broth and 1 tablespoon Chardonnay into the pot. Add cooked rice, corn, and peas. Do not stir. Seal and lock lid into place.
- **Step 6**

Select high pressure according to manufacturer's instructions; set timer for 5 minutes. Allow 10 minutes for pressure to build.
- **Step 7**

Release pressure using the quick-release method according to manufacturer's instructions, about 5 minutes. Unlock and remove the lid. Stir in cream, Parmesan cheese, garlic powder, oregano, thyme, marjoram, salt, and pepper. Serve immediately.

Nutrition Facts
Per Serving:
552.7 calories; protein 23.1g 46% DV; carbohydrates 50.7g 16% DV; fat 26.9g 42% DV; cholesterol 117.4mg 39% DV; sodium 849.5mg 34% DV.

Instant Pot Chicken and Mushrooms with Gravy

Prep: 10 mins Cook: 25 mins Additional: 25 mins Total: 1 hr

Servings: 3

Ingredients

- 6 tablespoons unsalted butter, divided
- 1 tablespoon extra-virgin olive oil
- 1 onion, diced
- 1 pinch salt

- 3 large boneless, skinless chicken breasts, trimmed of fat
- ¼ cup chicken stock, or more to taste

- 1 (16 ounce) package baby bella mushrooms, halved
- 1 tablespoon ranch seasoning mix
- 1 teaspoon steak sauce, or more to taste
- 1 teaspoon Worcestershire sauce, or more to taste
- 1 pinch freshly ground black pepper
- 2 tablespoons all-purpose flour

Directions
- **Step 1**

Turn on a multi-functional pressure cooker (such as Instant Pot) and select Saute function. Add 2 tablespoons butter and olive oil. Add onion and salt; stir occasionally until onion starts to brown.
- **Step 2**

Meanwhile, grease a skillet with 1 tablespoon butter and heat over high heat. Add chicken breasts and cook until browned, about 3 minutes per side.
- **Step 3**

Switch pressure cooker to Warm function. Pour in chicken stock and stir the pot to release any bits stuck on the bottom. Add mushrooms, ranch seasoning, steak sauce, Worcestershire sauce, and pepper. Stir until combined. Place chicken breasts on top, with a small pat of butter on each chicken breast.
- **Step 4**

Close and lock the lid. Select high pressure according to manufacturer's instructions; set timer for 6 minutes. Allow 10 to 15 minutes for pressure to build.
- **Step 5**

Release pressure using the natural-release method according to manufacturer's instructions, about 25 minutes. Transfer chicken breasts and mushrooms to a serving dish. Select Saute function to boil liquid in the pot.
- **Step 6**

Heat remaining 2 tablespoons butter in a saucepan over low heat. Stir in flour until a smooth, thick paste forms, 2 to 3 minutes. Whisk into the liquid in the pot and cook until thickened, 2 to 3 minutes. seasoning as desired and pour chicken and mushrooms.

Cook's Note:
Deglaze onions with a splash of beer, if preferred.

Nutrition Facts
Per Serving:
550.7 calories; protein 50g 100% DV; carbohydrates 14.5g 5% DV; fat 32.8g 51% DV; cholesterol 178.2mg 59% DV; sodium 424.3mg 17% DV.

Instant Pot Chocolate Cherry Cheesecake

Prep: 20 mins Cook: 50 mins Additional: 8 hrs 30 mins Total: 9 hrs 40 mins

Servings: 8

Ingredients

- 6 ounces chocolate cookie crumbs
- 1 serving cooking spray
- 2 tablespoons melted butter
- Cheesecake Batter:
- 2 (8 ounce) packages cream cheese, at room temperature
- 2 large eggs eggs
- ⅔ cup white sugar

- ½ cup vanilla and honey Greek yogurt, at room temperature
- 2 tablespoons cornstarch
- 1 tablespoon black onyx cocoa powder (from Savory Spice Shop)
- ¼ cup miniature semisweet chocolate chips
- ½ cup morello cherries, sliced in half and drained

Directions
- **Step 1**

Preheat the oven to 325 degrees F (165 degrees C).
- **Step 2**

Pulse the chocolate wafers in a blender until finely ground. Spray the bottom of a cheesecake pan with cooking spray. Pour crumbs into the bottom of the pan and pour melted butter on top. Mix and lightly press crust over the bottom of the pan and slightly up the edges.
- **Step 3**

Bake crust in the preheated oven until lightly browned, about 8 minutes. Remove from oven and cool completely.

- **Step 4**

Combine cream cheese, eggs, sugar, yogurt, cornstarch, and cocoa powder in a bowl; beat with an electric blender until creamy. Fold in mini chocolate chips.
- **Step 5**

Pour some of the cheesecake filling into the cooled crust. Top with a handful of sliced morello cherries. Repeat layers until all cherries and filling have been added.
- **Step 6**

Pour 1/2 cup of water into a multi-functional pressure cooker (such as Instant Pot). Add an elevated rack and set cheesecake pan on top of the rack. Close and lock the lid. Select high pressure according to manufacturer's instructions; set timer for 31 minutes. Allow 10 to 15 minutes for pressure to build.
- **Step 7**

Release pressure using the natural-release method according to manufacturer's instructions, about 12 minutes. Unlock and remove the lid. Remove cheesecake and let cool. Cover and refrigerate before serving, 8 hours to overnight.

Nutrition Facts
Per Serving:
444.8 calories; protein 8.5g 17% DV; carbohydrates 41g 13% DV; fat 28.9g 44% DV; cholesterol 117.3mg 39% DV; sodium 332.1mg 13% DV.

Instant Pot Clam Chowder

Prep: 20 mins Cook: 35 mins Additional: 10 mins Total: 1 hr 5 mins

Servings: 6

Ingredients

- 3 (5 ounce) cans baby clams
- 6 thick slices bacon, cut lengthwise first, then into 1-inch pieces
- ½ cup diced onion
- ½ cup diced celery
- 2 cloves garlic, minced
- 2 cups diced russet potatoes
- ½ cup shredded carrots, loosely packed

- ¼ teaspoon freshly ground black pepper
- 2 sprigs thyme
- 1 cup half-and-half

Directions
- **Step 1**

Drain clams into a colander set over a measuring cup. Reserve clam juice (there should be just over 2 cups liquid).
- **Step 2**

Turn on a multi-functional pressure cooker (such as Instant Pot) and select Saute function. Cook bacon until fat has rendered and bacon is crispy, about 5 minutes. Remove bacon to a paper-towel-lined plate; set aside.
- **Step 3**

Remove and discard all but 1 tablespoon of bacon grease. Cook onion and celery in the bacon grease until onion is soft and translucent, about 5 minutes. Add garlic and cook until fragrant, about 1 minute.

- **Step 4**

Pour 1/4 cup clam juice into the pan and bring to a boil while scraping the browned bits of food off the bottom of the pan with a wooden spoon. Mix in potatoes, carrots, pepper, thyme, and remaining clam juice. Close and lock the lid. Select high pressure according to manufacturer's instructions; set timer for 4 minutes. Allow 10 to 15 minutes for pressure to build.
- **Step 5**

Release pressure using the natural-release method according to manufacturer's instructions, about 5 minutes. Release remaining pressure carefully using the quick-release method, about 5 minutes. Unlock and remove the lid.
- **Step 6**

Remove 3/4 cup of the potatoes and mash with a fork. Return the mashed potatoes to the pot and stir. Turn on Saute mode. Add clams and half-and-half to the pot and cook until heated through but not boiling. Ladle into bowls and top with bacon.

Nutrition Facts
Per Serving:
278.1 calories; protein 25.4g 51% DV; carbohydrates 17.7g 6% DV; fat 11.4g 18% DV; cholesterol 76.2mg 25% DV; sodium 403.9mg 16% DV.

Instant Pot Low Country Boil

Prep: 15 mins Cook: 35 mins Additional: 5 mins Total:55 mins

Servings: 4

Ingredients

- 1 (12 ounce) package andouille sausage, sliced
- 1 ½ pounds baby red potatoes, halved
- 1 medium onion, chopped
- 4 teaspoons seafood seasoning (such as Old Bay)
- 1 (12 fluid ounce) can or bottle beer
- 3 ears corn, husked and cut into thirds
- 12 ounces frozen shell-on shrimp

Directions
- **Step 1**

Combine andouille sausage, potatoes, and onion in a multi-functional pressure cooker (such as Instant Pot). Sprinkle seafood seasoning over the top. Pour in beer. Lay corn pieces on top. Close and lock the lid. Select high pressure according to manufacturer's instructions; set timer for 1 minute. Allow 20 minutes for pressure to build.
- **Step 2**

Release pressure carefully using the quick-release method according to manufacturer's instructions, about 2 minutes. Unlock and remove the lid. Stir in shrimp. Close and lock the lid.
- **Step 3**

Select high pressure according to manufacturer's instructions; set timer for 0 minutes. Allow 10 minutes for pressure to build.
- **Step 4**

Release pressure carefully using the quick-release method according to manufacturer's instructions, about 2 minutes. Unlock and remove the lid.

Cook's Note:

Make sure you use frozen shrimp to prevent overcooking.

Nutrition Facts

Per Serving:

564.7 calories; protein 30.1g 60% DV; carbohydrates 48.3g 16% DV; fat 26g 40% DV; cholesterol 176.4mg 59% DV; sodium 1481.8mg 59% DV.

Instant Pot Chicken Soup

Prep: 30 mins Cook:38 mins Additional: 10 mins Total: 1 hr 18 mins

Servings: 8

Ingredients

- 1 tablespoon olive oil
- 5 stalks celery, diced
- 1 large onion, diced
- 2 small heads garlic, peeled and chopped
- 1 (32 fluid ounce) container chicken bone broth
- 1 (32 fluid ounce) container chicken broth
- 4 eaches boneless chicken thighs, cut into 1-inch pieces
- 2 eaches boneless skinless chicken breasts, cut into 1-inch pieces
- 1 (8 ounce) package baby carrots
- 2 tablespoons herbes de Provence
- 1 tablespoon chicken broth base (such as Superior Touch™ Better Than Bouillon™)
- 1 ½ teaspoons red pepper flakes
- 1 pinch salt and ground black pepper to taste
- 2 eaches bay leaves

Directions
- **Step 1**

Turn on a multi-functional pressure cooker (such as Instant Pot) and select Saute function. Add oil, celery, onion, and garlic. Saute until slightly softened, 3 to 5 minutes.
- **Step 2**

Mix bone broth, chicken broth, chicken thighs, chicken breasts, carrots, herbes de Provence, broth base, red pepper flakes, salt, pepper, and bay leaves into the pot. Close

and lock the lid. Select low pressure. Set timer for 25 minutes. Allow 10 to 15 minutes for pressure to build.
* **Step 3**
Release pressure using the natural-release method according to manufacturer's instructions, 10 to 40 minutes. Remove bay leaves before serving.

Nutrition Facts
Per Serving:
176.3 calories; protein 17.7g 35% DV; carbohydrates 9.4g 3% DV; fat 7.4g 11% DV; cholesterol 54.6mg 18% DV; sodium 1190.3mg 48% DV

Instant Pot Brown Butter

Cook: 15 mins Additional: 5 mins Total: 20 mins

Servings: 8

Ingredients

* ½ cup cold salted butter

Directions
* **Step 1**
Add butter to a multi-functional pressure cooker (such as Instant Pot). Close and lock the lid. Seal the vent. Select high pressure according to manufacturer's instructions; set timer for 2 minutes. Allow 10 to 15 minutes for pressure to build.
* **Step 2**
Release any pressure carefully using the quick-release method according to manufacturer's instructions; there may not be any built-up pressure, and that's okay. Unlock and remove the lid.
* **Step 3**
Quickly remove the pot insert from the base and swirl the butter inside until it is pale golden yellow with brown flecks collected in the bottom. Immediately pour brown butter into a container and allow to cool.

Cook's Note:
Brown butter adds extra depth of flavor to cookies, pancakes, muffins, popcorn, etc. When it's this easy to make, you can have it on hand for every one of those "secret ingredient" moments.

Nutrition Facts
Per Serving:
101.7 calories; protein 0.1g; carbohydratesg; fat 11.5g 18% DV; cholesterol 30.5mg 10% DV; sodium 81.7mg 3% DV.

Instant Pot Buckwheat Minestra

Prep: 30 mins Cook: 30 mins Additional: 10 mins Total: 1 hr 10 mins

Servings: 8

Ingredients

- 2 tablespoons extra-virgin olive oil
- 4 carrot, (7-1/2")s carrots, diced
- 1 medium onion, diced
- ½ red bell pepper, diced
- 1 celery stalk, diced
- ½ bunch flat-leaf parsley, chopped
- 1 large clove garlic, minced
- ½ cup raw buckwheat groats
- ½ cup red lentils
- 3 ½ small (3 ounce) potatoes, diced
- 1 medium zucchini, cubed
- ½ (12 ounce) package green beans, trimmed and cut into bite-sized pieces
- 5 cups low-sodium vegetable broth
- ¼ cup prepared hummus
- 1 tablespoon sambal oelek (chile paste)
- 1 pinch salt and ground black pepper to taste
- 4 tablespoons nutritional yeast

Directions

- **Step 1**

Turn on a multi-functional pressure cooker (such as Instant Pot) and select Saute function. Add oil. Cook and stir carrots, onion, bell pepper, celery, parsley, and garlic until vegetables are fragrant and onion is translucent, about 8 minutes. Turn off Saute function.

- **Step 2**

Add buckwheat and lentils; mix to coat with the oil and vegetables. Add potatoes, zucchini, and green beans. Pour in broth; stir to mix. Close and lock the lid. Select high pressure according to manufacturer's instructions; set timer for 10 minutes. Allow 10 to 15 minutes for pressure to build.

- **Step 3**

Release pressure using the natural-release method according to manufacturer's instructions, 10 to 40 minutes. Open lid and stir in hummus and sambal oelek. Season with salt and pepper. Divide soup among 8 bowls. Top each with 1/2 tablespoon nutritional yeast. Serve warm.

Cook's Note:

If you don't have sambal oelek, use Sriracha or any chile sauce.

Nutrition Facts

Per Serving:
215.3 calories; protein 9.3g 19% DV; carbohydrates 35.9g 12% DV; fat 5.2g 8% DV; cholesterolmg; sodium 232.3mg 9% DV

Instant Pot Korean BBQ Tacos

Prep: 15 mins Cook: 1 hr Additional: 5 mins Total: 1 hr 20 mins

Servings: 12

Ingredients

- 1 tablespoon butter
- ½ onion, sliced

- 10 cloves garlic, diced
- 1 (1 inch) piece ginger root, peeled and grated
- 2 tablespoons seasoned rice vinegar
- 3 pounds chuck roast, trimmed and cut into several large pieces
- ½ cup brown sugar
- ⅓ cup soy sauce
- 1 tablespoon sesame oil
- 1 tablespoon chile-garlic paste
- 1 pinch salt and ground black pepper to taste

Directions
- **Step 1**

Turn on a multi-functional pressure cooker (such as Instant Pot) and select Saute function. Add butter and onion and cook until soft, about 5 minutes. Add garlic and ginger and cook until aromatic, about 30 seconds more. Deglaze the pot with vinegar and scrape the bottom. Add chuck pieces, brown sugar, soy sauce, sesame oil, chile-garlic paste, salt, and black pepper.
- **Step 2**

Close and lock the lid; be sure vent is closed. Select high pressure according to manufacturer's instructions; set timer for 45 minutes. Allow 10 to 15 minutes for pressure to build.
- **Step 3**

Release pressure carefully using the quick-release method according to manufacturer's instructions, about 5 minutes. Unlock and remove the lid. Remove beef and shred.

Nutrition Facts
Per Serving:
241 calories; protein 13.9g 28% DV; carbohydrates 12.5g 4% DV; fat 15g 23% DV; cholesterol 54.1mg 18% DV; sodium 516.1mg 21% DV

Instant Pot Spinach and Mushroom Orzo

Prep:5 mins Cook: 15 mins Additional: 5 mins Total: 25 mins

Servings: 2

Ingredients

- ¾ cup chicken broth
- ½ cup tricolor orzo
- 1 tablespoon butter
- 2 cloves garlic, minced
- ½ cup julienned fresh spinach
- 2 ounces sliced portobello mushrooms
- ½ teaspoon salt
- ¼ teaspoon ground black peppe

Directions
- **Step 1**

Combine chicken broth and orzo in a multi-functional pressure cooker (such as Instant Pot); stir to combine. Close and lock the lid. Select high pressure according to manufacturer's instructions; set timer for 5 minutes. Allow 10 to 15 minutes for pressure to build.
- **Step 2**

Release pressure carefully using the quick-release method according to manufacturer's instructions, about 5 minutes. Unlock and remove the lid. Switch to Saute function. Stir in butter, minced garlic, spinach, and mushrooms. Season with salt and pepper.

Nutrition Facts
Per Serving:
253.9 calories; protein 8.5g 17% DV; carbohydrates 40.6g 13% DV; fat 6.8g 11% DV;
cholesterol 17.5mg 6% DV; sodium 1069.3mg 43% DV

Quick Instant Pot Baked Beans

Prep: 5 mins Cook: 20 mins Additional: 5 mins Total: 30 mins
Servings: 6

Ingredients

- 8 slices bacon, chopped
- 2 (15 ounce) cans baked beans with pork
- ½ cup ketchup
- 6 tablespoons brown sugar
- ½ teaspoon dry mustard powder

Directions
- **Step 1**

Turn on a multi-functional pressure cooker (such as Instant Pot) and select Saute
function. Add bacon and cook until browned and crispy but not burned, about 6 minutes.
Transfer bacon to a baking sheet lined with paper towels. Allow grease to drain.
- **Step 2**

Pour off some liquid from the beans, clearing at least 1 inch from the top of the can, but
leaving some liquid. Add beans and remaining liquid, ketchup, brown sugar, and mustard
to the Instant Pot . Mix in bacon. Close and lock the lid. Select high pressure according to
manufacturer's instructions; set timer for 3 minutes. Allow 10 to 15 minutes for pressure
to build.
- **Step 3**

Release pressure carefully using the quick-release method according to manufacturer's
instructions, about 5 minutes. Unlock and remove the lid.

Nutrition Facts
Per Serving:
269.7 calories; protein 11.6g 23% DV; carbohydrates 48.2g 16% DV; fat 5.8g 9% DV;
cholesterol 13.4mg 5% DV; sodium 987.9mg 40% DV.

Instant Pot Pickled Jalapeno Rings

Prep: 10 mins Cook: 10 mins Additional: 5 mins Total: 25 mins

Servings: 16

Ingredients

- 1 pound fresh jalapenos
- 1 cup white distilled vinegar
- ½ cup water
- 1 tablespoon minced garlic
- 1 tablespoon sugar
- 1 teaspoon sea salt

Directions
- **Step 1**

Slice jalapenos into thin rings using a mandoline.
- **Step 2**

Combine jalapeno rings, vinegar, water, garlic, sugar, and sea salt in a multi-functional pressure cooker (such as Instant Pot). Close and lock the lid. Select high pressure according to manufacturer's instructions; set timer for 0 minutes. Allow 10 minutes for pressure to build.

- **Step 3**

Release pressure carefully using the quick-release method according to manufacturer's instructions, about 5 minutes. Unlock and remove the lid.
- **Step 4**

Ladle jalapeno rings and cooking liquid between 2 pint-sized jars and immediately place in the refrigerator to cool.

Nutrition Facts
Per Serving:
12.6 calories; protein 0.4g 1% DV; carbohydrates 2.6g 1% DV; fat 0.2g; cholesterolmg; sodium 110.6mg 4% DV

Instant Pot Chicken and Wild Rice Bowls

Prep: 15 mins Cook: 45 mins Additional: 20 mins Total: 1 hr 20 mins

Servings: 6

Ingredients

- 1 tablespoon olive oil
- 1 (8 ounce) package sliced fresh mushrooms
- ½ cup diced onion
- 3 cloves garlic, minced
- 2 cups low-sodium chicken broth
- 1 small firm apple, cored and chopped
- 1 ½ cups uncooked wild and brown rice blend (such as Lundberg Wild Blend)
- ½ cup sweetened dried cranberries (such as Craisins)
- 1 teaspoon ground thyme
- 1 pinch salt and ground black pepper to taste
- 1 ¼ pounds skinless, boneless chicken thighs
- 2 tablespoons chopped fresh parsley

Directions
- **Step 1**

Turn on a multi-functional pressure cooker (such as Instant Pot) and select Saute function. Heat olive oil in the pot until hot and add mushrooms and onion. Cook and stir for about 3 minutes. Stir in garlic and cook until fragrant, about 30 seconds. Turn the pressure cooker off.
- **Step 2**

Pour chicken broth into the pot and stir in apple, rice, cranberries, thyme, salt, and pepper. Place chicken thighs on top of the rice mixture, but do not stir. Close and lock the

lid; set the pressure valve to Sealing. Select high pressure according to manufacturer's instructions; set timer for 30 minutes. Allow 10 to 15 minutes for pressure to build.
*   **Step 3**
Release pressure using the natural-release method according to manufacturer's instructions for 15 minutes. Release remaining pressure carefully using the quick-release method. Unlock and remove the lid.
*   **Step 4**
Transfer chicken thighs to a cutting board and cut or shred into bite-sized pieces. Return to the pot and stir. Garnish with parsley and serve in bowls.
Cook's Note:
If there's too much liquid after cooking is complete, just turn to the Saute function and cook down for a few minutes. If you'd like a little more liquid, stir in some chicken broth. Just adapt to your preference.

Nutrition Facts
Per Serving:
384.7 calories; protein 24.3g 49% DV; carbohydrates 44.2g 14% DV; fat 12.8g 20% DV; cholesterol 60.2mg 20% DV; sodium 123.1mg 5% DV

Instant Pot Guinness Corned Beef

Prep: 30 mins Cook: 1 hr 55 mins Additional: 10 mins Total: 2 hrs 35 mins

Servings: 12

Ingredients

*   2 cups water
*   1 (12 fluid ounce) can or bottle dark beer (such as Guinness)
*   4 cloves garlic, minced
*   1 (3 pound) corned beef brisket with spice packet
*   1 cup brown sugar
*   10 eaches baby red potatoes, quartered
*   4 large carrots, peeled and cut into matchstick pieces
*   1 onion, peeled and cut into bite-sized pieces
*   ½ head cabbage, coarsely chopped

Directions
*   **Step 1**
Combine water, beer, and garlic in a multi-functional pressure cooker (such as Instant Pot). Place trivet inside.
*   **Step 2**
Rub all sides of brisket with brown sugar. Place on the trivet and sprinkle spice packet on top. Close and lock the lid.
*   **Step 3**
Select high pressure according to manufacturer's instructions; set timer for 90 minutes. Allow 10 to 15 minutes for pressure to build.
*   **Step 4**
Release pressure carefully using the quick-release method according to manufacturer's instructions, about 5 minutes. Unlock and remove the lid. Transfer brisket to a baking sheet.
*   **Step 5**
Cover brisket with aluminum foil; let rest for 15 minutes.

- **Step 6**

Meanwhile, remove the trivet from the pot. Place potatoes, carrots, onion, and cabbage in the bottom of the pressure cooker. Close and lock the lid.
- **Step 7**

Select high pressure according to manufacturer's instructions; set timer for 5 minutes. Allow 10 to 15 minutes for pressure to build.
- **Step 8**

Release pressure carefully using the quick-release method according to manufacturer's instructions, about 5 minutes. Unlock and remove the lid. Serve vegetables with rested brisket.

Nutrition Facts
Per Serving:
260.3 calories; protein 10.9g 22% DV; carbohydrates 31.5g 10% DV; fat 9.6g 15% DV; cholesterol 48.7mg 16% DV; sodium 599mg 24% DV

Instant Pot Sweet and Spicy Chicken Thighs

Prep: 5 mins Cook: 25 mins Additional: 5 mins Total:35 mins

Servings: 4

Ingredients

- ⅓ cup chicken broth
- ¼ cup soy sauce
- ¼ cup honey
- 4 cloves garlic, minced
- ½ teaspoon red pepper flakes

- 1 pinch freshly ground black pepper to taste
- 1 ½ pounds boneless, skinless chicken thighs
- 1 tablespoon water
- 2 teaspoons cornstarch

Directions
- **Step 1**

Whisk chicken broth, soy sauce, honey, garlic, red pepper flakes, and pepper together in a multi-functional pressure cooker (such as Instant Pot). Add chicken thighs and turn to coat with the sauce. Close and lock the lid. Select high pressure according to manufacturer's instructions; set timer for 8 minutes. Allow 10 to 15 minutes for pressure to build.
- **Step 2**

Release pressure carefully using the quick-release method according to manufacturer's instructions, about 5 minutes. Unlock and remove the lid. Remove chicken thighs and set aside, keeping them warm.
- **Step 3**

Select Saute function. Stir together water and cornstarch in a small bowl and add slurry to Instant Pot . Cook and stir until sauce has thickened and reduced, about 5 minutes. Return chicken thighs to the sauce and toss to coat.

Nutrition Facts
Per Serving:
367.4 calories; protein 30g 60% DV; carbohydrates 21.4g 7% DV; fat 17.8g 27% DV; cholesterol 106.5mg 36% DV; sodium 1096.5mg 44% DV.

Instant Pot Galbi (Korean-Style Short Ribs)

Prep: 20 mins Cook: 55 mins Additional: 1 hr 10 mins Total: 2 hrs 25 mins

Servings: 6

Ingredients

- 3 pounds beef short ribs
- 1 Asian pear - peeled, cored, and coarsely chopped
- 1 small onion, chopped
- 4 cloves garlic, chopped
- ½ tablespoon peeled and coarsely chopped fresh ginger
- 1 cup low-sodium soy sauce, divided
- ¼ cup rice wine
- ¼ cup water
- ¼ cup brown sugar
- 2 tablespoons sesame oil, divided
- ½ teaspoon ground black pepper
- 2 eaches carrots, peeled and cut in chunks
- 5 eaches radishes, peeled and cut into chunks
- ¼ cup white sugar
- ½ bunch green onions, chopped, or to taste
- 1 tablespoon sesame seeds, or to taste

Directions

- **Step 1**

Soak ribs in a large bowl of water for 1 hour.

- **Step 2**

Meanwhile, combine Asian pear, onion, garlic, and ginger in a blender or food processor; puree until smooth. Transfer mixture to a mixing bowl. Add 3/4 cup soy sauce, rice wine, water, brown sugar, 1 tablespoon sesame oil, and pepper and mix to create the sauce.

- **Step 3**

Drain ribs and dry them well. Trim off excess fat. Place ribs in a multi-functional pressure cooker (such as Instant Pot) and add carrots and radishes. Pour Asian pear sauce on top. Close and lock the lid. Select Meat function according to manufacturer's instructions; set timer for 35 minutes. Allow 10 to 15 minutes for pressure to build.

- **Step 4**

Release pressure using the natural-release method according to manufacturer's instructions, 10 to 40 minutes. Unlock and remove the lid. Transfer meat and vegetables to a plate and set aside.

- **Step 5**

Select the Saute function on your Instant Pot . Stir in remaining soy sauce, remaining sesame oil, and white sugar. Cook, stirring occasionally, until sugar has melted and sauce has thickened, about 10 minutes. Return ribs and vegetables to the pot to get nice and saucy.

- **Step 6**

Garnish ribs and vegetables with green onions and sesame seeds.

Nutrition Facts
Per Serving:
656.6 calories; protein 25.2g 50% DV; carbohydrates 30.6g 10% DV; fat 47.1g 73% DV; cholesterol 93.2mg 31% DV; sodium 1588.5mg 64% DV

Instant Pot Red Beans and Rice with Sausage

Prep 10 mins Cook: 1 hr Additional: 20 mins Total: 1 hr 30 mins

Servings: 12

Ingredients

- 1 tablespoon vegetable oil
- 14 ounces andouille sausage, sliced into rounds
- 1 medium onion, chopped
- 1 green bell pepper, chopped
- 3 stalks celery, chopped
- 1 clove garlic, minced
- 2 teaspoons Creole seasoning (such as Tony Chachere's)
- 1 teaspoon ground thyme
- 1 teaspoon oregano
- 1 pound dried red beans
- 4 cups chicken broth
- 1 tablespoon hot sauce (such as Louisiana)
- 1 bay leaf
- 4 cups hot cooked rice
- ¼ cup chopped fresh flat-leaf parsley
- 3 eaches green onions, chopped

Directions

- **Step 1**

Turn on a multi-functional pressure cooker (such as Instant Pot) and select Saute function. Add oil and let heat about 30 seconds. Add sausage and cook for 5 minutes. Transfer to a plate using a slotted spoon and set sausage aside.

- **Step 2**

Add onion, bell pepper, and celery to the Instant Pot and cook for 3 minutes. Add garlic, Creole seasoning, thyme, and oregano; cook 2 minutes more. Turn pot off.

- **Step 3**

Add beans, broth, hot sauce, and bay leaf to the Instant Pot with the vegetables. Close and lock the lid. Select high pressure and set the timer for 30 minutes. Allow 10 minutes for pressure to build.

- **Step 4**

Release pressure using the natural-release method according to manufacturer's instructions, 10 to 40 minutes. Unlock and remove the lid.

- **Step 5**

Remove bay leaf from the pot and discard. Add reserved cooked sausage. Select Saute function. Cook, stirring frequently to mash some of the beans and thicken the mixture, for about 10 minutes. Turn off pot and let stand for 10 minutes.

- **Step 6**

Serve beans over hot cooked rice garnished with parsley and green onions.

Nutrition Facts
Per Serving:
326.3 calories; protein 15.1g 30% DV; carbohydrates 41.2g 13% DV; fat 11.3g 17% DV; cholesterol 21mg 7% DV; sodium 815mg 33% DV

Instant Pot Chicken Congee

Prep: 10 mins Cook: 50 mins Additional: 15 mins Total: 1 hr 15 mins

Servings: 6

Ingredients

- 1 cup uncooked short-grain white rice
- 1 tablespoon olive oil
- 14 ounces boneless, skinless chicken breast
- 6 cups chicken broth
- 1 (2 inch) piece grated fresh ginger
- 1 ear fresh corn, husked
- 1 pinch salt and ground black pepper to taste
- Topping:
- 3 eaches spring onions, sliced
- 6 teaspoons black sesame seeds
- 6 teaspoons spicy chili crisp sauce

Directions
- **Step 1**

Rinse rice under cold running water until the water runs clear. Set aside.
- **Step 2**

Turn on a multi-functional pressure cooker (such as Instant Pot) and select Saute function. Heat oil and brown chicken on all sides, about 8 minutes, making sure each side is browned before flipping. Add a few tablespoons of chicken broth to the Instant Pot and scrape off any browned bits from the bottom with a wooden spatula. Turn off Saute function. Add drained rice, ginger, and remaining broth.
- **Step 3**

Cut the kernels from the corn cob and break cob into 3 pieces. Add corn kernels and cob pieces to the pot. Close and seal the lid. Select Porridge function and set timer for 30 minutes. Allow 10 to 15 minutes for pressure to build.
- **Step 4**

Release pressure using the natural-release method according to manufacturer's instructions, about 15 minutes. Open the lid and discard the corn cob pieces. Remove chicken breast. Shred chicken with two forks and return to the congee. Season with salt and pepper and mix well.
- **Step 5**

Divide congee amongst 6 bowls. Top each bowl with equal amounts of sliced spring onions, sesame seeds, and chili crisp.

Nutrition Facts
Per Serving:
299.4 calories; protein 18.3g 37% DV; carbohydrates 32.5g 11% DV; fat 9.7g 15% DV; cholesterol 43.7mg 15% DV; sodium 1272.2mg 51% DV.

Instant Pot Red Beans and Rice with Sausage

Prep:10 mins Cook:1 hr Additional: 20 mins Total: 1 hr 30 mins

Servings: 12

Ingredients
- 1 tablespoon vegetable oil
- 14 ounces andouille sausage, sliced into rounds
- 1 medium onion, chopped
- 1 green bell pepper, chopped
- 3 stalks celery, chopped

- 1 clove garlic, minced
- 2 teaspoons Creole seasoning (such as Tony Chachere's)
- 1 teaspoon ground thyme
- 1 teaspoon oregano
- 1 pound dried red beans
- 4 cups chicken broth
- 1 tablespoon hot sauce (such as Louisiana)
- 1 bay leaf
- 4 cups hot cooked rice
- ¼ cup chopped fresh flat-leaf parsley
- 3 eaches green onions, chopped

Directions

- **Step 1**

Turn on a multi-functional pressure cooker (such as Instant Pot) and select Saute function. Add oil and let heat about 30 seconds. Add sausage and cook for 5 minutes. Transfer to a plate using a slotted spoon and set sausage aside.

- **Step 2**

Add onion, bell pepper, and celery to the Instant Pot and cook for 3 minutes. Add garlic, Creole seasoning, thyme, and oregano; cook 2 minutes more. Turn pot off.

- **Step 3**

Add beans, broth, hot sauce, and bay leaf to the Instant Pot with the vegetables. Close and lock the lid. Select high pressure and set the timer for 30 minutes. Allow 10 minutes for pressure to build.

- **Step 4**

Release pressure using the natural-release method according to manufacturer's instructions, 10 to 40 minutes. Unlock and remove the lid.

- **Step 5**

Remove bay leaf from the pot and discard. Add reserved cooked sausage. Select Saute function. Cook, stirring frequently to mash some of the beans and thicken the mixture, for about 10 minutes. Turn off pot and let stand for 10 minutes.

- **Step 6**

Serve beans over hot cooked rice garnished with parsley and green onions.

Nutrition Facts

Per Serving:

326.3 calories; protein 15.1g 30% DV; carbohydrates 41.2g 13% DV; fat 11.3g 17% DV; cholesterol 21mg 7% DV; sodium 815mg 33% DV.

Instant Pot Caldillo

Prep: 15 mins Cook: 1 hr 5 mins Additional: 10 mins Total: 1 hr 30 mins

Servings: 8

Ingredients

- 2 tablespoons olive oil
- 2 pounds cubed beef stew meat
- 1 onion, diced
- 4 cups beef broth
- 4 eaches russet potatoes, peeled and diced
- 1 (14.5 ounce) can fire-roasted diced tomatoes
- 1 (8 ounce) can chopped green chiles, drained (such as Hatch)
- 2 teaspoons Mexican oregano
- 2 teaspoons minced garlic
- 2 teaspoons cumin
- 1 teaspoon dried chipotle chile powder
- 1 teaspoon chili powder
- ½ teaspoon ground black pepper

Directions

- **Step 1**

Turn on a multi-functional pressure cooker (such as Instant Pot) and select Saute function. Heat olive oil and sear beef cubes until browned on all sides, 5 to 8 minutes. Remove browned beef from the pot and set aside. Add onion and cook until soft and translucent, about 5 minutes. Turn off Saute function.

- **Step 2**

Return beef to the pot with onions. Mix in beef broth, potatoes, diced tomatoes, green chiles, oregano, garlic, cumin, chipotle chile powder, chili powder, and pepper. Close and lock the lid. Select high pressure according to manufacturer's instructions; set timer for 45 minutes. Allow 10 to 15 minutes for pressure to build.

- **Step 3**

Release pressure using the natural-release method according to manufacturer's instructions, 10 to 40 minutes.

Nutrition Facts

Per Serving:

370 calories; protein 23.1g 46% DV; carbohydrates 25.4g 8% DV; fat 19.3g 30% DV; cholesterol 62.6mg 21% DV; sodium 919.6mg 37% DV

Instant Pot Tomato Soup

Prep: 20 mins Cook: 30 mins Additional: 5 mins Total: 55 mins

Servings: 4

Ingredients

- 1 tablespoon olive oil
- 4 stalks celery, chopped
- 1 cup chopped carrot
- 1 small yellow onion, chopped
- 2 cloves garlic, chopped
- 4 cups vegetable broth
- 1 (14.5 ounce) can fire-roasted diced tomatoes
- 1 (14.5 ounce) can crushed San Marzano tomatoes
- 3 tablespoons tomato paste
- 2 teaspoons dried basil
- 1 pinch salt and ground black pepper to taste
- ¼ cup butter
- ¼ cup all-purpose flour
- 1 cup milk
- ½ cup grated Parmesan cheese
- 1 tablespoon raw cane sugar
- 1 teaspoon red pepper flakes

Directions

- **Step 1**

Turn on a multi-functional pressure cooker (such as Instant Pot) and select Saute function. Add olive oil, celery, carrot, onion, and garlic. Cook for 5 minutes, stirring occasionally.

- **Step 2**

Stir in vegetable broth, diced and crushed tomatoes, tomato paste, basil, salt, and pepper. Close and lock the lid. Select high pressure according to manufacturer's instructions; set timer for 6 minutes. Allow 10 to 15 minutes for pressure to build.

- **Step 3**

Meanwhile, melt butter in a small saucepan over low heat. Stir in flour until a smooth, thick paste forms, about 3 minutes.

- **Step 4**

Release pressure naturally for 2 minutes according to manufacturer's instructions. Release remaining pressure by opening the valve to vent.

- **Step 5**

Use an immersion blender to carefully puree the hot soup. Select Saute function again; set timer for 3 minutes. Add flour paste, stirring continuously. Add milk, Parmesan cheese, sugar, and red pepper flakes. Season with more salt and pepper if needed. Stir to combine until the timer ends.

Cook's Notes:

The cane sugar helps cut the acidity, but you can leave it out.
You can use a regular blender to puree the soup. The soup will be extremely hot, so work in batches and be careful when blending.

Nutrition Facts

Per Serving:
379.4 calories; protein 11.9g 24% DV; carbohydrates 39.8g 13% DV; fat 20.2g 31% DV; cholesterol 44.2mg 15% DV; sodium 1321.1mg 53% DV.

Instant Pot Chicken Marsala

Prep: 10 mins Cook: 15 mins Total: 25 mins

Servings: 6

Ingredients

- ¼ cup all-purpose flour
- ½ teaspoon salt, or to taste
- ¼ teaspoon freshly ground black pepper
- 1 ½ pounds skinless, boneless chicken breast halves
- ¼ cup oil
- 2 cups sliced fresh mushrooms
- ½ cup dry Marsala wine
- ¼ cup butter

Directions

- **Step 1**

Combine flour, salt, and pepper in a shallow dish. Dredge chicken breasts through flour mixture.

- **Step 2**

Turn on a multi-functional pressure cooker (such as Instant Pot), select Saute function, and allow pot to heat up. Add oil. Add chicken and cook until lightly browned, 3 about minutes. Turn chicken over and add mushrooms. Cook, stirring mushrooms occasionally, until other side of the chicken is lightly browned, about 3 more minutes. Pour Marsala wine around chicken. Close and lock the lid, and simmer until chicken is no longer pink in the center and the juices run clear, about 5 minutes.

- **Step 3**

Remove chicken from the pot and place on a serving platter. Add butter to the pot. Turn off heat and stir butter into sauce until fully blended. Pour sauce over chicken breasts and serve immediately.

Nutrition Facts
Per Serving:
322 calories; protein 23.7g 47% DV; carbohydrates 7.9g 3% DV; fat 19.2g 30% DV; cholesterol 78.9mg 26% DV; sodium 299.7mg 12% DV.

Instant Pot Lebanese Lentil Soup (Shorbat Adas)

Prep: 25 mins Cook: 25 mins Additional: 5 mins Total: 55 mins

Servings: 4

Ingredients

- 2 tablespoons extra-virgin olive oil
- 1 onion, finely chopped
- 1 Yukon Gold potato, peeled and diced
- 1 carrot, peeled and diced
- 1 tomato, diced
- 2 rib (blank)s celery ribs, diced
- 1 clove garlic, chopped, or more to taste
- 1 ½ teaspoons kosher salt
- ¾ teaspoon ground cumin
- ⅛ teaspoon ground cinnamon
- ⅛ teaspoon allspice
- 4 cups low-sodium vegetable broth
- 2 cups water
- 1 ½ cups red lentils
- 2 fruit, without seeds lemons
- 2 eaches pita bread, cut into squares
- 1 cooking spray
- 1 pinch salt

Directions
- **Step 1**
Preheat the oven to 400 degrees F (200 degrees C).
- **Step 2**
Turn on a multi-functional pressure cooker (such as Instant Pot) and select Saute function. Heat olive oil in the pot. Add onion, potato, carrot, tomato, celery, and garlic; cook and stir until starting to soften, 3 to 5 minutes. Sprinkle salt, cumin, cinnamon, and allspice over the vegetables and stir until fragrant.
- **Step 3**
Pour in stock, water, and lentils. Close and lock the lid. Select high pressure according to manufacturer's instructions; set timer for 10 minutes. Allow 10 to 15 minutes for pressure to build.
- **Step 4**
Meanwhile, spread pita squares on a lined baking sheet. Spray with cooking spray and season with salt.
- **Step 5**
Bake in the preheated oven until toasted, about 8 minutes.
- **Step 6**

Release pressure carefully using the quick-release method according to manufacturer's instructions, about 5 minutes. Unlock and remove the lid. Puree soup using an immersion blender. Stir in juice of 1 lemon.
- **Step 7**

Divide soup among bowls and scatter a handful of pita chips over each. Cut the second lemon into wedges and serve alongside.

Cook's Note:
This soup tends to thicken as it sits. You can thin leftovers with some water when reheating.

Nutrition Facts
Per Serving:
456.2 calories; protein 23.2g 46% DV; carbohydrates 76.7g 25% DV; fat 8.9g 14% DV; cholesterolmg; sodium 1139.3mg 46% DV.

Instant Pot Chicken and Rice Stracciatella

Prep: 10 mins Cook: 20 mins Additional: 5 mins Total: 35 mins

Servings: 4

Ingredients

- 6 cups chicken broth
- 1 ½ cups diced rotisserie chicken meat
- ¼ cup long grain rice
- 3 large eggs eggs
- 3 tablespoons finely grated Parmigiano-Reggiano cheese
- 1 pinch freshly ground black pepper to taste
- 1 teaspoon chopped fresh parsley

Directions
- **Step 1**

Combine chicken broth, chicken, and rice in a multi-functional pressure cooker (such as Instant Pot). Close and lock the lid. Select high pressure according to manufacturer's instructions; set timer for 4 minutes. Allow 10 to 15 minutes for pressure to build.
- **Step 2**

Meanwhile, whisk eggs and Parmigiano-Reggiano cheese together in a small bowl. Season with black pepper. Set aside.
- **Step 3**

Release pressure carefully using the quick-release method according to manufacturer's instructions, about 5 minutes. Unlock and remove the lid. Change pressure cooker setting to Saute. Pour egg mixture into the broth in a slow steady stream while whisking. Cook for 1 minute. Serve immediately and garnish with parsley.

Nutrition Facts
Per Serving:
227.7 calories; protein 22g 44% DV; carbohydrates 11.7g 4% DV; fat 9.3g 14% DV; cholesterol 191.3mg 64% DV; sodium 1895.5mg 76% DV.

Instant Pot Roasted Melting Sweet Potatoes

Prep: 5 mins Cook: 20 mins Additional: 5 mins Total: 30 mins

Servings: 2

Ingredients

- ½ cup butter
- 1 pound sweet potatoes, peeled and cut into 1-inch slices
- ¾ cup vegetable broth
- 1 teaspoon ground thyme
- 1 teaspoon salt
- ½ teaspoon ground black pepper

Directions

- **Step 1**

Turn on a multi-functional pressure cooker (such as Instant Pot) and select Saute function. Melt butter. Add sweet potato rounds in a single layer and cook until golden, about 4 minutes. Flip and cook for 4 minutes more. Pour vegetable broth over the sweet potatoes and sprinkle with thyme, salt, and pepper.

- **Step 2**

Close and lock lid. Select high pressure according to manufacturer's instructions; set timer for 2 minutes. Allow 10 to 15 minutes for pressure to build.

- **Step 3**

Release pressure carefully using the quick-release method according to manufacturer's instructions, about 5 minutes. Unlock and remove lid.

Nutrition Facts
Per Serving:
616.7 calories; protein 4.5g 9% DV; carbohydrates 48.4g 16% DV; fat 46.4g 71% DV; cholesterol 122mg 41% DV; sodium 1787.6mg 72% DV

Instant Pot Risotto

Prep: 5 mins Cook: 20 mins Additional: 5 mins Total: 30 mins

Servings: 3

Ingredients

- 1 cube chicken bouillon (such as Knorr)
- 2 cups hot water
- 2 tablespoons extra-virgin olive oil
- ¼ cup finely diced onion
- 1 clove garlic, minced
- 1 cup Arborio rice
- ¼ cup white wine
- 2 tablespoons butter
- ¼ cup grated Parmigiano-Reggiano cheese
- 2 teaspoons chopped fresh parsley

Directions

- **Step 1**

Dissolve the chicken bouillon cube in the hot water and set aside.

- **Step 2**

Turn on a multi-functional pressure cooker (such as Instant Pot) and select Saute function. Add olive oil to the pot. Add onion and cook for 1 minute. Add garlic and rice and stir until each grain of rice is coated with the oil mixture. Cook until rice is slightly toasted, about 2 minutes. Pour in white wine and simmer for about 30 seconds. Stir in chicken broth.

- **Step 3**

Turn off Saute function. Close and lock the lid. Select high pressure according to manufacturer's instructions; set timer for 6 minutes. Allow 5 to 10 minutes for pressure to build.

- **Step 4**

Release pressure carefully using the quick-release method according to manufacturer's instructions, about 5 minutes. Unlock and remove the lid. Add butter; stir until risotto is creamy, about 1 minute. Stir in Parmigiano-Reggiano cheese until melted and well combined. Serve sprinkled with parsley.

Nutrition Facts
Per Serving:
446.5 calories; protein 7.7g 15% DV; carbohydrates 57.2g 18% DV; fat 18.7g 29% DV; cholesterol 26.4mg 9% DV; sodium 547.4mg 22% DV

Instant Pot Classic Hummus

Prep: 10 mins Cook: 45 mins Additional: 5 mins Total: 1 hr

Servings: 8

Ingredients

- 1 cup dry garbanzo beans
- 3 cups vegetable broth
- ⅓ cup lemon juice
- 3 tablespoons tahini
- 2 tablespoons olive oil
- 2 cloves garlic, chopped
- 1 teaspoon ground cumin
- ½ teaspoon salt

Directions
- **Step 1**

Combine garbanzo beans with vegetable broth in a multi-functional pressure cooker (such as Instant Pot). Close and lock the lid. Select high pressure according to manufacturer's instructions; set timer for 35 minutes. Allow 10 to 15 minutes for pressure to build.

- **Step 2**

Release pressure carefully using the quick-release method according to manufacturer's instructions, about 5 minutes. Unlock and remove lid.

- **Step 3**

Strain garbanzo beans, saving 2/3 cup liquid. Place garbanzo beans in the bowl of a food processor; add lemon juice, tahini, olive oil, and garlic. Blend until smooth and creamy, about 3 minutes. Scrape bowl and add reserved 2/3 cup liquid, cumin, and salt; blend for 1 minute more.

Nutrition Facts
Per Serving:
170.2 calories; protein 6.3g 13% DV; carbohydrates 19.5g 6% DV; fat 8.2g 13% DV; cholesterolmg; sodium 331mg 13% DV

Instant Pot Pork Stew

Prep: 10 mins Cook: 50 mins Additional: 10 mins Total: 1 hr 10 mins

Servings: 8

Ingredients

- 2 tablespoons olive oil
- 2 pounds pork shoulder, cut into 6 pieces
- 1 pinch salt and ground black pepper to taste
- 2 tablespoons all-purpose flour
- 1 cup red wine
- 1 cup beef broth
- 2 tablespoons tomato paste
- 1 onion, cut into large chunks
- 4 stalks celery, cut into 1-inch pieces
- ½ pound baby carrots
- 2 cloves garlic, chopped
- 2 leaf (blank)s bay leaves

Directions

- **Step 1**

Turn on a multi-functional pressure cooker (such as Instant Pot) and select Saute function. Heat oil for 1 minute. Season pork with salt and pepper. Add to the pot. Cook and stir until browned evenly on all sides, 4 to 5 minutes. Add flour and cook and stir for 1 to 2 minutes. Deglaze the pot by adding wine, broth, and tomato paste, scraping up all the browned bits from the bottom.

- **Step 2**

Close and lock the lid. Select high pressure according to manufacturer's instructions; set timer for 15 minutes. Allow 10 to 15 minutes for pressure to build.

- **Step 3**

Release pressure carefully using the quick-release method according to manufacturer's instructions, about 5 minutes. Unlock and remove the lid. Stir in onion, celery, carrots, garlic, and bay leaves. Close and lock the lid. Select high pressure according to manufacturer's instructions; set timer for 15 minutes. Allow 5 minutes for pressure to build.

- **Step 4**

Release pressure carefully using the quick-release method according to manufacturer's instructions, about 5 minutes.

Nutrition Facts
Per Serving:
197.8 calories; protein 15.9g 32% DV; carbohydrates 8.9g 3% DV; fat 8.4g 13% DV; cholesterol 42.6mg 14% DV; sodium 219.6mg 9% DV

Instant Pot Chicken Drumsticks

Prep:20 mins Cook: 25 mins Additional: 8 hrs 20 mins Total: 9 hrs 5 mins

Servings: 6

Ingredients

- 1 ½ cups orange juice
- 1 lime, juiced
- 1 lemon, juiced
- 1 tablespoon chili powder
- 2 cloves garlic, crushed
- 1 teaspoon ground cumin

- 1 teaspoon dried oregano
- 1 teaspoon garlic salt
- ½ teaspoon ground chipotle powder
- 6 eaches chicken drumsticks
- ½ onion, sliced and separated into rings
- 2 tablespoons chopped fresh cilantro

Directions
- **Step 1**

Combine orange juice, lime juice, lemon juice, chili powder, garlic, cumin, oregano, garlic salt, and chipotle powder in a bowl. Pour into a resealable plastic bag and add chicken drumsticks, onion, and cilantro. Seal the bag and refrigerate for at least 8 hours to overnight, turning the bag frequently.
- **Step 2**

Pour marinade into a multi-functional pressure cooker (such as Instant Pot). Place the rack inside the pot and place drumsticks on top. Close and lock the lid. Select high pressure according to manufacturer's instructions; set timer for 15 minutes. Allow 10 to 15 minutes for pressure to build.
- **Step 3**

Release pressure using the natural-release method for 15 minutes. Release remaining pressure using the quick-release method according to manufacturer's instructions, about 5 minutes. Unlock and remove the lid.

Cook's Note:

If crispy chicken is desired, place drumsticks under a broiler and cook for 4 minutes, turning after 2 minutes.

Nutrition Facts
Per Serving:
239.3 calories; protein 16.7g 34% DV; carbohydrates 18.7g 6% DV; fat 11.6g 18% DV; cholesterol 60.5mg 20% DV; sodium 507.7mg 20% DV.

Instant Pot Vanilla Extract

Prep: 10 mins Cook: 40 mins Additional: 5 mins Total: 55 mins

Servings: 96

Ingredients

- 3 eaches vanilla beans
- 2 cups vodka
- 1 cup water

Directions
- **Step 1**

Split vanilla beans with a very sharp knife.
- **Step 2**

Pour vodka into a mason jar and add vanilla beans. Place a lid loosely on the jar.
- **Step 3**

Place a trivet in a multi-functional pressure cooker (such as Instant Pot) and set the mason jar on top of the trivet. Pour water into the pot.
- **Step 4**

Close and lock the lid. Select high pressure according to manufacturer's instructions; set timer for 30 minutes. Allow 10 to 15 minutes for pressure to build.

- **Step 5**

Release pressure carefully using the quick-release method according to manufacturer's instructions, about 5 minutes. Unlock and remove the lid.

- **Step 6**

Transfer mixture, including vanilla beans, into a glass bottle, and seal tightly.

Cook's Notes:

Instead of quick-releasing the pressure, you can also allow the mixture to steep longer and the pressure to naturally release.

Madagascar vanilla beans are rich and creamy--some have notes reminiscent of tobacco, while Tahitian vanilla beans have notes akin to bourbon and Mexican vanilla beans are more spicy and robust.

Nutrition Facts

Per Serving:

13.1 calories; proteing; carbohydrates 0.4g; fatg; cholesterolmg; sodium 0.1mg

Instant Pot Farro

Prep: 5 mins Cook: 20 mins Additional: 10 mins Total: 35 mins

Servings: 6

Ingredients

- 2 ½ cups water
- 1 cup farro
- ½ teaspoon salt

Directions

- **Step 1**

Combine water, farro, and salt in a multi-functional pressure cooker (such as Instant Pot). Close and lock the lid. Select high pressure according to manufacturer's instructions; set timer for 10 minutes. Allow 10 to 15 minutes for pressure to build.

- **Step 2**

Release pressure naturally according to manufacturer's instructions for 10 minutes. Release remaining pressure through the vent. Unlock and remove the lid. Drain any excess liquid that was not absorbed.

Nutrition Facts

Per Serving:

99.3 calories; protein 3.4g 7% DV; carbohydrates 22.6g 7% DV; fat 0.8g 1% DV; cholesterolmg; sodium 197.6mg 8% DV

Instant Pot Vegetable Soup

Prep: 30 mins Cook: 25 mins Additional: 10 mins Total: 1 hr 5 mins

Servings: 4

Ingredients

- 1 tablespoon olive oil
- 2 medium carrots - peeled, halved lengthwise, and sliced
- 2 stalks celery, sliced
- 1 brown onion, diced
- ¼ teaspoon salt
- 4 cloves garlic, diced
- ½ red chile pepper, sliced
- 1 pound Yukon gold potatoes, scrubbed and quartered
- 1 (28 ounce) can fire-roasted diced tomatoes
- 1 bunch kale, stemmed and coarsely chopped
- 1 small zucchini, diced
- 4 cups vegetable broth
- 1 bay leaf
- 1 teaspoon lemon zest, or to taste
- 1 teaspoon chopped fresh parsley, or to taste

Directions

- **Step 1**

Turn on a multi-functional pressure cooker (such as Instant Pot) and select Saute function.

- **Step 2**

Pour olive oil into the hot cooker and add carrots, celery, onion, and salt. Cook and stir for 2 minutes. Stir in garlic and red chile pepper; saute for 2 minutes. Add potatoes, tomatoes, kale, and zucchini. Pour in vegetable broth, add bay leaf, and stir to combine. Close and lock the lid.

- **Step 3**

Select high pressure according to manufacturer's instructions; set timer for 10 minutes. Allow 10 to 15 minutes for pressure to build.

- **Step 4**

Release pressure using the natural-release method according to manufacturer's instructions, about 5 minutes. Release remaining pressure carefully using the quick-release method according to manufacturer's instructions, about 5 minutes more. Unlock and remove the lid. Serve soup in bowls and top with lemon zest and parsley.

Nutrition Facts
Per Serving:
311.6 calories; protein 10.4g 21% DV; carbohydrates 59.2g 19% DV; fat 5g 8% DV; cholesterolmg; sodium 1229.7mg 49% DV

Instant Pot Beef Burritos

Prep:15 mins Cook: 25 mins Additional: 5 mins Total: 45 mins

Servings: 8

Ingredients

- 1 pound 85% lean ground beef
- 1 teaspoon kosher salt
- ½ teaspoon ground black pepper
- 1 small onion, diced
- 1 tablespoon olive oil
- 1 cup uncooked long grain rice
- 1 (15 ounce) can black beans, drained and rinsed
- 1 (14.5 ounce) can fire-roasted diced tomatoes, drained
- 1 (14.5 ounce) can vegetable broth
- 2 (1 ounce) packets taco seasoning
- ¼ cup chopped cilantro, or to taste
- 8 (10 inch) burrito-size tortillas, or as needed
- 2 cups shredded Mexican cheese blend

- 2 eaches tomatoes, diced, or more to taste
- 1 avocado, diced, or more to taste
- ¼ cup sour cream, or to taste
- 2 eaches green onions, chopped, or to taste

Directions
- **Step 1**

Turn on a multi-functional pressure cooker (such as Instant Pot) and select Saute function; if available, select "more" option. Add ground beef, salt, and pepper. Cook and stir beef until browned and crumbly, 5 to 7 minutes. Add onion and cook until starting to soften, 1 to 3 minutes more. Add olive oil and rice. Cook and stir until some grains start to turn golden brown, about 2 minutes. Stir in beans, tomatoes, broth, and taco seasoning.
- **Step 2**

Close and lock the lid. Select high pressure according to manufacturer's instructions; set timer for 7 minutes. Allow 10 to 15 minutes for pressure to build.
- **Step 3**

Release pressure carefully using the quick-release method according to manufacturer's instructions, about 5 minutes. Unlock and remove the lid. Fluff burrito bowl filling with a fork and add cilantro.
- **Step 4**

Serve filling in tortillas with Mexican cheese blend. Garnish with fresh tomatoes, avocado, sour cream, and green onions.

Cook's Note:
Substitute chicken broth for the vegetable broth if preferred.

Nutrition Facts
Per Serving:
684.5 calories; protein 29.6g 59% DV; carbohydrates 77g 25% DV; fat 27.7g 43% DV; cholesterol 67.7mg 23% DV; sodium 1804.8mg 72% DV

Instant Pot Chili

Prep: 20 mins Cook: 30 mins Additional: 10 mins Total: 1 hr

Servings: 8

Ingredients

- 1 tablespoon vegetable oil
- 1 pound lean ground beef
- 1 large onion, diced
- 4 cloves garlic, crushed
- ½ teaspoon salt
- ¼ cup chili powder
- 1 tablespoon ground cumin
- 1 teaspoon dried oregano
- 1 ½ cups water
- 4 (15 ounce) cans kidney beans, drained
- 1 (28 ounce) can crushed tomatoes
- 2 tablespoons tomato paste

Directions
- **Step 1**

Turn on a multi-functional pressure cooker (such as Instant Pot) and select Saute function. Add ground beef. Cook and stir until browned and crumbly, 5 to 7 minutes. Drain and discard grease. Transfer cooked beef to a separate container.

- **Step 2**

Pour oil into the Instant Pot and select Saute function. Add onion, garlic, and salt. Cook until softened, 5 to 7 minutes. Make a hole in the center of the mixture and add chili powder, cumin, and oregano. Let spices sit for 30 seconds, then stir into the onion. Return cooked beef to the pot and add water. Stir, being sure to scrape any browned bits from the bottom.

- **Step 3**

Stir beans, crushed tomatoes, and tomato paste into the beef mixture. Close and lock the lid. Select Chili function and set the timer for 10 minutes. Allow 10 to 15 minutes for pressure to build.

- **Step 4**

Release pressure using the natural-release method according to manufacturer's instructions, 10 to 40 minutes. Unlock and remove the lid.

Cook's Notes:

Use any kind of canned beans you like. You can substitute tomato sauce for the crushed tomatoes.

To save preparation time, I do the following the night before: Brown the beef, drain, and place in a covered container in the refrigerator. Chop the onion and place in a covered container in the refrigerator. Measure the spices and place in a covered container.

Nutrition Facts

Per Serving:

362.6 calories; protein 25.1g 50% DV; carbohydrates 45.1g 15% DV; fat 10.6g 16% DV; cholesterol 39.5mg 13% DV; sodium 837.6mg 34% DV

Instant Pot Moroccan Chicken Tagine

Prep: 25 mins Cook: 35 mins Additional: 3 hrs 10 mins Total: 4 hrs 10 mins

Servings: 6

Ingredients

- 2 tablespoons minced fresh garlic
- 1 ¼ teaspoons paprika
- ¾ teaspoon ground ginger
- ¾ teaspoon ground turmeric
- ⅛ teaspoon saffron powder
- 1 ½ pounds skinless, boneless chicken breasts, cut into bite-sized pieces
- 1 preserved lemon
- 2 tablespoons extra-virgin olive oil
- 2 tablespoons butter
- 2 medium red onions, sliced
- 1 cinnamon stick
- 1 cup pitted and halved Mediterranean olives
- 1 cup chicken broth
- 1 tablespoon chopped fresh flat-leaf parsley
- 1 tablespoon chopped fresh cilantro

Directions

- **Step 1**

Combine garlic, paprika, ginger, turmeric, and saffron in a large bowl. Add chicken pieces and mix until coated with spices. Cover and refrigerate, 3 to 4 hours or overnight.

- **Step 2**

Cut preserved lemon into quarters. Remove pulp from the peel and remove seeds from pulp. Mince pulp and set aside. Cut lemon peel into strips and set aside.
- **Step 3**

Turn on a multi-functional pressure cooker (such as Instant Pot) and select Saute function. Heat olive oil and butter in the cooker; add chicken. Cook chicken until browned, about 3 minutes per side. Transfer chicken to a plate, reserving drippings in the pot.
- **Step 4**

Place onions and lemon pulp into the hot pot and cook, stirring occasionally, until onions have softened, about 5 minutes. Add cinnamon stick, place chicken on top, and scatter olives and lemon peel over the chicken. Pour in chicken broth. Close and lock the lid. Select high pressure according to manufacturer's instructions; set timer for 10 minutes. Allow 10 to 15 minutes for pressure to build.
- **Step 5**

Release pressure using the natural-release method according to manufacturer's instructions, about 10 minutes. Unlock and remove the lid carefully, turning it away from you. Transfer contents to a large serving bowl. Sprinkle with parsley and cilantro and serve immediately.

Cook's Note:

You can use any skinless, boneless cut of chicken that you'd like.

Nutrition Facts

Per Serving:

257.2 calories; protein 24.6g 49% DV; carbohydrates 8.7g 3% DV; fat 13.8g 21% DV; cholesterol 75.8mg 25% DV; sodium 2538.4mg 102% DV

Easy Instant Pot Baby Back Ribs

Prep: 20 mins Cook: 50 mins Additional: 20 mins Total: 1 hr 30 mins

Servings: 6

Ingredients

- 1 cup water
- ½ cup apple cider vinegar
- 1 tablespoon liquid smoke flavoring
- 1 rack baby back pork ribs
- 1 pinch salt and freshly ground black pepper to taste
- 1 (12 ounce) bottle barbeque sauce, divided

Directions
- **Step 1**

Combine water, vinegar, and liquid smoke in the pot of a multi-functional pressure cooker (such as Instant Pot). Place rack in the bottom of the pot.
- **Step 2**

Season baby back pork ribs with salt and pepper on both sides. Cut rack in half. Place ribs in a teepee formation onto the rack. Pour a little barbeque sauce onto each half and let run down the sides. Close and lock the lid.
- **Step 3**

Select Meat setting according to manufacturer's instructions; set timer for 30 minutes. Allow 10 to 15 minutes for pressure to build.
* **Step 4**

Wait 15 minutes before releasing pressure carefully using the quick-release method according to manufacturer's instructions, about 5 minutes. Unlock and remove the lid.
* **Step 5**

Set an oven rack about 6 inches from the heat source and preheat the oven's broiler. Line a baking pan with aluminum foil. Place ribs onto the prepared baking pan and slather with barbeque sauce.

* **Step 6**

Cook under the broiler for 5 minutes. Remove and immediately add more sauce.

Nutrition Facts
Per Serving:
291.4 calories; protein 12g 24% DV; carbohydrates 20.5g 7% DV; fat 17.1g 26% DV; cholesterol 58.4mg 20% DV; sodium 704.7mg 28% DV.

Instant Pot Corn Chowder

Prep: 10 mins Cook: 35 mins Additional: 15 mins Total: 1 hr

Servings: 8

Ingredients

* 2 tablespoons butter
* 1 onion, diced
* 4 cloves garlic, minced
* 4 cups fresh corn kernels
* 4 cups peeled and diced potatoes
* 4 cups vegetable broth
* ½ teaspoon fresh thyme leaves
* ½ teaspoon paprika
* 1 teaspoon salt
* 1 teaspoon ground black pepper
* 1 cup heavy cream

Directions
* **Step 1**

Turn on a multi-functional pressure cooker (such as Instant Pot) and select Saute function. Add butter and melt. Stir in onion and garlic; cook until onion is soft and translucent, about 5 minutes. Turn off Saute function.
* **Step 2**

Add corn, potatoes, vegetable broth, thyme, paprika, salt, and pepper to the pot; stir to combine. Close and lock the lid. Select high pressure according to manufacturer's instructions; set timer for 15 minutes. Allow 10 to 15 minutes for pressure to build.
* **Step 3**

Release pressure using the natural-release method according to manufacturer's instructions, about 15 minutes. Release any remaining pressure carefully using the quick-release method according to manufacturer's instructions. Unlock and remove the lid. Remove 1 cup of potatoes and corn to a bowl. Mash with a fork and return to the pot.
* **Step 4**

Select Saute function again and pour in heavy cream. Cook until soup has thickened to desired consistency.

Cook's Note:
Frozen corn may be substituted for fresh, if desired.

Nutrition Facts
Per Serving:
277.9 calories; protein 5.5g 11% DV; carbohydrates 33.6g 11% DV; fat 15.2g 23% DV;
cholesterol 48.4mg 16% DV; sodium 569.6mg 23% DV

Instant Pot Southern-Style Green Beans from a Can

Prep: 10 mins Cook: 30 mins Additional: 5 mins Total: 45 mins

Servings: 8

Ingredients

- 8 ounces thick cut bacon, cut into 1 inch pieces
- 1 cup diced yellow onion
- 2 tablespoons cider vinegar
- 4 (15 ounce) cans cut green beans, with liquid
- 2 teaspoons sea salt, or to taste
- ½ teaspoon black pepper
- 1 ½ pounds daikon (white radish), peeled and chopped

Directions
- **Step 1**

Turn on a multi-functional pressure cooker (such as Instant Pot) and select Saute function. Add bacon and cook until almost crispy, about 8 minutes. Take your time cooking the bacon in order to render out all the fat. Add onions and cook, stirring frequently, until soft and translucent, about 3 minutes.
- **Step 2**

Pour in vinegar and scrape up the brown bits from the bottom of the pot. Pour in beans and their liquid; season with salt and pepper. Stir in radishes. Close and lock the lid. Select high pressure according to manufacturer's instructions; set timer for 5 minutes. Allow 10 to 15 minutes for pressure to build.
- **Step 3**

Release pressure carefully using the quick-release method according to manufacturer's instructions, about 5 minutes. Unlock and remove the lid.

Cook's Note:
Recipe Notes
If you want to make a smaller batch, scale down the Ingredients but the cook time remains the same.

Nutrition Facts
Per Serving:
101.5 calories; protein 5g 10% DV; carbohydrates 11.3g 4% DV; fat 4.3g 7% DV;
cholesterol 10mg 3% DV; sodium 996.4mg 40% DV

Instant Pot Cheesy Broccoli Rice

Prep: 5 mins Cook: 40 mins Additional: 10 mins Total: 55 mins

Servings: 4

Ingredients

- 1 tablespoon butter
- ¼ cup chopped onion
- 1 cup uncooked white rice
- 1 ½ cups chicken broth, divided
- 1 head broccoli, chopped
- ½ cup fat-free half-and-half
- 1 teaspoon garlic salt
- ½ teaspoon Italian seasoning
- ¼ teaspoon black pepper
- 1 cup shredded Cheddar cheese, divided

Directions
- **Step 1**

Turn on a multi-functional pressure cooker (such as Instant Pot) and select Saute function. Add butter and stir until melted. Add onion and saute until golden brown, about 5 minutes. Stir in rice and pour in 1 1/4 cup chicken broth or as much as needed to cover rice. Close and lock the lid. Select rice setting according to manufacturer's instructions; set timer for 12 minutes. Allow 10 to 15 minutes for pressure to build.
- **Step 2**

Release pressure carefully using the quick-release method according to manufacturer's instructions, about 5 minutes. Unlock and remove the lid. Add chopped broccoli and stir to combine. If rice looks dry, add remaining 1/4 cup chicken broth. Close lid and seal the vent. Select steam and set the timer for 5 minutes.
- **Step 3**

Release pressure carefully using the quick-release method according to manufacturer's instructions, about 5 minutes. Pour in half-and-half, garlic salt, Italian seasoning, pepper, and 3/4 cup Cheddar cheese. Stir to combine.
- **Step 4**

Set an oven rack about 6 inches from the heat source and preheat the oven's broiler. Grease an 8-inch square casserole dish.
- **Step 5**

Transfer broccoli mixture to the prepared casserole dish and top with remaining Cheddar cheese. Broil until cheese is golden brown, about 5 minutes.

Nutrition Facts
Per Serving:
370.8 calories; protein 13.8g 28% DV; carbohydrates 48.5g 16% DV; fat 13.5g 21% DV; cholesterol 41.1mg 14% DV; sodium 1155.1mg 46% DV.

Instant Pot Refried Beans

Prep: 5 mins Cook: 50 mins Additional: 10 mins Total: 1 hr 5 mins

Servings: 10

Ingredients

- ¼ cup vegetable oil
- 1 medium white onion, chopped
- 2 cloves garlic
- 1 teaspoon dried Mexican oregano
- 1 pound dried pinto beans
- 8 cups water
- 2 teaspoons salt

Directions
- **Step 1**

Turn on a multi-functional pressure cooker (such as Instant Pot) and select Saute function. Add oil, onion, garlic, and oregano; cook for 5 minutes. Add beans and water; stir. Close and lock the lid. Choose high pressure and set timer for 35 minutes. Allow 10 to 15 minutes for pressure to build.
- **Step 2**

Release pressure using the natural-release method according to manufacturer's instructions, 10 to 40 minutes.
- **Step 3**

Remove the lid and check a bean; if not yet tender, close and lock the lid and cook another 5 minutes at high pressure.
- **Step 4**

Drain beans, reserving 2 cups of liquid. Return beans to pot and add salt and 1 cup reserved liquid. Puree using a stick blender, adding additional cooking liquid as needed. Keep warm using the slow cooker function.

Nutrition Facts
Per Serving:
211.5 calories; protein 9.9g 20% DV; carbohydrates 29.7g 10% DV; fat 6g 9% DV; cholesterolmg; sodium 476.8mg 19% DV.

Instant Pot Tomato and Beef Sauce

Prep: 10 mins Cook: 40 mins Additional: 10 mins Total: 1 hr

Servings: 6

Ingredients

- 1 pound lean ground beef
- 1 teaspoon salt
- ½ teaspoon freshly ground black pepper
- 1 large onion, finely diced
- 4 cloves garlic, minced
- 2 teaspoons Italian seasoning
- ¼ cup dry red wine
- 1 (24 ounce) container crushed tomatoes
- 1 (28 ounce) can whole peeled San Marzano tomatoes, crushed with a fork
- 2 teaspoons lemon juice

Directions
- **Step 1**

Turn on a multi-functional pressure cooker (such as Instant Pot). Select Saute function and the setting to low. Add ground beef and season with salt and pepper. Cook until browned and crumbly, about 5 minutes. Drain and set aside. Add onion, garlic, and

Italian seasoning to the pot and saute until tender, about 5 minutes. Turn Saute function off.
• **Step 2**
Select Saute function again and the setting to high heat. Saute for an additional 4 to 5 minutes, stirring infrequently to allow brown bits to form on the bottom of the pot. Pour in red wine to deglaze. Add both tomatoes and browned beef mixture; stir to combine.
• **Step 3**
Close and lock the lid. Select high pressure according to manufacturer's instructions; set timer for 10 minutes. Allow 10 to 15 minutes for pressure to build.

• **Step 4**
Release pressure using the natural-release method according to manufacturer's instructions, about 5 minutes. Release any additional pressure carefully using the quick-release method, about 5 minutes. Unlock and remove the lid. Add lemon juice and simmer for 3 to 4 minutes.

Cook's Note:
You can use 1 tablespoon each basil, oregano, parsley, and a pinch of red pepper flakes if you don't have the Italian seasoning.

Nutrition Facts
Per Serving:
234.1 calories; protein 16.9g 34% DV; carbohydrates 17.3g 6% DV; fat 11g 17% DV; cholesterol 44.2mg 15% DV; sodium 757.8mg 30% DV.

Instant Pot Turkey Stock

Prep: 5 mins Cook: 1 hr Additional: 8 hrs 15 mins Total: 9 hrs 20 mins

Servings: 10

Ingredients

- 1 leftover turkey carcass from a 12 pound turkey
- 1 large onion, cut into wedges
- 2 large carrots, sliced
- 2 ribs celery, sliced
- 10 cups water

Directions
• **Step 1**
Combine turkey carcass, onion, carrots, celery, and water in a multi-functional pressure cooker (such as an Instant Pot . Close and lock the lid. Select high pressure according to manufacturer's instructions; set timer for 45 minutes. Allow 15 minutes for pressure to build.
• **Step 2**
Release pressure carefully using the quick-release method according to manufacturer's instructions, about 15 minutes.
• **Step 3**
Pour liquid through a strainer and discard all solids. Refrigerate for 8 hours or overnight. Skim fat from the top and discard. Use stock within 3 days or freeze for up to 3 months.

Nutrition Facts
Per Serving:
25.4 calories; protein 0.9g 2% DV; carbohydrates 3.2g 1% DV; fat 1.1g 2% DV; cholesterol 2.9mg 1% DV; sodium 29.3mg 1% DV.

Instant Pot Chicken Pot Pie Stew

Prep: 10 mins Cook: 40 mins Additional: 30 mins Total: 1 hr 20 mins

Servings: 10

Ingredients

- 2 pounds skinless, boneless chicken breasts, or more to taste
- 6 cups chicken broth, divided
- 2 tablespoons butter
- 1 large onion, chopped
- 1 tablespoon garlic powder
- 1 tablespoon Italian seasoning
- 1 teaspoon salt and ground black pepper to taste

- 1 (16 ounce) package uncooked wide egg noodles
- 1 cup water as needed
- 1 (16 ounce) package frozen mixed vegetables
- 1 (10.5 ounce) can cream of chicken soup
- 1 cup sour cream

Directions

- **Step 1**

Turn on a multi-functional pressure cooker (such as Instant Pot) and add chicken and 2 cups broth. Close and lock the lid and seal the vent. Choose manual high pressure and set timer for 10 minutes. Allow 10 to 15 minutes for pressure to build.

- **Step 2**

Release pressure using the natural-release method according to manufacturer's instructions for 10 minutes. Release remaining pressure carefully using the quick-release method according to manufacturer's instructions, about 5 minutes. Unlock and remove the lid.

- **Step 3**

Remove chicken, shred, and set aside. Pour broth into a bowl and reserve.

- **Step 4**

Turn the empty Instant Pot to Saute and melt butter. Add onion to melted butter and saute 2 to 3 minutes. Add shredded chicken, reserved broth, and remaining broth. Stir in garlic powder, Italian seasoning, salt, and pepper. Place egg noodles on top and press down to submerge; if necessary, add more water just to cover the noodles.

- **Step 5**

Close and lock the lid and seal the vent. Choose manual high pressure and set timer for 4 minutes. Allow 10 to 15 minutes for pressure to build.

- **Step 6**

Release pressure using the natural-release method according to manufacturer's instructions for 5 minutes. Release remaining pressure carefully using the quick-release method according to manufacturer's instructions, about 5 minutes. Unlock and remove the lid.

- **Step 7**

Add frozen vegetables, cream of chicken soup, and sour cream to the pot. Stir to combine and replace the lid. Wait 5 minutes for vegetables to warm through.

Nutrition Facts
Per Serving:
476.6 calories; protein 25.5g 51% DV; carbohydrates 49.6g 16% DV; fat 19.5g 30% DV; cholesterol 111.6mg 37% DV; sodium 1354.1mg 54% DV.

Instant Pot Protein-Packed Vegetarian Chili

Prep: 10 mins Cook: 20 mins Additional: 5 mins Total: 35 mins

Servings: 6

Ingredients

- 2 teaspoons olive oil
- 1 cup chopped onion
- ½ cup chopped green bell pepper
- ½ cup chopped red bell pepper
- 2 cloves garlic, minced
- 1 pound vegetarian ground beef substitute (such as Beyond Meat Beyond Beef)
- 1 (15 ounce) can chili beans
- 1 (14.5 ounce) can diced tomatoes
- 2 tablespoons chili powder

Directions
- **Step 1**

Turn on a multi-functional pressure cooker (such as Instant Pot) and select Saute function. Add oil, onion, and bell peppers. Saute until tender, about 3 minutes. Add garlic and cook until fragrant, about 30 seconds. Add ground beef substitute. Stir, breaking up into crumbles. Add beans, tomatoes, and chili powder. Hit Cancel.
- **Step 2**

Close and lock the lid. Select high pressure according to manufacturer's instructions; set timer for 5 minutes. Allow 10 to 15 minutes for pressure to build.
- **Step 3**

Release pressure carefully using the quick-release method according to manufacturer's instructions, about 5 minutes. Unlock and remove the lid. Serve immediately.

Nutrition Facts
Per Serving:
225.4 calories; protein 19.1g 38% DV; carbohydrates 26g 8% DV; fat 6.1g 9% DV; cholesterol 0.3mg; sodium 743.3mg 30% DV.

Instant Pot Split Pea Soup

Prep: 20 mins Cook: 40 mins Additional: 15 mins Total: 1 hr 15 mins

Servings: 6

Ingredients

- 2 tablespoons butter
- 1 tablespoon olive oil
- 1 onion, diced
- 3 stalks celery, diced

- 2 leaf (blank)s bay leaves
- ½ teaspoon dried thyme
- 3 carrot, (7-1/2")s carrots, chopped
- 6 slices bacon, chopped
- 4 cloves garlic, minced

- ½ teaspoon salt
- ¼ teaspoon ground black pepper
- 6 cups chicken broth
- 1 pound green split peas, rinsed and sorted

Directions

• Step 1

Turn on a multi-functional pressure cooker (such as Instant Pot) and select Saute function. Let warm up and add butter and olive oil. Add onion, celery, bay leaves, and thyme. Cook, stirring occasionally, until onion starts to turn translucent, about 5 minutes.

• Step 2

Add carrots, bacon, garlic, salt, and pepper. Cook until fragrant, about 1 minute. Add broth and bring to a simmer. Stir in split peas. Close and lock the lid; set release knob to Sealing position.

• Step 3

Select Manual/Pressure Cook setting according to manufacturer's instructions; set timer for 18 minutes. Allow 10 to 15 minutes for pressure to build.

• Step 4

Release pressure using the natural-release method according to manufacturer's instructions, about 15 minutes. Turn steam release knob to Venting and use quick-release function for the remaining pressure. Carefully open lid. Remove bay leaves. Taste and seasonings as desired.

Cook's Note:

For a vegetarian version, substitute vegetable broth for the chicken broth and 1 teaspoon liquid smoke for the bacon.

Nutrition Facts

Per Serving:
408.4 calories; protein 24g 48% DV; carbohydrates 53.6g 17% DV; fat 11.6g 18% DV; cholesterol 26.3mg 9% DV; sodium 1649.9mg 66% DV.

Instant Pot Cabbage and Beef Soup

Prep: 15 mins Cook: 40 mins Additional: 20 mins Total: 1 hr 15 mins

Servings: 6

Ingredients

- 1 tablespoon olive oil
- 1 pound ground beef
- 1 teaspoon dried oregano
- 1 teaspoon dried thyme
- 1 cup chopped carrot
- 1 cup chopped Yukon Gold potato
- ½ onion, chopped
- 2 cloves garlic, chopped
- 8 cups water

- 1 (14.5 ounce) can Italian-style stewed tomatoes, drained and diced
- ½ head cabbage, cored and coarsely chopped
- 8 teaspoons vegetable bouillon base (such as Better Than Bouillon)
- 1 teaspoon salt, or to taste
- ½ teaspoon ground black pepper, or to taste

Directions
- **Step 1**

Turn on a multi-functional pressure cooker (such as Instant Pot) and select Saute function for medium heat. When the display reads "Hot," add olive oil to coat the bottom of the pot. Add beef, oregano, and thyme; cook and stir until browned, breaking it apart as it cooks, 5 to 7 minutes. Add carrot, potato, onion, and garlic. Cook to soften, stirring frequently, about 5 minutes. Turn off Saute mode.
- **Step 2**

Stir water, tomatoes with their juices, cabbage, vegetable base, salt, and pepper into the pot. Stir briefly together.
- **Step 3**

Close and lock the lid. Select high pressure according to manufacturer's instructions; set timer for 20 minutes. Allow 10 to 15 minutes for pressure to build.
- **Step 4**

Release pressure using the natural-release method according to manufacturer's instructions for 15 minutes. Release remaining pressure carefully using the quick-release method according to manufacturer's instructions, about 5 minutes. Unlock and remove the lid; stir. Serve while hot.

Nutrition Facts
Per Serving:
237.1 calories; protein 15.5g 31% DV; carbohydrates 18.5g 6% DV; fat 11.6g 18% DV; cholesterol 47.3mg 16% DV; sodium 626.9mg 25% DV.

Instant Pot Piccata Israeli Couscous

Prep: 10 mins Cook: 15 mins Additional: 5 mins Total: 30 mins

Servings: 4

Ingredients

- 1 tablespoon butter
- 1 teaspoon olive oil
- 2 tablespoons diced shallot
- 1 tablespoon lemon zest
- 1 clove garlic, minced
- 1 cup Israeli couscous
- 1 ½ cups low-sodium chicken broth
- 2 tablespoons fresh lemon juice
- 2 tablespoons capers
- 1 teaspoon caper brine
- 2 tablespoons chopped fresh parsley
- 1 tablespoon grated Parmesan cheese, or more to taste
- 4 wedge (blank)s lemon wedges

Directions
- **Step 1**

Turn on a multi-functional pressure cooker (such as an Instant Pot), and select Saute function. Heat butter and oil until butter is melted. Add shallot, lemon zest, and garlic; cook until garlic is translucent, 1 to 2 minutes. Add couscous and cook, stirring occasionally, until lightly browned and toasted, about 2 minutes. Turn off Saute function.
- **Step 2**

Pour in chicken broth and lemon juice. Close and lock the lid. Select high pressure according to manufacturer's instructions; set timer for 5 minutes. Allow 10 to 15 minutes for pressure to build.

- **Step 3**

Carefully release pressure using the quick-release method according to manufacturer's instructions, about 5 minutes. Unlock and remove the lid, and stir in the capers and caper brine.
- **Step 4**

Garnish with parsley and Parmesan cheese. Serve with lemon wedges.

Nutrition Facts

Per Serving:
60.7 calories; protcin 2.3g 5% DV; carbohydrates 4.1g 1% DV; fat 4.7g 7% DV; cholesterol 10.2mg 3% DV; sodium 234.9mg 9% DV.

Instant Pot Pilau Rice

Prep: 10 mins Cook: 20 mins Additional: 10 mins Total: 40 mins

Servings: 6

Ingredients

- 1 tablespoon vegetable oil
- ½ teaspoon cumin seeds
- ¼ cup diced red onion
- ¾ tablespoon garam masala
- ½ teaspoon ground turmeric
- ½ teaspoon salt
- 1 ½ cups vegetable broth
- 1 cup uncooked basmati rice, rinsed and drained
- ½ cup frozen peas and carrots
- 1 bay leaf

Directions
- **Step 1**

Turn on a multi-functional pressure cooker (such as Instant Pot) and select Saute function. Heat oil in the pot. Add cumin seeds and stir until they just start to pop. Stir in onion and cook until they begin to soften, about 2 minutes. Season with garam masala, turmeric, and salt. Add vegetable broth, rice, frozen peas and carrots, and bay leaf; stir until well combined.
- **Step 2**

Close and lock the lid. Select high pressure according to manufacturer's instructions; set timer for 5 minutes. Allow 10 to 15 minutes for pressure to build.
- **Step 3**

Release pressure using the natural-release method according to manufacturer's instructions, 10 to 40 minutes. Manually release any remaining pressure. Unlock and remove the lid. Remove bay leaf. Taste rice and seasoning if necessary before serving.

Nutrition Facts

Per Serving:
151.2 calories; protein 3.2g 6% DV; carbohydrates 28.5g 9% DV; fat 3.1g 5% DV; cholesterolmg; sodium 321.3mg 13% DV.

Instant Pot Mexican Quinoa

Prep: 15 mins Cook: 15 mins Additional: 10 mins Total: 40 mins

Servings: 4

Ingredients

- 1 tablespoon olive oil
- 1 small onion, chopped
- 1 jalapeno pepper, minced, or to taste
- 3 cloves garlic, chopped
- 1 (15 ounce) can black beans, drained and rinsed
- 1 (14.5 ounce) can fire-roasted diced tomatoes
- ¾ cup corn kernels
- ¾ teaspoon salt, or to taste
- ½ teaspoon ground cumin
- ½ teaspoon smoked paprika
- ¼ teaspoon chili powder
- ⅛ teaspoon black pepper
- 1 cup dry quinoa
- 1 cup vegetable broth, or as needed
- 2 tablespoons chopped cilantro, or to taste
- 1 lime, juiced
- 1 avocado, diced

Directions
- **Step 1**

Turn on a multi-functional pressure cooker (such as Instant Pot) and select Saute function. Add oil, onion, jalapeno pepper, and garlic. Saute until onion is softened, about 2 minutes. Add black beans, tomatoes, and corn; mix well. Season with salt, cumin, paprika, chili powder, and black pepper. Add quinoa and toss until well combined. Pour in broth and mix.
- **Step 2**

Close and lock the lid; set valve to the sealing position. Select high pressure according to manufacturer's instructions; set timer for 1 minute. Allow 10 to 15 minutes for pressure to build.
- **Step 3**

Release pressure using the natural-release method according to manufacturer's instructions, 10 to 40 minutes. Open the pot and fluff quinoa using a fork. Add cilantro and lime juice. Stir in avocado.

Nutrition Facts
Per Serving:
442.1 calories; protein 16g 32% DV; carbohydrates 66g 21% DV; fat 14.2g 22% DV; cholesterolmg; sodium 1245mg 50% DV.

Instant Pot Beef Stew with Frozen Meat

Prep: 25 mins Cook: 1 hr 5 mins Additional: 15 mins Total: 1 hr 45 mins

Servings: 8

Ingredients

- 2 tablespoons avocado oil
- 1 large onion, finely diced
- 3 cloves garlic, finely chopped
- ¼ cup dry red wine
- 2 cups beef broth
- 1 teaspoon dried thyme

- 1 teaspoon dried parsley
- 1 teaspoon dried oregano
- 1 bay leaf
- 1 teaspoon salt, or to taste
- ½ teaspoon freshly ground black pepper, or to taste
- 1 tablespoon tomato paste
- 2 (1 pound) packages cubed beef stew meat, frozen
- 6 medium carrots, sliced
- 5 large potatoes, peeled and cut into large cubes
- 3 stalks celery, sliced
- 2 tablespoons water
- 1 tablespoon cornstarch

Directions
- **Step 1**

Turn on a multi-functional pressure cooker (such as Instant Pot) and select Saute function. Pour in oil. Cook onions and garlic in the hot oil until soft and translucent, about 5 minutes. Pour in wine and continue sauteing until wine has reduced by half, 4 to 5 minutes.
- **Step 2**

Add beef broth, thyme, parsley, oregano, bay leaf, salt, and pepper; stir to combine. Mix in tomato paste. Place frozen meat into the pot and add carrots, potatoes, and celery. Close and lock the lid. Select Meat/Stew function and set timer for 45 minutes. Allow 10 to 15 minutes for pressure to build.
- **Step 3**

Release pressure using the natural-release method according to manufacturer's instructions, about 10 minutes. Carefully move the vent to release the remainder of the pressure, about 5 minutes. Unlock and remove the lid.
- **Step 4**

Mix water and cornstarch together in a small bowl and pour slowly into the pot. Press the Saute button and cook stew until slightly thickened, about 3 minutes.

Nutrition Facts
Per Serving:
586.3 calories; protein 36.3g 73% DV; carbohydrates 49.1g 16% DV; fat 26.4g 41% DV; cholesterol 98.6mg 33% DV; sodium 634.7mg 25% DV

Instant Pot Venison Chili

Prep: 10 mins Cook: 40 mins Additional: 5 mins Total: 55 mins

Servings: 6

Ingredients

- 1 ½ pounds ground venison
- 1 medium onion, chopped
- 2 eaches jalapeno peppers, seeded and chopped
- 2 (15.5 ounce) cans chili beans, undrained
- 1 (28 ounce) can crushed tomatoes
- 1 (15.5 ounce) can kidney beans, drained
- 1 cup water
- 1 tablespoon chili powder
- 2 teaspoons ground cumin
- ½ teaspoon dried oregano
- ¼ teaspoon garlic powder
- ¼ teaspoon onion powder

Directions
- **Step 1**

Turn on a multi-functional pressure cooker (such as Instant Pot) and select Low Saute function. Add venison and cook for 5 minutes, breaking it up with a spoon as it cooks. Add onion and jalapeno peppers; cook and stir until softened, about 3 minutes. Cancel Saute mode.
- **Step 2**

Add chili beans, crushed tomatoes, kidney beans, water, chili powder, cumin, oregano, garlic powder, and onion powder to the pot. Close and lock the lid. Select high pressure according to manufacturer's instructions; set timer for 20 minutes. Allow 10 to 15 minutes for pressure to build.
- **Step 3**

Release pressure carefully using the quick-release method according to manufacturer's instructions, about 5 minutes. Unlock and remove the lid.

Nutrition Facts
Per Serving:
367.5 calories; protein 37.8g 76% DV; carbohydrates 50.4g 16% DV; fat 4.7g 7% DV; cholesterol 86.2mg 29% DV; sodium 1037.6mg 42% DV.

Instant Pot Cream of Asparagus Soup

Prep: 10 mins Cook: 15 mins Additional: 20 mins Total: 45 mins

Servings: 4

Ingredients

- 1 tablespoon olive oil
- 4 slices bacon, diced
- ½ onion, diced
- 3 cloves garlic, minced
- 2 pounds asparagus, cut into 1 1/2-inch pieces
- 2 ½ cups chicken broth
- 1 teaspoon salt
- ½ teaspoon ground black pepper
- 1 cup heavy whipping cream

Directions
- **Step 1**

Turn on a multi-functional pressure cooker (such as Instant Pot), select Saute function, and add olive oil. Add bacon to warmed oil and saute for 2 minutes. Stir in onion and continue cooking until onion is soft and translucent, about 5 minutes. Add garlic and asparagus. Cook 1 to 2 minutes.
- **Step 2**

Pour chicken broth over asparagus mixture and bring to a boil. Turn Saute mode off and press the Manual mode. Close and lock the lid. Select High pressure according to manufacturer's instructions; set timer for 5 minutes. Allow 10 to 15 minutes for pressure to build.
- **Step 3**

Release pressure using the natural-release method according to manufacturer's instructions, 10 to 40 minutes. Unlock and remove the lid.
- **Step 4**

Puree asparagus mixture with an immersion blender until smooth. Mix in cream and select Saute function. Cook until soup is warmed through, but not boiling. Taste and season with salt and pepper.

Nutrition Facts
Per Serving:
355.9 calories; protein 10.8g 22% DV; carbohydrates 14.9g 5% DV; fat 29.8g 46% DV; cholesterol 95.2mg 32% DV; sodium 1545.4mg 62% DV.

Instant Pot Sweet Baby Back Ribs

Prep: 10 mins Cook: 45 mins Additional: 20 mins Total: 1 hr 15 mins
Servings: 8

Ingredients

2 racks baby back pork ribs
Dry Rub:
- ¼ cup dark brown sugar
- 2 tablespoons garlic salt (such as Lawry's)
- 2 tablespoons chili powder
Cooking Liquid:
- 1 cup beef broth
- 12 fluid ounces root beer
- 2 tablespoons apple cider vinegar

- 1 teaspoon ground black pepper
- 1 teaspoon cayenne pepper, or to taste

- 1 teaspoon liquid smoke flavoring
- 1 cup barbecue sauce (such as Sweet Baby Ray's), or more to taste

Directions
- **Step 1**

Use a butter knife to cut into an edge of the rib racks. Use a paper towel to grab and lift off the silvery membranes.
- **Step 2**

Combine brown sugar, garlic salt, chili powder, black pepper, and cayenne pepper in bowl. Coat the ribs generously with the dry rub.
- **Step 3**

Place the trivet inside the Instant Pot . Pour in broth, root beer, vinegar, and liquid smoke. Place ribs on the trivet on their sides, with one inside the other. Close and lock the lid and make sure the vent is sealed. Select manual high pressure and set the timer for 30 minutes. Allow 10 to 15 minutes for pressure to build.
- **Step 4**

Release pressure using the natural-release method according to manufacturer's instructions for 15 minutes. Release remaining pressure carefully using the quick-release method according to manufacturer's instructions, about 5 minutes. Unlock and remove the lid.
- **Step 5**

Set an oven rack about 6 inches from the heat source and preheat the oven's broiler on the highest heat setting. Place a rack 6 inches from the heat source.
- **Step 6**

Transfer ribs to a broiling pan and generously coat with barbecue sauce.
- **Step 7**

Cook in the broiler until barbeque sauce is bubbly and caramelized, 5 to 7 minutes.

Nutrition Facts
Per Serving:
384.7 calories; protein 18.8g 38% DV; carbohydrates 24.8g 8% DV; fat 23.1g 36% DV; cholesterol 87.8mg 29% DV; sodium 1910.9mg 76% DV.

Instant Pot Celery Soup

Prep: 20 mins Cook: 25 mins Additional: 15 mins Total: 1 hr

Servings: 4

Ingredients

- 2 tablespoons olive oil
- 2 pounds celery, sliced
- 1 large onion, sliced
- 3 cloves garlic, sliced
- ½ pound potatoes, peeled and chopped
- 4 cups vegetable broth
- ¼ teaspoon salt
- ⅛ teaspoon ground black pepper

Directions
- **Step 1**

Combine olive oil, celery, onion, and garlic in a multi-functional pressure cooker (such as Instant Pot). Select Saute function and cook, stirring occasionally, for 5 minutes. Add potatoes, broth, salt, and pepper and stir. Close and lock the lid and set the steamer valve to Sealing.
- **Step 2**

Select high pressure according to manufacturer's instructions; set timer for 10 minutes. Allow 10 to 15 minutes for pressure to build.
- **Step 3**

Release pressure using the natural-release method according to manufacturer's instructions, about 15 minutes. Unlock and remove the lid.
- **Step 4**

Use an electric hand mixer or blender to puree the soup until smooth. Serve while warm or let cool and serve as a chilled soup on a hot day.

Nutrition Facts
Per Serving:
188.2 calories; protein 4.3g 9% DV; carbohydrates 25.9g 8% DV; fat 7.7g 12% DV; cholesterolmg; sodium 792.4mg 32% DV.

Instant Pot Orange Chicken

Prep: 15 mins Cook: 35 mins Additional: 20 mins Total: 1 hr 10 mins

Servings: 8

Ingredients

- 3 pounds skinless, boneless chicken
- 2 tablespoons oil

- ¾ cup orange juice
- 1 (8 ounce) can tomato sauce
- ¼ cup white sugar
- ¼ cup blackstrap molasses
- ¼ cup soy sauce
- 4 cloves garlic, minced
- 1 orange, zested and juiced, divided
- 1 tablespoon grated fresh ginger
- 1 tablespoon rice wine
- 3 tablespoons cornstarch

Directions
- **Step 1**

Blot chicken with paper towels until completely dry. Cut into 1- to 2-inch chunks.
- **Step 2**

Turn on a multi-functional pressure cooker (such as Instant Pot), select Saute function, and click to to the highest heat. When the pot is hot, add oil and heat until shimmering. Add chicken and saute until it starts to get golden, stirring constantly so it doesn't stick to the bottom of the pot, for 2 to 3 minutes. Pour 3/4 cup orange juice into the pot and bring to a boil while scraping all the browned bits of food off the bottom of the pan with a wooden spoon.
- **Step 3**

Add tomato sauce, sugar, molasses, soy sauce, garlic, orange zest, ginger, and rice wine; gently stir until all **Ingredients** are combined and coated in sauce. Cancel Saute function.
- **Step 4**

Close and lock the lid, and make sure the vent is closed. Select high pressure according to manufacturer's instructions; set timer for 5 minutes. Allow 10 to 15 minutes for pressure to build.
- **Step 5**

Allow the Instant Pot to remain on for 10 minutes with the Keep Warm function. Release pressure carefully using the quick-release method according to manufacturer's instructions, about 5 minutes. Unlock and remove the lid. Select Saute function and click to to the lowest heat.
- **Step 6**

Combine 3 tablespoons freshly squeezed orange juice with cornstarch in a medium bowl; whisk until combined with no lumps. Add to the Instant Pot and stir to combine. Cook, stirring gently, until sauce thickens, about 3 minutes. Simmer for 2 to 3 minutes more.
- **Step 7**

Cancel Saute function and let stand until sauce thickens further, 5 to 7 minutes. Serve.

Nutrition Facts
Per Serving:
296.2 calories; protein 34.3g 69% DV; carbohydrates 22.3g 7% DV; fat 7g 11% DV; cholesterol 87.9mg 29% DV; sodium 674.3mg 27% DV.

Instant Pot Creamy Vanilla Rice Pudding

Prep: 5 mins Cook: 30 mins Additional: 10 mins Total: 45 mins

Servings: 8

Ingredients

- 3 cups cooked short-grain rice
- 2 ¼ cups milk, divided
- ½ cup white sugar
- ¼ teaspoon salt
- 2 eaches egg yolks, whisked well
- ¼ cup heavy cream

- 1 teaspoon vanilla extract

- 1 pinch ground cinnamon, or as needed

Directions

- **Step 1**

Combine cooked rice, 2 cups milk, sugar, and salt in a multi-functional pressure cooker (such as Instant Pot) and stir well. Close and lock the lid. Select porridge function according to manufacturer's instructions and seal the vent. Set timer for 20 minutes. Allow 10 to 15 minutes for pressure to build.

- **Step 2**

Release pressure using the natural-release method according to manufacturer's instructions, 10 to 40 minutes. Unlock and carefully remove the lid.

- **Step 3**

Whisk egg yolks together well in a bowl. Add a small amount of cooked porridge and whisk quickly into yolks. Pour mixture into the pot and stir to combine well with rice. Add heavy cream, remaining milk, and vanilla extract. Stir to combine completely.

- **Step 4**

Serve rice pudding in individual bowls garnished with cinnamon.

Nutrition Facts

Per Serving:
214 calories; protein 4.7g 10% DV; carbohydrates 36.3g 12% DV; fat 5.3g 8% DV; cholesterol 66.9mg 22% DV; sodium 105.7mg 4% DV.

Instant Pot Gyros

Prep: 5 mins Cook: 55 mins Additional: 5 mins Total: 1 hr 5 mins

Servings: 16

Ingredients

- 4 pounds pork butt, cut into 2-inch cubes
- 3 tablespoons Greek seasoning (such as Cavender's)
- 1 teaspoon paprika

- 2 cloves garlic, minced
- 1 cup chicken broth
- 2 teaspoons olive oil

Directions

- **Step 1**

Turn on a multi-functional pressure cooker (such as Instant Pot) and select the Saute function. Place cubed pork in the pot and cook until starting to brown, about 5 minutes. Turn pot off.

- **Step 2**

Add Greek seasoning, paprika, garlic, and chicken broth to the pot with the pork. Close and lock the lid. Select Manual and set timer for 35 minutes. Allow 10 minutes for pressure to build.

- **Step 3**

Release pressure carefully using the quick-release method according to manufacturer's instructions, about 5 minutes. Unlock and remove the lid.

- **Step 4**

Heat oil in a large skillet over medium-high heat. Transfer pork to the skillet using a slotted spoon and cook for 5 minutes or until most of the liquid has evaporated and pork has a nice crisp on it.

Nutrition Facts
Per Serving:
249.9 calories; protein 14.8g 30% DV; carbohydrates 1.2g; fat 20.7g 32% DV; cholesterol 65.2mg 22% DV; sodium 1654.1mg 66% DV.

Instant Pot Bang Bang Shrimp Pasta

Prep: 10 mins Cook: 25 mins Additional: 5 mins Total: 40 mins

Servings: 6

Ingredients

- 1 pound dry spaghetti
- 4 cups water
- 2 cloves garlic, minced
- 1 tablespoon olive oil
- 1 teaspoon salt
- 1 pound large shrimp, peeled and deveined
- ¾ cup mayonnaise
- ¾ cup Thai sweet red chili sauce
- ¼ cup lime juice
- 1 teaspoon chile-garlic sauce (such as Sriracha)
- 2 eaches green onions, chopped

Directions
- **Step 1**

Break spaghetti noodles in half and place in a multi-functional pressure cooker (such as Instant Pot). Add water, garlic, olive oil, and salt. Close and lock the lid. Select high pressure according to manufacturer's instructions; set timer for 6 minutes. Allow 10 to 15 minutes for pressure to build.
- **Step 2**

Release pressure carefully using the quick-release method according to manufacturer's instructions, about 5 minutes. Unlock and remove the lid.
- **Step 3**

Combine shrimp, mayonnaise, chili sauce, lime juice, and Sriracha in a bowl; mix until well coated. Pour into the pot and select Saute function. Add chopped green onions and cook until shrimp are pink and green onions are tender, about 7 minutes.

Nutrition Facts
Per Serving:
612.2 calories; protein 22.6g 45% DV; carbohydrates 71.9g 23% DV; fat 26.1g 40% DV; cholesterol 125.5mg 42% DV; sodium 1061.4mg 43% DV.

Instant Pot Chocolate Cheesecake

Prep:25 mins Cook: 1 hr 3 mins Additional: 7 hrs 20 mins Total: 8 hrs 48 mins

Servings: 10

Ingredients

Crust:
- 2 (4.8 ounce) packages graham crackers, crushed
- 5 tablespoons butter

Filling:
- 1 (8 ounce) package cream cheese, softened
- 1 (8 ounce) package Neufchatel cheese, softened
- ¾ cup white sugar
- 2 large eggs eggs

Glaze:
- 1 (12 ounce) package frozen sweet cherries
- 2 tablespoons apricot jam
- 2 tablespoons white sugar

- 1 pinch kosher salt

- 2 teaspoons vanilla extract
- ¼ cup heavy whipping cream
- 1 (8 ounce) package semisweet chocolate chips
- 2 tablespoons all-purpose flour

- 1 tablespoon water
- 1 tablespoon cornstarch

Directions

- **Step 1**

Wrap the bottom and sides of an 8-inch springform pan with aluminum foil.

- **Step 2**

Combine graham cracker crumbs, butter, and salt in a bowl; mix thoroughly. Pour into the prepared pan; press tightly onto the bottom and up the sides of the pan using the bottom of a measuring cup. Freeze crust until firm, 10 to 15 minutes.

- **Step 3**

Beat cream cheese, Neufchatel cheese, and 3/4 cup sugar in a bowl with an electric mixer until creamy, about 4 minutes. Beat in eggs one at a time; add vanilla. Beat in heavy cream.

- **Step 4**

Melt chocolate chips in a microwave-safe glass or ceramic bowl in 15-second intervals, stirring after each melting, 1 to 2 minutes. Beat melted chocolate into the cream cheese mixture. Fold in flour.

- **Step 5**

Pour chocolate cream cheese mixture over the chilled crust. Cover tightly with aluminum foil.

- **Step 6**

Pour 1 1/2 cup water into the pot of an electric pressure cooker (such as Instant Pot). Place the steam rack in the pot; set springform pan on top. Close and lock the lid. Set timer for 45 minutes. Set to high pressure according to manufacturer's instructions, 10 to 15 minutes.

- **Step 7**

Release pressure naturally according to manufacturer's instructions, 10 to 12 minutes. Cool cheesecake to room temperature, about 1 hour.

- **Step 8**

Combine cherries, apricot jam, and 2 tablespoons sugar in a saucepan over medium heat. Simmer until cherries are heated through and release some of their juices, 5 to 7 minutes.

- **Step 9**

Mix water and cornstarch in a small bowl until smooth. Stir into the cherry mixture until thick and glossy, 2 to 3 minutes. Remove from heat; cool glaze to room temperature.

- **Step 10**

Pour glaze over cheesecake and refrigerate until firm, at least 6 hours or overnight. Remove the springform ring and transfer cheesecake to a serving platter.

Cook's Notes:

Substitute evaporated milk for the cream if desired.
I couldn't get the trivet to fit, so I used a small metal bowl upside down inside the pot as a "support" for the springform pan. Worked great!

Nutrition Facts

Per Serving:
567.8 calories; protein 9.4g 19% DV; carbohydrates 64.8g 21% DV; fat 32g 49% DV; cholesterol 102.3mg 34% DV; sodium 419.7mg 17% DV.

Instant Pot Dark Chocolate Brownies

Prep:15 mins Cook: 40 mins Additional: 20 mins Total:1 hr 15 mins

Servings: 4

Ingredients

- 5 ounces dark chocolate (such as Lindt 78% Cocoa), chopped into small pieces
- 6 tablespoons unsalted butter
- 1 cup superfine sugar
- 2 tablespoons Greek yogurt
- 1 tablespoon vanilla extract
- 3 large eggs eggs
- ¾ cup all-purpose flour
- 1 tablespoon unsweetened cocoa powder
- 1 teaspoon baking soda
- ½ teaspoon salt

Directions

- **Step 1**

Heat chocolate and butter in a glass bowl placed inside a saucepan of simmering water. Stir frequently, scraping down the sides with a rubber spatula to avoid scorching, until chocolate is melted and glossy, about 5 minutes.

- **Step 2**

Let melted chocolate cool to room temperature, about 10 minutes. Add sugar; whisk thoroughly. Mix in yogurt and vanilla extract until combined. Beat in eggs 1 at a time using the whisk. Sift in flour, cocoa powder, baking soda, and salt; gently fold into the chocolate mixture until batter is thick and smooth. Do not overmix.

- **Step 3**

Butter a 6-inch round cake pan with 2-inch sides. Pour batter into the pan and seal top with a sheet of aluminum foil.

- **Step 4**

Set a trivet inside the pot of an electric pressure cooker (such as Instant Pot). Add 1 cup water. Make sure the steam release handle is in Sealing position according to manufacturers' instructions. Arrange long strips of aluminum foil crosswise under the cake pan; hold the ends to lower cake onto the trivet. Keep foil strips folded down to prevent contact with the lid.

- **Step 5**

Close and lock the lid. Select high pressure according to manufacturer's instructions; set timer for 25 minutes. Allow 10 to 15 minutes for pressure to build. Release pressure

using the natural-release method according to manufacturer's instructions, about 10 minutes.
*   **Step 6**
Check a toothpick inserted into the brownie comes out clean. Cook at high pressure for 3 minutes more if needed. Release pressure using the quick-release method, about 5 minutes. Let brownie cool before cutting.

Cook's Notes:
Sour cream can be substituted for the Greek yogurt, if desired.
If you like, you can add chopped walnuts/chocolate chunks at the end of •**Step 2**.

Nutrition Facts
Per Serving:
693.9 calories; protein 9.9g 20% DV; carbohydrates 90.6g 29% DV; fat 33.5g 52% DV; cholesterol 188.5mg 63% DV; sodium 667.9mg 27% DV.

Instant Pot Curried Chicken Thighs

Prep:10 mins Cook: 50 mins Additional: 15 mins Total:1 hr 15 mins

Servings: 4

Ingredients

*   4 (6 ounce) chicken thighs
*   2 teaspoons mild yellow curry powder (such as Savory Spice)
*   1 teaspoon honey powder (such as Savory Spice)
*   ¾ teaspoon salt
*   ½ teaspoon ground black pepper
*   2 tablespoons olive oil
*   1 tablespoon butter
*   1 small onion, cut in half and thinly sliced
*   4 cloves garlic, minced
*   1 tablespoon minced fresh ginger root
*   1 (14.5 ounce) can diced tomatoes
*   1 tablespoon tomato powder
*   ½ cup coconut milk
*   1 teaspoon ground cumin
*   1 tablespoon mild yellow curry powder (such as Savory Spice)

Directions
*   **Step 1**
Season chicken thighs with 2 teaspoons curry powder, honey powder, salt, and black pepper.
*   **Step 2**
Turn on a multi-functional pressure cooker (such as Instant Pot) and select Saute function. Heat oil and butter. Add chicken and cook until browned, 2 to 3 minutes per side. Transfer to a plate. Add onion; cook and stir until soft and translucent, about 5 minutes. Add garlic and ginger; cook until fragrant, about 2 minutes. Return chicken to Instant Pot . Add tomatoes and tomato powder. Close and lock the lid.
*   **Step 3**
Select high pressure according to manufacturer's instructions; set timer for 20 minutes. Allow 10 to 15 minutes for pressure to build.
*   **Step 4**
Release pressure using the natural-release method according to manufacturer's instructions, for 10 minutes. Switch to the quick-release method according to

manufacturer's instructions and release remaining pressure for about 5 minutes. Unlock and remove the lid.
- **Step 5**

Turn on Saute function. Add coconut milk, cumin, and remaining curry powder to the pot. Cook until sauce has thickened, about 5 minutes.

Cook's Note:
I love using tomato powder as it has a robust taste, and while tomato paste may be used, I prefer tomato powder as I don't have to worry about leftover tomato paste. Honey powder is dehydrated honey, and while honey may be used I prefer honey powder as it is not sticky. Both may be found at the Savory spice shop, or your local grocer may carry them.

Nutrition Facts
Per Serving:
471.6 calories; protein 31g 62% DV; carbohydrates 11.2g 4% DV; fat 33.8g 52% DV; cholesterol 113.4mg 38% DV; sodium 721.3mg 29% DV.

Instant Pot Asparagus Risotto

Prep:10 mins Cook:30 mins Additional: 10 mins Total:50 mins

Servings: 4

Ingredients

- 3 tablespoons unsalted butter
- 2 eaches shallots, finely chopped
- 2 cloves garlic, minced
- 1 pound asparagus spears, trimmed and cut into 1-inch pieces
- ½ cup dry white wine
- 1 ½ cups Arborio rice
- 3 ½ cups chicken broth
- ½ cup heavy cream
- ½ teaspoon salt
- ¼ teaspoon ground black pepper
- ¼ teaspoon dried thyme
- ½ cup shredded Parmesan cheese
- 2 tablespoons lemon juice

Directions
- **Step 1**

Turn on a multi-functional pressure cooker (such as Instant Pot) and select Saute function. Add butter and melt. Stir in shallots and garlic; cook for 2 minutes. Remove shallots and garlic with a slotted spoon and set aside. Add asparagus and saute in butter for 2 minutes; remove and set aside on a plate.
- **Step 2**

Return shallots and garlic to the Instant Pot and pour in wine. Stir well, scraping the bottom of the pot with a wooden or plastic spoon, for 30 seconds. Stir in rice and saute in the wine mixture for 2 1/2 minutes, stirring constantly and scraping the bottom of the pot to loosen any brown bits. Stir in chicken broth, cream, salt, pepper, and thyme. Cancel Saute function.
- **Step 3**

Close and lock the lid. Select high pressure according to manufacturer's instructions; set timer for 6 minutes. Allow 10 to 15 minutes for pressure to build.
- **Step 4**

Release pressure carefully using the quick-release method according to manufacturer's instructions, about 5 minutes. Unlock and remove the lid. Gradually stir in Parmesan cheese and lemon juice, stirring until cheese is melted. Stir in reserved asparagus pieces. Allow risotto to thicken in the pot, uncovered, for 3 to 4 minutes before serving.

Nutrition Facts
Per Serving:
611.4 calories; protein 14.5g 29% DV; carbohydrates 81.3g 26% DV; fat 23.1g 36% DV; cholesterol 76.2mg 25% DV; sodium 1498.2mg 60% DV.

Instant Pot Chilorio

Prep: 25 mins Cook: 30 mins Additional: 25 mins Total:1 hr 20 mins

Servings: 10

Ingredients

- 2 ½ pounds pork shoulder, trimmed and cut into 1-inch cubes
- 4 eaches oranges, juiced
- 1 (14.25 ounce) can low-sodium chicken broth
- 1 onion, sliced and separated into rings
- 1 teaspoon dried oregano
- 3 peppers dried ancho chiles (poblanos), stemmed and torn into small pieces

- 2 cups boiling water
- ¼ cup apple cider vinegar
- 1 jalapeno, seeded and chopped
- 2 garlic clove (blank)s garlic cloves
- 2 tablespoons chopped cilantro
- ¼ teaspoon ground cumin

Directions
- **Step 1**

Combine pork, orange juice, broth, onion, and oregano in the inner pot of an electric pressure cooker (such as Instant Pot). Close and lock the lid. Select high pressure according to manufacturer's instructions; set timer for 20 minutes. Allow 10 to 15 minutes for pressure to build.
- **Step 2**

Release pressure using the natural-release method according to manufacturer's instructions, 10 to 40 minutes. Unlock and remove lid.
- **Step 3**

Remove pork from the pot and drain. Transfer to a serving dish.
- **Step 4**

Place ancho chiles in a heat-proof bowl. Pour boiling water over chiles and soak for 15 minutes. Drain chiles, reserving soaking water.
- **Step 5**

Combine 1/2 cup chile soaking water, soaked ancho chiles, apple cider vinegar, jalapeno pepper, garlic, cilantro, and cumin in a blender. Blend to form a thick sauce. Pour sauce over pork and mix well.

You can get a second wind out of your Instant Pot Chilorio with these Torta Sandwiches by user Betty Soup:

Stir together 1 thinly sliced red onion, 3 tablespoons cider vinegar, and 1 teaspoon sugar in a small bowl. Let stand at least 1 hour. Drain. Reheat 1 1/3 cups pork and sauce, covered, in a 2-quart saucepan over medium heat, 5 to 7 minutes. Mash 1 avocado and spread over the bottom half of 4 toasted buns. Top each bun with 1/3 cup pork and sauce and red onion mixture.

Nutrition Facts
Per Serving:
309.1 calories; protein 16.6g 33% DV; carbohydrates 14.9g 5% DV; fat 20.7g 32% DV; cholesterol 65.5mg 22% DV; sodium 1339.7mg 54% DV.

Instant Pot Sweet Potato Chipotle Soup

Prep:20 mins Cook: 25 mins Additional: 5 mins Total: 50 mins

Servings: 4

Ingredients

- 2 tablespoons olive oil
- 1 small onion, chopped
- 2 cloves garlic, chopped
- 1 ½ pounds sweet potatoes, peeled and cut into 1 1/2-inch pieces
- 1 teaspoon smoked paprika
- 1 teaspoon ground chipotle pepper, or more to taste
- 1 pinch salt to taste
- 3 teaspoons vegetable bouillon base (such as Better Than Bouillon)
- 3 cups hot water
- ½ cup fresh orange juice
- ⅓ cup heavy cream

 Directions
 • **Step 1**
Turn on a multi-functional pressure cooker (such as Instant Pot) and select Saute function; heat olive oil. Saute onion and garlic for 1 to 2 minutes. Add sweet potatoes, smoked paprika, chipotle pepper, and salt. Stir for 1 minute then turn cooker off.
 • **Step 2**
Dissolve vegetable bouillon in hot water. Pour into the pot with orange juice and scrape up any browned bits from the bottom of the pot. Close and lock the lid. Select high pressure according to manufacturer's instructions; set timer for 10 minutes. Allow 10 to 15 minutes for pressure to build.
 • **Step 3**
Release pressure carefully using the quick-release method according to manufacturer's instructions, about 5 minutes. Unlock and remove the lid.
 • **Step 4**
Blend soup using an immersion blender until smooth. Stir in heavy cream. Taste and salt if needed.

Cook's Notes:
Substitute coconut milk for the cream to make it vegan.
Feel free to use any vegetable stock.
If you do not have an immersion blender, blend soup in a blender in batches.

Nutrition Facts
Per Serving:
299.5 calories; protein 3.7g 7% DV; carbohydrates 40.5g 13% DV; fat 14.3g 22% DV; cholesterol 27.2mg 9% DV; sodium 150.9mg 6% DV

Instant Pot Salsa Verde

Prep:5 mins Cook: 20 mins Additional: 15 mins Total:40 mins

Servings: 32
Ingredients

- 1 ¼ pounds tomatillos, husked and quartered
- 2 large jalapenos, halved lengthwise
- 1 medium onion, peeled and quartered
- ¼ cup water

- 2 teaspoons minced garlic
- ¼ cup firmly packed fresh cilantro
- 1 tablespoon lime juice
- 1 teaspoon salt

Directions
- **Step 1**

Combine tomatillos, jalapenos, onion, water, and garlic in the inner pot of a multi-functional pressure cooker (such as Instant Pot). Close and lock the lid. Select high pressure according to manufacturer's instructions; set timer for 10 minutes. Allow 10 to 15 minutes for pressure to build.
- **Step 2**

Release pressure carefully using the quick-release method according to manufacturer's instructions, about 5 minutes. Unlock and remove the lid. Let cool for 10 minutes.
- **Step 3**

Stir in cilantro, lime juice, and salt. Blend until smooth using an immersion blender.
- **Step 4**

Transfer mixture to 2 pint-sized canning jars with lids. Refrigerate until cool and thickened.

Cook's Note:
You can control the heat of the salsa verde by choosing how many seeds of the jalapenos you use (if any).

Nutrition Facts
Per Serving:
7.8 calories; protein 0.2g 1% DV; carbohydrates 1.5g 1% DV; fat 0.2g; cholesterolmg; sodium 73.3mg 3% DV.

Instant Pot Colorado Chile Verde

Prep:15 mins Cook: 50 mins Additional: 15 mins Total:1 hr 20 mins

Servings: 8

Ingredients

- 1 tablespoon olive oil
- 1 pound chicken breasts, cubed, or more to taste
- ½ large onion, diced
- 2 eaches roasted Hatch chile peppers - seeded, de-veined, and diced, or more to taste
- 3 cloves garlic, minced
- 1 tablespoon ground cumin
- ½ teaspoon salt
- ½ teaspoon freshly ground black pepper
- 2 cups chicken broth
- 1 (16 ounce) jar salsa verde (green salsa)
- 1 (15.5 ounce) can white beans, drained and rinsed
- 2 ears corn, kernels cut from cob
- ¼ cup minced cilantro
- ¼ cup all-purpose flour
- 1 tablespoon potato starch
- 2 tablespoons cold water
- 1 lime, cut into wedges

Directions

- **Step 1**

Turn on a multi-functional pressure cooker (such as Instant Pot), select Saute function, and add olive oil. Add chicken breast, onion, chile peppers, garlic, cumin, salt, and pepper to hot oil. Saute until chicken is browned and onions are soft and translucent, about 5 minutes. Add chicken broth, salsa verde, white beans, corn kernels, and cilantro; mix well. Turn off Saute mode.

- **Step 2**

Close and lock the lid. Select high pressure according to manufacturer's instructions; set timer for 30 minutes. Allow 10 to 15 minutes for pressure to build.

- **Step 3**

Release pressure using the natural-release method according to manufacturer's instructions, about 15 minutes. Unlock and remove the lid. Select Saute function. Stir in flour and cook chile until it thickens, 1 to 2 minutes. If you like a thicker consistency, mix potato starch and water in a small bowl and stir into chile with the flour. Serve with lime wedges.

Nutrition Facts

Per Serving:
337.2 calories; protein 26.8g 54% DV; carbohydrates 48.6g 16% DV; fat 4.2g 6% DV; cholesterol 33.8mg 11% DV; sodium 666.4mg 27% DV

Instant Pot Beef Panang Curry

Prep: 10 mins Cook: 25 mins Additional: 15 mins Total: 50 mins

Servings: 4

Ingredients

- 2 teaspoons vegetable oil
- 2 tablespoons Panang-style red curry paste
- 1 pound beef top sirloin, thinly sliced
- ¾ cup coconut milk, or as needed
- 1 medium onion, sliced
- 1 green bell pepper, sliced
- 1 red bell pepper, sliced

- 1 tablespoon peanut butter
- 1 tablespoon coconut sugar
- ½ tablespoon fish sauce
- ⅓ cup finely chopped Thai basil

Directions
- **Step 1**

Turn on a multi-functional pressure cooker (such as Instant Pot) and select Saute function. Add oil and curry paste to the hot pot; cook and stir for 1 minute. Add sirloin strips and saute for 2 to 3 minutes. Mix in coconut milk. Cancel Saute mode. Close and lock the lid.
- **Step 2**

Select high pressure according to manufacturer's instructions; set timer for 5 minutes. Allow 10 to 15 minutes for pressure to build.
- **Step 3**

Release pressure using the natural-release method according to manufacturer's instructions, for 10 minutes. Release remaining pressure carefully using the quick-release method according to manufacturer's instructions, about 5 minutes.
- **Step 4**

Unlock and remove the lid. Select Saute function. Mix in onion, bell peppers, peanut butter, coconut sugar, and fish sauce. Simmer until flavors are well combined, about 5 minutes. Taste and add more coconut milk if curry is too spicy. Sprinkle with Thai basil before serving.

Nutrition Facts
Per Serving:
293.8 calories; protein 26.1g 52% DV; carbohydrates 12.2g 4% DV; fat 21.7g 33% DV; cholesterol 38.9mg 13% DV; sodium 352.4mg 14% DV

Instant Pot Orange Chicken

Prep:15 mins Cook: 35 mins Additional: 20 mins Total: 1 hr 10 mins

Servings:8

Ingredients

- 3 pounds skinless, boneless chicken
- 2 tablespoons oil
- ¾ cup orange juice
- 1 (8 ounce) can tomato sauce
- ¼ cup white sugar
- ¼ cup blackstrap molasses
- ¼ cup soy sauce
- 4 cloves garlic, minced
- 1 orange, zested and juiced, divided
- 1 tablespoon grated fresh ginger
- 1 tablespoon rice wine
- 3 tablespoons cornstarch

Directions
- **Step 1**

Blot chicken with paper towels until completely dry. Cut into 1- to 2-inch chunks.
- **Step 2**

Turn on a multi-functional pressure cooker (such as Instant Pot), select Saute function, and click to to the highest heat. When the pot is hot, add oil and heat until shimmering. Add chicken and saute until it starts to get golden, stirring constantly so it doesn't stick to the bottom of the pot, for 2 to 3 minutes. Pour 3/4 cup orange juice into the pot and bring

to a boil while scraping all the browned bits of food off the bottom of the pan with a wooden spoon.
- **Step 3**

Add tomato sauce, sugar, molasses, soy sauce, garlic, orange zest, ginger, and rice wine; gently stir until all **Ingredients** are combined and coated in sauce. Cancel Saute function.
- **Step 4**

Close and lock the lid, and make sure the vent is closed. Select high pressure according to manufacturer's instructions; set timer for 5 minutes. Allow 10 to 15 minutes for pressure to build.
- **Step 5**

Allow the Instant Pot to remain on for 10 minutes with the Keep Warm function. Release pressure carefully using the quick-release method according to manufacturer's instructions, about 5 minutes. Unlock and remove the lid. Select Saute function and click to to the lowest heat.
- **Step 6**

Combine 3 tablespoons freshly squeezed orange juice with cornstarch in a medium bowl; whisk until combined with no lumps. Add to the Instant Pot and stir to combine. Cook, stirring gently, until sauce thickens, about 3 minutes. Simmer for 2 to 3 minutes more.
- **Step 7**

Cancel Saute function and let stand until sauce thickens further, 5 to 7 minutes. Serve.

Nutrition Facts
Per Serving:
296.2 calories; protein 34.3g 69% DV; carbohydrates 22.3g 7% DV; fat 7g 11% DV; cholesterol 87.9mg 29% DV; sodium 674.3mg 27% DV.

Instant Pot Coconut-Orange Rice Pudding

Prep:10 mins Cook: 6 mins Additional: 10 mins Total: 26 mins

Servings: 4

Ingredients

- 2 cups unsweetened vanilla-flavored almond milk, divided
- 1 cup orange juice
- 1 cup Arborio rice
- ¼ teaspoon salt
- 1 egg, lightly beaten
- 1 teaspoon orange extract
- ⅓ cup cream of coconut (such as Coco Lopez)
- 1 teaspoon grated orange zest

Directions
- **Step 1**

Combine 1 3/4 cups almond milk, orange juice, rice, and salt in the pot of an electric pressure cooker (such as Instant Pot). Seal pressure cooker, choose the "Manual" setting and high pressure. Set the timer for 4 minutes.
- **Step 2**

Allow pressure to release naturally for 10 minutes; release any remaining pressure with the quick-release valve.

- **Step 3**

Whisk the remaining 1/4 cup milk, egg, and orange extract together in a small bowl. Add 1/2 cup of the the cooked rice; stir constantly until well combined. Pour mixture into the pot; select "Saute" mode. Add cream of coconut and orange zest. Cook and stir until egg is set, about 2 minutes. Stir.

Cook's Note:

If you don't have vanilla almond milk, you may substitute other types of milk, but I'd recommend you then add a little vanilla extract (maybe 1/4 to 1/2 teaspoon).
If you want your pudding a little thinner, stir in a little milk at the end; if you'd like it thicker, just cook down a bit using the "Saute" button.

Nutrition Facts
Per Serving:
374.2 calories; protein 5.9g 12% DV; carbohydrates 70.8g 23% DV; fat 7.1g 11% DV; cholesterol 46.5mg 16% DV; sodium 257.1mg 10% DV.

Instant Pot Asparagus Risotto

Prep: 10 mins Cook: 30 min Additional: 10 mins Total: 50 mins

Servings: 4

Ingredients

- 3 tablespoons unsalted butter
- 2 eaches shallots, finely chopped
- 2 cloves garlic, minced
- 1 pound asparagus spears, trimmed and cut into 1-inch pieces
- ½ cup dry white wine
- 1 ½ cups Arborio rice
- 3 ½ cups chicken broth
- ½ cup heavy cream
- ½ teaspoon salt
- ¼ teaspoon ground black pepper
- ¼ teaspoon dried thyme
- ½ cup shredded Parmesan cheese
- 2 tablespoons lemon juice

Directions
- **Step 1**

Turn on a multi-functional pressure cooker (such as Instant Pot) and select Saute function. Add butter and melt. Stir in shallots and garlic; cook for 2 minutes. Remove shallots and garlic with a slotted spoon and set aside. Add asparagus and saute in butter for 2 minutes; remove and set aside on a plate.
- **Step 2**

Return shallots and garlic to the Instant Pot and pour in wine. Stir well, scraping the bottom of the pot with a wooden or plastic spoon, for 30 seconds. Stir in rice and saute in the wine mixture for 2 1/2 minutes, stirring constantly and scraping the bottom of the pot to loosen any brown bits. Stir in chicken broth, cream, salt, pepper, and thyme. Cancel Saute function.
- **Step 3**

Close and lock the lid. Select high pressure according to manufacturer's instructions; set timer for 6 minutes. Allow 10 to 15 minutes for pressure to build.
- **Step 4**

Release pressure carefully using the quick-release method according to manufacturer's instructions, about 5 minutes. Unlock and remove the lid. Gradually stir in Parmesan cheese and lemon juice, stirring until cheese is melted. Stir in reserved asparagus pieces. Allow risotto to thicken in the pot, uncovered, for 3 to 4 minutes before serving.

Nutrition Facts
Per Serving:
611.4 calories; protein 14.5g 29% DV; carbohydrates 81.3g 26% DV; fat 23.1g 36% DV; cholesterol 76.2mg 25% DV; sodium 1498.2mg 60% DV.

Instant Pot Roasted Garlic

Prep: 5 mins Cook: 20 mins Additional: 15 mins Total: 40 mins

Servings: 4

Ingredients

- 1 cup water, or as needed
- 1 bulb garlic
- 1 tablespoon olive oil, or as needed
- 1 pinch salt

Directions
- **Step 1**
Place the steamer basket in the bottom of a multi-functional pressure cooker (such as Instant Pot). Add water up to the bottom of the steamer basket.
- **Step 2**
Cut 1/4 inch off the top of the garlic bulb and place into the steamer basket. Drizzle with olive oil and sprinkle with salt. Close and lock the lid. Select Poultry function according to manufacturer's instructions; set timer for 10 minutes. Allow 10 to 15 minutes for pressure to build.
- **Step 3**
Release pressure using the natural-release method according to manufacturer's instructions, about 10 minutes. Unlock and remove the lid. Remove garlic and cool until easily handled, about 5 minutes. Squeeze garlic pulp into a glass jar and refrigerate.

Cook's Note:
Double or triple the recipe if desired. You can cook as many garlic bulbs as will fit in the basket.

Nutrition Facts
Per Serving:
51.2 calories; protein 0.9g 2% DV; carbohydrates 4.6g 2% DV; fat 3.4g 5% DV; cholesterolmg; sodium 42.9mg 2% DV

Instant Pot Sweet Baby Back Ribs

Prep: 10 mins Cook: 45 mins Additional: 20 mins Total: 1 hr 15 mins

Servings: 8

Ingredients

2 racks baby back pork ribs
- Dry Rub:
- ¼ cup dark brown sugar
- 2 tablespoons garlic salt (such as Lawry's)
- 2 tablespoons chili powder
- 1 teaspoon ground black pepper
- 1 teaspoon cayenne pepper, or to taste
- Cooking Liquid:
- 1 cup beef broth
- 12 fluid ounces root beer
- 2 tablespoons apple cider vinegar
- 1 teaspoon liquid smoke flavoring
- 1 cup barbecue sauce (such as Sweet Baby Ray's), or more to taste

Directions
- **Step 1**

Use a butter knife to cut into an edge of the rib racks. Use a paper towel to grab and lift off the silvery membranes.
- **Step 2**

Combine brown sugar, garlic salt, chili powder, black pepper, and cayenne pepper in bowl. Coat the ribs generously with the dry rub.
- **Step 3**

Place the trivet inside the Instant Pot . Pour in broth, root beer, vinegar, and liquid smoke. Place ribs on the trivet on their sides, with one inside the other. Close and lock the lid and make sure the vent is sealed. Select manual high pressure and set the timer for 30 minutes. Allow 10 to 15 minutes for pressure to build.
- **Step 4**

Release pressure using the natural-release method according to manufacturer's instructions for 15 minutes. Release remaining pressure carefully using the quick-release method according to manufacturer's instructions, about 5 minutes. Unlock and remove the lid.
- **Step 5**

Set an oven rack about 6 inches from the heat source and preheat the oven's broiler on the highest heat setting. Place a rack 6 inches from the heat source.
- **Step 6**

Transfer ribs to a broiling pan and generously coat with barbecue sauce.
- **Step 7**

Cook in the broiler until barbeque sauce is bubbly and caramelized, 5 to 7 minutes.

Nutrition Facts
Per Serving:
384.7 calories; protein 18.8g 38% DV; carbohydrates 24.8g 8% DV; fat 23.1g 36% DV; cholesterol 87.8mg 29% DV; sodium 1910.9mg 76% DV

Instant Pot Tomato-Spinach Risotto

Prep: 10 mins Cook: 25 mins Additional: 5 mins Total: 40 mins

Servings: 8

Ingredients

- 1 tablespoon olive oil
- ½ cup finely diced onion
- 2 cloves garlic, minced
- 2 cups Arborio rice
- 5 cups reduced-sodium chicken broth, divided
- 1 (14.5 ounce) can diced tomatoes
- 1 teaspoon dried basil
- 1 (6 ounce) package fresh baby spinach, chopped
- ⅓ cup grated Parmesan cheese
- 1 pinch salt and freshly ground black pepper to taste

Directions
- **Step 1**

Turn on a multi-functional pressure cooker (such as Instant Pot) and select Saute function. Add oil and onion and cook until soft, about 3 minutes. Add garlic and cook until fragrant, about 1 minute. Stir in rice and cook until opaque, stirring frequently, about 2 minutes. Stir in 4 cups broth, tomatoes, and basil. Close and lock the lid. Select high pressure and set timer for 6 minutes. Allow about 10 minutes for pressure to build.
- **Step 2**

Release pressure carefully using the quick-release method according to manufacturer's instructions, about 5 minutes. Unlock and remove the lid.
- **Step 3**

Select Saute function and stir in remaining broth. Check rice for doneness; if needed, continue stirring until tender.
- **Step 4**

Stir in spinach and Parmesan cheese; cook until wilted, about 1 minute. Season with salt and pepper to taste.

Nutrition Facts
Per Serving:
265.5 calories; protein 8.3g 17% DV; carbohydrates 50g 16% DV; fat 3g 5% DV; cholesterol 5.5mg 2% DV; sodium 237.9mg 10% DV

Instant Pot Shepherd's Pie with Potatoes and Yams

Prep: 20 mins Cook: 45 mins Additional: 10 mins Total: 1 hr 15 mins

Servings: 10

Ingredients

Topping:
- 1 cup low-sodium chicken broth
- 1 large yam, chopped
- 1 large russet potato, chopped

Meat Filling:
- 1 tablespoon vegetable oil
- ½ onion, chopped
- 2 cloves garlic, mashed
- 1 ⅛ pounds ground beef

- 1 teaspoon Himalayan pink salt
- ½ cup milk
- 3 tablespoons butter

- 1 pinch salt and ground black pepper to taste
- 6 medium (blank)s mushrooms, sliced
- 1 cup frozen corn
- 1 cup frozen green peas

- 1 crown broccoli, diced
- 1 carrot, chopped
- 1 stalk celery, chopped
- 1 (.87 ounce) package low-sodium gravy mix
- 1 tablespoon water, or as needed
- ½ cup shredded Cheddar cheese

Directions

- **Step 1**

Pour chicken broth into a multi-functional electric pressure cooker. Place a steamer rack into the pot. Add yam and potato; sprinkle pink salt on top. Close and lock the lid. Turn valve to Seal. Select high pressure according to manufacturer's instructions; set timer for 8 minutes. Allow 10 to 15 minutes for pressure to build.

- **Step 2**

Release pressure carefully using the quick-release method according to manufacturer's instructions, about 5 minutes. Unlock and remove lid. Remove yam, potato, and rack. Strain liquid into a glass measuring cup and reserve. Return yam and potato to pot. Add milk and butter; mash using a potato masher until smooth. Scrape mashed potato topping into a bowl using a silicone spatula.

- **Step 3**

Preheat the oven to 350 degrees F (175 degrees C).

- **Step 4**

Select Saute function on the pressure cooker. Heat oil on high mode. Add onion and garlic; saute until slightly tender, 1 to 2 minutes. Add ground beef, salt, and pepper. Cook and stir until filling is well combined, 2 to 3 minutes. Add mushrooms; saute until starting to soften, about 1 minute.

- **Step 5**

Stir corn, peas, broccoli, carrot, and celery into the pot with the filling. Pour in reserved potato liquid. Close and lock the lid. Set pot to Manual function. Select low pressure according to manufacturer's instructions; set timer for 3 minutes. Allow 5 to 10 minutes for pressure to build.

- **Step 6**

Release pressure carefully using the quick-release method according to manufacturer's instructions, about 5 minutes. Unlock and remove lid. Strain out excess liquid and discard; return filling to pot. Set pot to Saute mode.

- **Step 7**

Dissolve gravy mix in just enough water to dissolve the powder; add to the filling in the pot. Cook and stir until gravy thickens, about 2 minutes. Transfer filling to a baking dish and cover with the mashed topping. Sprinkle Cheddar cheese on top.

- **Step 8**

Bake in the preheated oven until cheese is melted, about 10 minutes.

- **Step 9**

Set oven rack about 6 inches from the heat source and preheat the oven's broiler. Broil shepherd's pie until top is browned, 3 to 5 minutes. Let sit for 5 minutes before serving.

Cook's Notes:

Ground turkey can be substituted for the ground beef.
Substitute salt and pepper with steak seasoning (such as The Keg(R)), if desired.
Broiling is optional.

Nutrition Facts

Per Serving:
308.6 calories; protein 14g 28% DV; carbohydrates 29.8g 10% DV; fat 15g 23% DV; cholesterol 47.1mg 16% DV; sodium 467mg 19% DV

Instant Pot Beef and Vegetable Soup

Prep: 30 mins Cook: 50 mins Additional: 10 mins Total: 1 hr 30 mins

Servings: 8

Ingredients

- 1 tablespoon olive oil
- 2 pounds boneless beef chuck roast, cut into cubes, or to taste
- 5 large carrots, chopped
- 1 large yellow onion, chopped
- 2 stalks celery, chopped
- 6 cups water
- 3 large turnips, peeled and diced
- 1 pound fresh green beans, trimmed and sliced
- 2 tablespoons tomato paste
- 2 tablespoons salt, or more to taste
- 2 tablespoons garlic powder, or more to taste
- 1 tablespoon onion powder, or more to taste
- 1 tablespoon celery seed
- 2 leaf (blank)s bay leaves
- 1 pinch ground black pepper to taste

Directions
- **Step 1**

Heat olive oil in a multi-functional pressure cooker (such as Instant Pot)
and select Saute function. Cook beef cubes until brown on all sides, 5 to 10 minutes.
Transfer to a plate. Cook carrots, onion, and celery until translucent, about 5 minutes.
Return beef to the pot; add water, turnips, green beans, tomato paste, salt, garlic powder,
onion powder, celery seed, and bay leaves.
- **Step 2**

Close and lock the lid. Select high pressure according to manufacturer's instructions; set
timer for 30 minutes. Allow 10 to 15 minutes for pressure to build.
- **Step 3**

Release pressure using the natural-release method according to manufacturer's
instructions, 10 to 40 minutes. Unlock and remove the lid. Taste the soup; add more salt,
garlic, onion, and pepper, if needed.

Cook's Note:
Sometimes we mix 1 tablespoon xanthan gum with some water to thicken it up.
Nutrition Facts
Per Serving:
264.8 calories; protein 16.4g 33% DV; carbohydrates 18.2g 6% DV; fat 14.7g 23% DV;
cholesterol 51.5mg 17% DV; sodium 1905.2mg 76% DV.

Instant Pot Midwest Goulash

Prep: 15 mins Cook: 10 mins Additional: 15 mins Total: 40 mins

Servings: 4

Ingredients

- 1 tablespoon olive oil
- 1 pound ground turkey
- 2 small carrots, grated
- ½ onion, diced
- ½ green bell pepper, diced
- 1 tablespoon Italian seasoning, or to taste
- 1 teaspoon garlic powder, or to taste
- 1 teaspoon seasoned salt (such as Lawry's), or to taste
- 1 teaspoon ground black pepper, or to taste
- 1 ½ cups water
- 1 tablespoon Worcestershire sauce
- 1 ½ teaspoons beef bouillon granules
- 2 cups elbow macaroni
- 1 teaspoon paprika
- 1 (15 ounce) can petite diced tomatoes
- 1 (8 ounce) can tomato sauce

Directions
- **Step 1**

Turn on a multi-functional pressure cooker (such as Instant Pot) and select Saute function. Add olive oil and turkey; cook until halfway browned and crumbly, 3 to 4 minutes. Add carrots, onion, bell pepper, Italian seasoning, garlic powder, seasoned salt, and black pepper.
- **Step 2**

Mix water with Worcestershire sauce and bouillon granules in a small bowl. Pour into meat mixture and mix well. Bring to a simmer. Add macaroni and paprika and stir. Add tomatoes and tomato sauce, making sure not to stir after this addition. Close and lock the lid.
 Set timer for 4 minutes. Allow about 10 minutes for pressure to build.

- **Step 3**

Release pressure carefully using the quick-release method according to manufacturer's instructions to prevent sauce from mixing with the steam, about 5 minutes. Unlock and remove the lid. Mix well.

Cook's Note:
You can also use Italian-seasoned diced tomatoes or stewed tomatoes instead of regular diced.
Nutrition Facts
Per Serving:
460.4 calories; protein 32.1g 64% DV; carbohydrates 53.1g 17% DV; fat 13.2g 20% DV; cholesterol 83.7mg 28% DV; sodium 1414.5mg 57% DV.

Instant Pot Egg Bites

Prep: 15 mins Cook: 13 mins Additional: 10 mins Total: 38 mins

Servings: 6

Ingredients

- 12 eaches eggs
- 1 teaspoon granulated garlic
- 1 ½ teaspoons salt, or to taste
- 1 ½ teaspoons ground black pepper, or to taste
- 1 cup chopped spinach
- ¾ cup shredded Muenster cheese

- ½ cup chopped onion

Directions
- **Step 1**

Beat eggs in a medium bowl until yellow and frothy. Add garlic, salt, and pepper.
- **Step 2**

Toss spinach, Muenster cheese, and onion together in a small bowl. Divide evenly among the cavities of a silicone egg mold. Pour beaten eggs into each cavity, filling each 3/4 full. Cover mold with aluminum foil.
- **Step 3**

Pour 1/2 cup water into a multi-functional pressure cooker (such as Instant Pot). Place egg mold inside. Close and lock the lid, sealing the vent. Select Steam function; set timer for 13 minutes.
- **Step 4**

Release pressure naturally according to manufacturer's instructions, 10 to 40 minutes.

Nutrition Facts
Per Serving:
187.1 calories; protein 14.8g 30% DV; carbohydrates 3g 1% DV; fat 13g 20% DV; cholesterol 340.9mg 114% DV; sodium 798.1mg 32% DV.

Instant Pot Pork Loin in Cranberry-Dijon Sauce

Prep: 10 mins Cook: 25 mins Additional: 20 mins Total: 55 mins

Servings: 4

Ingredients

- 1 pound boneless pork loin roast
- 1 pinch salt and pepper to taste
- 1 tablespoon butter
- 1 (14 ounce) can whole cranberry sauce
- ½ yellow onion, sliced
- 2 tablespoons Dijon mustard
- 2 tablespoons chopped fresh tarragon
- 1 packet dry onion soup mix
- 1 tablespoon cornstarch

Directions
- **Step 1**

Pat pork loin dry and season on all sides with salt and pepper.
- **Step 2**

Turn on a multi-functional pressure cooker (such as Instant Pot) and select Saute function. Add butter and let melt. Add pork loin and cook on all sides until just a little bit of color shows, about 1 minute per side. Turn off Saute function and add cranberry sauce, sliced onion, Dijon mustard, tarragon, and dry onion mix. Gently combine and spoon some of the sauce over the pork loin.
- **Step 3**

Close and lock the lid. Select high pressure according to manufacturers' instructions; set timer for 9 minutes. Allow 10 to 15 minutes for pressure to build.

- **Step 4**

Release pressure using the natural-release method according to manufacturer's instructions, about 10 minutes. Check internal temperature of the pork loin; an instant-read thermometer inserted into the center should read at least 180 degrees F (82 degrees C). Temperature will continue to rise slightly after the pork loin is removed from pot.

- **Step 5**

Place on a cutting board to allow to rest for 8 to 10 minutes before cutting into thin slices.

- **Step 6**

While pork loin is resting, select Saute function again and stir cornstarch into sauce. Whisk until sauce thickens, 2 to 5 minutes. Serve pork loin with cranberry-Dijon sauce.

Cook's Note:

I made this recently and did not have tarragon on hand. I substituted 1 to 2 teaspoons of dried marjoram and it was great.

Nutrition Facts

Per Serving:

384.5 calories; protein 19.5g 39% DV; carbohydrates 49.3g 16% DV; fat 12.2g 19% DV; cholesterol 61.2mg 20% DV; sodium 1091.3mg 44% DV.

Instant Pot Chicken Tinga

Prep: 5 mins Cook: 27 mins Additional: 20 mins Total: 52 mins

Servings: 6

Ingredients

- 1 tablespoon olive oil
- 1 large onion, sliced into petals
- 3 pounds skinless, boneless chicken breast halves
- 1 teaspoon dried Mexican oregano
- 6 peppers canned chipotle chile peppers in adobo sauce, finely chopped
- 1 (28 ounce) can crushed tomatoes
- 1 teaspoon salt
- 6 eaches tostada shells

Directions

- **Step 1**

Turn on a multi-functional pressure cooker (such as Instant Pot) and select Saute function. Add olive oil and onions. Cook until onions have softened, about 2 minutes. Turn off Saute function. Add chicken, oregano, chipotle peppers, tomatoes and salt.

- **Step 2**

Select high pressure according to manufacturer's instructions and set timer for 15 minutes. Allow 10 minutes for pressure to build.

- **Step 3**

Release pressure using the natural-release method according to manufacturer's instructions, 10 minutes. Unlock and remove the lid.

- **Step 4**

Transfer chicken to a cutting board to cool for 10 minutes. Shred chicken and return to the pot. Stir to combine. Spoon chicken tinga on tostadas using a slotted spoon and serve immediately.

Nutrition Facts

Per Serving:
380.4 calories; protein 50.3g 101% DV; carbohydrates 19.6g 6% DV; fat 10.6g 16% DV; cholesterol 129.3mg 43% DV; sodium 782mg 31% DV

Instant Pot Pineapple Chicken (Frozen Chicken Method)

Prep: 10 mins Cook: 30 mins Additional: 10 mins Total: 50 mins

Servings: 4

Ingredients

- 1 (19 ounce) can unsweetened pineapple chunks
- 3 tablespoons low-sodium soy sauce (such as Bragg)
- 2 tablespoons light-colored honey
- ½ teaspoon salt
- 4 (7 ounce) frozen skinless, boneless chicken breast halves
- 1 red bell pepper, seeded and cut into 1-inch pieces
- 2 tablespoons cornstarch
- ¼ teaspoon ground ginger
- ½ teaspoon red pepper flakes

Directions

- **Step 1**

Drain pineapple chunks and pour the juice into the bottom of a multi-functional pressure cooker (such as Instant Pot), reserving 2 tablespoons of the juice. Add soy sauce, honey, and salt; stir to combine. Place frozen chicken breasts into the pot, making sure that they are not touching.

- **Step 2**

Close and lock the lid. Select Poultry setting according to manufacturer's instructions; set timer for 10 minutes. Allow 10 to 15 minutes for pressure to build.

- **Step 3**

Release pressure using the natural-release method according to manufacturer's instructions, for 5 minutes, then release remaining pressure carefully using the quick-release method according to manufacturer's instructions, about 5 minutes. Unlock and remove the lid. Transfer chicken to a warm plate, cover, and let rest for 5 minutes.

- **Step 4**

Meanwhile, select Saute function on Instant Pot and select high temperature. Add bell pepper and saute for 5 minutes. Mix reserved 2 tablespoons pineapple juice with cornstarch and add slowly to the pot. Stir until mixture thickens. Mix in ginger.

- **Step 5**

Cut the chicken into 1 inch pieces and add to the pot along with the pineapple chunks. Heat through and serve.

Cook's Note:
I find that honey that is lighter in color is less sweet.

Nutrition Facts
Per Serving:
364.1 calories; protein 42.8g 86% DV; carbohydrates 36.4g 12% DV; fat 5g 8% DV; cholesterol 112.8mg 38% DV; sodium 790.7mg 32% DV.

Instant Pot Vegan Steel-Cut Oats with Apple and Cinnamon

Prep: 5 mins Cook: 20 mins Additional: 10 mins Total: 35 mins

Servings: 6

Ingredients

- 2 cups water
- 1 cup almond milk
- 1 cup steel-cut oats
- 2 tablespoons maple syrup
- 2 tablespoons flaxseed meal
- 1 apple, diced
- 1 teaspoon ground cinnamon
- 1 tablespoon chopped almonds, or more to taste

Directions

- **Step 1**

Combine water, almond milk, oats, maple syrup, flax seed meal, apple, cinnamon, and almonds in a multi-functional pressure cooker (such as Instant Pot). Close and lock the lid. Select high pressure according to manufacturer's instructions; set timer for 10 minutes. Allow 10 minutes for pressure to build.

- **Step 2**

Release pressure using the natural-release method according to manufacturer's instructions, 10 to 15 minutes. Unlock and remove the lid. Stir oatmeal thoroughly and serve immediately.

Cook's Notes:
You can use any non-dairy milk of your choice.
Instead of almonds you can also use chopped pecans, walnuts, or any choice of nuts.

Nutrition Facts
Per Serving:
110.4 calories; protein 2.7g 5% DV; carbohydrates 19.4g 6% DV; fat 2.9g 4% DV; cholesterolmg; sodium 31.4mg 1% DV.

Instant Pot Mexican Lentil Soup

Prep: 10 mins Cook: 20 mins Additional: 10 mins Total: 40 mins

Servings: 8

Ingredients

- 1 tablespoon olive oil
- 1 large carrot, peeled and sliced
- 1 small onion, chopped
- 1 yellow bell pepper, chopped
- 1 fresh jalapeño chile pepper, seeded and chopped
- 2 cloves garlic, minced
- 5 cups low-sodium chicken broth
- 1 (16 ounce) jar picante sauce
- 1 ¼ cups dry lentils

- 1 tablespoon taco seasoning
- 1 teaspoon cumin

- ½ cup chopped fresh cilantro
- 1 tablespoon lime juice

Directions
- **Step 1**

Turn on a multi-functional pressure cooker (such as Instant Pot) and select Saute function. Add olive oil and let heat for 1 minute. Add carrot, onion, bell pepper, and jalapeno; saute for 2 minutes. Add garlic and saute for 30 seconds. Hit Cancel.
- **Step 2**

Add broth, picante sauce, lentils, taco seasoning, and cumin. Stir to combine. Close and lock the lid. Select high pressure according to manufacturer's instructions; set timer for 6 minutes. Allow 10 minutes for pressure to build.
- **Step 3**

Release pressure using the natural-release method according to manufacturer's instructions, about 10 minutes. Remove the lid and stir in cilantro and lime juice. Ladle into bowls and serve immediately.

Nutrition Facts
Per Serving:
173.1 calories; protein 11.3g 23% DV; carbohydrates 26.3g 9% DV; fat 2.6g 4% DV; cholesterol 2.5mg 1% DV; sodium 526.3mg 21% DV.

Instant Pot Butternut Squash and Pear Soup

Prep: 10 mins Cook: 40 mins Additional: 10 mins Total: 1 hr

Servings: 6

Ingredients

- 1 (3 pound) butternut squash
- 1 cup water
- 1 tablespoon olive oil
- ½ medium onion, quartered
- 2 cloves garlic, peeled

- 2 eaches ripe pears - peeled, cored, and chopped into 1-inch chunks
- 1 ½ teaspoons salt
- ¾ teaspoon ground sage
- 4 cups chicken broth
- ½ cup heavy cream

Directions
- **Step 1**

Cut butternut squash into 4 pieces and remove seeds. Pour water into the bottom of a multi-functional electric pressure cooker and place trivet inside. Place squash on trivet, close lid, and set seal valve. Select high pressure according to manufacturer's instructions; set timer for 10 minutes. Allow 10 to 15 minutes for pressure to build.
- **Step 2**

Release pressure carefully using the quick-release method according to manufacturer's instructions, about 5 minutes. Unlock and remove the lid. Drain out the water and wipe the bottom of the pot dry. Remove squash skin and discard. Roughly chop any large pieces into smaller 1- to 2-inch chunks. Set aside.
- **Step 3**

Select the Saute function and heat olive oil. Saute onion and garlic for 1 to 2 minutes. Add pears, salt, and sage; cook for 1 to 2 minutes more. Turn pressure cooker off. Add

the squash and chicken broth. Close lid and seal valve. Select high pressure; set timer for 5 minutes. Allow 10 to 15 minutes for pressure to build.
- **Step 4**

Release pressure manually and remove lid. Blend soup until smooth using an immersion blender. Stir in heavy cream.

Cook's Notes:
Use vegetable broth to make it vegetarian.
If you do not have an immersion blender, blend soup in batches in a blender.

Nutrition Facts
Per Serving:
240.1 calories; protein 3.9g 8% DV; carbohydrates 37.7g 12% DV; fat 10.3g 16% DV; cholesterol 31.2mg 10% DV; sodium 1376.1mg 55% DV.

Instant Pot Cajun Jambalaya

Prep: 30 mins Cook: 25 mins Additional: 5 mins Total: 1 hr

Servings: 4

Ingredients

- 1 cup uncooked white rice
- 1 cup chicken broth
- 1 tablespoon grapeseed oil
- 2 eaches chicken breasts, chopped in small pieces
- 2 link (raw dimensions: 4" long x 7/8" dia), cookeds andouille sausages, sliced
- 2 ribs celery, chopped
- 1 small green bell pepper, seeded and chopped
- 1 small onion, chopped
- 1 (14.5 ounce) can fire-roasted tomatoes
- 2 teaspoons Creole seasoning
- 1 teaspoon Cajun seasoning
- 12 eaches large shrimp, peeled and deveined

Directions
- **Step 1**

Rinse rice. Combine wet rice and chicken broth in a multi-functional pressure cooker (such as Instant Pot). Close and lock the lid and set valve to sealing. Choose Rice function. Allow 10 to 15 minutes for pressure to build.
- **Step 2**

Release pressure carefully using the quick-release method according to manufacturer's instructions, about 5 minutes. Unlock and remove the lid. Transfer rice to a bowl and keep warm.
- **Step 3**

Rinse out pot liner and choose Saute function. Add grapeseed oil, chicken, and sausage; saute until browned, 5 to 7 minutes. Add celery, bell pepper, and onion. Saute 1 more minute. Add tomatoes, Creole seasoning, and Cajun seasoning. Add shrimp and cook just until tails curl up, 1 to 3 minutes. Serve jambalaya on top of or mixed into the cooked rice.

Nutrition Facts
Per Serving:

380 calories; protein 27.9g 56% DV; carbohydrates 47.5g 15% DV; fat 7.9g 12% DV; cholesterol 133.1mg 44% DV; sodium 1016mg 41% DV.

Instant Pot Butter Chicken from Frozen

Prep: 10 mins Cook: 45 mins Additional: 20 mins Total: 1 hr 15 mins

Servings: 3

Ingredients

- 6 tablespoons salted butter, divided
- 3 cloves garlic, minced
- ⅓ cup diced onion
- 9 ounces frozen cubed chicken
- 1 (8 ounce) can tomato sauce
- ¼ cup heavy whipping cream
- 1 tablespoon tandoori seasoning
- 2 teaspoons garam masala
- 1 pinch cayenne pepper
- ¼ cup chopped fresh cilantro, or to taste

Directions

- **Step 1**

Turn on a multi-functional pressure cooker (such as Instant Pot), select Saute function, and add butter. Add onion and garlic to melted butter; saute until fragrant, 3 to 5 minutes. Add frozen chicken, then pour tomato sauce on top. Hit Cancel.

- **Step 2**

Close and lock the lid. Select high pressure according to manufacturer's instructions; set timer for 30 minutes. Allow 10 to 15 minutes for pressure to build.

- **Step 3**

Release pressure using the natural-release method according to manufacturer's instructions, for 15 minutes. Then use the quick-release method to release remaining pressure, about 5 minutes. Unlock and remove the lid.

- **Step 4**

Add whipping cream, tandoori seasoning, garam masala, and cayenne pepper; stir to combine. Serve immediately garnished with cilantro.

Nutrition Facts
Per Serving:
400.3 calories; protein 18.8g 38% DV; carbohydrates 9.6g 3% DV; fat 33g 51% DV; cholesterol 132.1mg 44% DV; sodium 610mg 24% DV

Instant Pot Wheat Berries

Prep: 5 mins Cook: 40 mins Additional: 10 mins Total: 55 mins

Servings: 10

Ingredients

- 6 eaches water
- 2 cups wheat berries
- ½ teaspoon kosher salt, or to taste

Directions
- **Step 1**

Turn on a multi-functional pressure cooker (such as Instant Pot). Add water and wheat berries; stir once. Close and lock the lid. Select Manual pressure according to manufacturer's instructions and set timer for 27 minutes. Allow 10 to 15 minutes for pressure to build.
- **Step 2**

Release pressure using the natural-release method according to manufacturer's instructions, about 10 minutes. Release remaining pressure carefully using the quick-release method according to manufacturer's instructions, about 5 minutes. Unlock and remove the lid.
- **Step 3**

Drain wheat berries and mix in salt.

Cook's Note:

Place a thin hand towel over the Instant Pot(R) vent before flicking it open. I like setting my Instant Pot(R) on a cool stove with the overhead vent on to pull the steam out of the house.

Nutrition Facts

Per Serving:
125.6 calories; protein 4.8g 10% DV; carbohydrates 27.3g 9% DV; fat 0.6g 1% DV; cholesterolmg; sodium 102.4mg 4% DV.

Instant Pot Bahn Flan (Vietnamese Flan)

Prep: 15 mins Cook: 35 mins Additional: 4 hrs 10 mins Total: 5 hrs

Servings: 3

Ingredients

- 2 cups milk
- 1 ⅔ cups white sugar, divided
- 4 large eggs
- 1 large egg yolk
- 1 teaspoon vanilla extract

Directions
- **Step 1**

Warm milk in a saucepan over medium heat. Add 2/3 cup sugar and stir to dissolve, about 3 minutes. Make sure milk does not boil; turn off heat if necessary.
- **Step 2**

Whisk eggs and egg yolk by hand; do not overmix. Pour slowly into the warm milk-sugar mixture and stir continuously over low heat for 1 1/2 minutes.
- **Step 3**

Strain through a tightly woven mesh strainer into a bowl to remove any solids that may have formed. Add vanilla extract to the bowl; mix until well combined. Set aside.
- **Step 4**

Pour 1 cup sugar into a wide skillet over medium heat. Stir occasionally with a wooden spoon until sugar has evenly melted and turned a golden caramel color, about 5 minutes. Immediately remove from heat and pour into a pressure cooker-safe cake pan, coating the bottom with liquid sugar. Pour in custard. Cover tightly with aluminum foil.

- **Step 5**

Place a trivet in the bottom of a multi-functional pressure cooker (such as Instant Pot) and add 1 cup water. Place the cake pan onto the trivet and close and lock the lid. Seal the valve and select high pressure according to manufacturer's instructions; set timer for 9 minutes. Allow 10 to 15 minutes for pressure to build.

- **Step 6**

Release pressure using the natural-release method according to manufacturer's instructions, for 10 minutes, then turn the valve to Venting to release remaining pressure. Unlock and remove the lid. Remove the trivet and pan.

- **Step 7**

Allow to cool for 1 hour, then chill for at least 3 to 4 hours, or overnight. Slide knife carefully around the edges and hold the bottom securely as you invert onto a large serving dish; the caramel should drip over the flan and onto the plate.

Cook's Note:
You can also make 3 individual flans in ramekins. Set cook time to 6 minutes if using ramekins.

Nutrition Facts
Per Serving:
628.4 calories; protein 14.6g 29% DV; carbohydrates 119.6g 39% DV; fat 11.3g 17% DV; cholesterol 329.3mg 110% DV; sodium 162.8mg 7% DV.

Instant Pot Chicken Paprikash with Egg Noodles

Prep: 10 mins Cook: 50 mins Additional: 10 mins Total: 1 hr 10 mins

Servings: 8

Ingredients

- 2 pounds skinless, boneless chicken thighs
- 1 pinch salt and ground black pepper to taste
- 3 tablespoons olive oil
- 1 large onion, diced
- 2 large garlic cloves, minced
- 2 cups chicken stock
- 2 tablespoons paprika
- 1 teaspoon salt
- ¼ teaspoon ground black pepper
- 1 bay leaf
- 1 (12 ounce) package wide egg noodles
- 2 tablespoons cornstarch
- 1 ½ tablespoons water, or as needed
- 1 cup heavy whipping cream
- 2 tablespoons sour cream

Directions
- **Step 1**

Pat chicken dry; season with salt and pepper.

- **Step 2**

Turn on a multi-functional pressure cooker (such as Instant Pot) and select Saute function. Heat olive oil. Add the chicken in 2 batches and cook until browned, 2 to 3 minutes per side. Remove from pot and set aside.

- **Step 3**

Add onion and garlic to the pot. Saute, stirring frequently, until onion is translucent, about 5 minutes. Add chicken stock, paprika, salt, pepper, and bay leaf and mix with a wooden spoon. Return chicken to the pot.

- **Step 4**

Close and lock the lid. Set steam release valve to Sealing position and press Manual and high pressure. Set the timer for 10 minutes. Allow 10 to 15 minutes for pressure to build.

- **Step 5**

Release pressure carefully using the quick-release method according to manufacturer's instructions, about 5 minutes. Unlock and remove the lid. Stir in egg noodles. Close and lock lid; select High pressure and set the timer for 3 minutes. Allow 10 to 15 minutes for pressure to build.

- **Step 6**

Immediately release the pressure manually, about 5 minutes. Select Saute function. Mix cornstarch with water in a bowl and pour into the pot. Add heavy cream and sour cream. Mix thoroughly and turn off heat.

Nutrition Facts
Per Serving:
517.5 calories; protein 25.1g 50% DV; carbohydrates 36.2g 12% DV; fat 30.3g 47% DV; cholesterol 141.6mg 47% DV; sodium 559.4mg 22% DV.

Instant Pot Shrimp Broth

Prep: 5 mins Cook: 1 hr 10 mins Additional: 15 mins Total: 1 hr 30 mins

Servings: 6

Ingredients

- 4 cups shrimp shells from 2 pounds of shrimp
- 10 eaches baby carrots
- 1 onion, halved and root end removed
- 1 stalk celery, cut into thirds
- 2 cloves garlic, halved
- 1 tablespoon distilled white vinegar
- 1 teaspoon salt
- 1 teaspoon ground black pepper
- 5 cups water

Directions

- **Step 1**

Combine shrimp shells, baby carrots, onion, celery, garlic, vinegar, salt, pepper, and water in a multi-functional pressure cooker (such as Instant Pot). Close and lock the lid. Select Manual function according to manufacturer's instructions; set timer for 60 minutes. Allow 10 minutes for pressure to build.

- **Step 2**

Release pressure using the natural-release method according to manufacturer's instructions, about 10 minutes. Release remaining pressure carefully using the quick-release method according to manufacturer's instructions, about 5 minutes. Unlock and remove the lid. Pour liquid through a strainer and discard all solids.

Cook's Note:
Shrimp broth can be stored in the refrigerator up to 3 days.

Nutrition Facts
Per Serving:
18.6 calories; protein 0.6g 1% DV; carbohydrates 4.3g 1% DV; fat 0.1g; cholesterolmg;
sodium 400.7mg 16% DV.

Instant Pot Beef Pho

Prep: 20 mins Cook: 53 mins Additional: 35 mins Total: 1 hr 48 mins

Servings: 6

Ingredients

- 3 pounds beef soup bones
- 3 eaches whole cloves
- 3 eaches whole star anise pods
- 1 (1/2 inch) piece cinnamon stick
- 1 teaspoon olive oil
- 1 large onion, chopped
- 1 (2 inch) piece ginger, peeled
- ½ pound chuck roast
- 2 tablespoons fish sauce

- 1 tablespoon raw sugar
- 2 teaspoons kosher salt
- 9 cups water
- ½ pound top round beef
- 12 ounces dry rice stick noodles
- ¼ cup chopped cilantro
- 2 medium (4-1/8" long)s green onions, chopped

Directions
- **Step 1**

Set an electric pressure cooker (such as Instant Pot) on "Saute" mode. Add beef bones
with water to cover; bring to a boil. Boil vigorously for 3 minutes; drain. Transfer bones
to a plate. Dry out the pot and return it to the pressure cooker.
- **Step 2**

Set cooker on "Saute" mode. Add cloves, star anise, and cinnamon stick to the bottom of
the pot. Toast, turning once to avoid burning, until aromatic, about 5 minutes. Transfer to
a bowl.
- **Step 3**

Pour olive oil into the hot pot. Add chopped onion and ginger; cook and stir until
softened and starting to brown, about 10 minutes.
- **Step 4**

Place the beef bones, toasted spices, chuck roast, fish sauce, sugar, and salt in the pot.
Pour in 9 cups of water, filling the pot 3/4 full. Seal pressure cooker and bring to high
pressure according to manufacturer's instructions; cook for 30 minutes. Release pressure
through natural-release method for 20 minutes.
- **Step 5**

Remove the chuck roast from the pot. Pour the stock through a sieve into another pot.
Discard the bones and spices. Put the pot on the stove, cover, and keep hot over low heat.
- **Step 6**

Place top round into the freezer for 15 minutes. Place rice noodles in a bowl with warm
water to cover; soak until pliable, about 15 minutes. Drain the noodles.
- **Step 7**

Remove the top round from the freezer and slice it as thinly as possible, cutting against
the grain for best results. Slice the chuck roast.
- **Step 8**

Put a small pile of rice noodles in the middle of a soup bowl. Top with cilantro and green onions. Arrange slices of raw top round and chuck roast around the noodles. Pour in the hot stock, carefully, until the bowl is full. Repeat for additional servings.

Editor's Note:
Consuming raw beef may increase your risk of foodborne illness, especially if you have certain medical conditions.
Nutrition data for this recipe includes the full amount of beef bones and aromatics. The actual amount consumed will vary.

Nutrition Facts
Per Serving:
366.8 calories; protein 17.5g 35% DV; carbohydrates 52.1g 17% DV; fat 8.7g 14% DV; cholesterol 40.2mg 13% DV; sodium 1050.1mg 42% DV.

Instant Pot Chicken Breasts

Prep: 5 mins Cook: 25 mins Additional: 25 mins Total: 55 mins

Servings: 6

Ingredients

- 1 pound boneless, skinless chicken breasts, halved horizontally
- 1 teaspoon Italian seasoning
- ½ teaspoon garlic salt
- ¼ teaspoon ground black pepper
- 1 tablespoon butter
- 1 tablespoon vegetable oil
- ½ cup chicken broth

Directions
- **Step 1**

Sprinkle both sides of chicken with Italian seasoning, garlic salt, and pepper.
- **Step 2**

Turn on a multi-functional pressure cooker (such as Instant Pot) and select Saute function. When pot is hot, add butter and oil and allow to butter to melt. Add chicken, working in batches if necessary, and cook until golden brown, about 3 minutes per side. Pour broth over chicken and press Cancel.
- **Step 3**

Close and lock the lid. Select high pressure according to manufacturer's instructions; set timer for 3 minutes. Allow 10 minutes for pressure to build.
- **Step 4**

Release pressure using the natural-release method according to manufacturer's instructions for 20 minutes. Release remaining pressure carefully using the quick-release method, about 5 minutes. Unlock and remove the lid.

Nutrition Facts
Per Serving:
123.6 calories; protein 15.9g 32% DV; carbohydrates 0.4g; fat 6.1g 9% DV; cholesterol 48.7mg 16% DV; sodium 299.2mg 12% DV.

Instant Pot Chicken and Farro Soup

Prep: 15 mins Cook: 30 mins Additional: 15 mins Total: 1 hr

Servings: 6

Ingredients

- 2 tablespoons avocado oil
- 2 cups carrots that have been sliced lengthwise and cut into 3/4-inch slices
- 1 cup sliced celery with leaves
- 1 leek, halved lengthwise and sliced
- 1 ½ teaspoons minced garlic
- 2 tablespoons tomato paste
- 1 teaspoon ground thyme
- 1 teaspoon dried oregano
- 1 teaspoon dried parsley
- 1 teaspoon salt
- ½ teaspoon ground black pepper
- 5 cups low-sodium chicken broth
- 1 cup farro, rinsed
- 1 pound skinless, boneless chicken breasts, trimmed

Directions
- **Step 1**

Turn on a multi-functional pressure cooker (such as Instant Pot) and select Saute function. Heat oil in the hot pot and add carrots, celery, and leek. Cook, stirring frequently, until vegetables start to soften, 3 to 4 minutes. Add garlic and cook until just fragrant, about 30 seconds. Add tomato paste and cook for 1 minute. Stir in thyme, oregano, parsley, salt, and pepper. Pour broth into the pot, add farro, and stir. Push chicken breasts down into the liquid. Close and lock the lid.
- **Step 2**

Select high pressure according to manufacturer's instructions; set timer for 12 minutes. Allow 10 to 15 minutes for pressure to build.
- **Step 3**

Release pressure using the natural-release method according to manufacturer's instructions for 10 minutes. Release remaining pressure carefully using the quick-release method according to manufacturer's instructions, about 5 minutes. Unlock and remove the lid. Transfer chicken to a clean work surface and roughly chop; return to the pot and stir. Taste and salt. Serve.

Nutrition Facts
Per Serving:
279.2 calories; protein 22.9g 46% DV; carbohydrates 32g 10% DV; fat 7.9g 12% DV; cholesterol 46.4mg 16% DV; sodium 613.6mg 25% DV.

Instant Pot Mongolian Chicken

Prep: 10 mins Cook: 20 mins Additional: 15 mins Total: 45 mins

Servings: 6

Ingredients

* 2 tablespoons olive oil
* 4 eaches boneless chicken breast, cut into cubes
* 1 cup chicken broth
* ½ cup brown sugar
* ½ cup soy sauce
* 1 carrot, chopped
* 4 eaches garlic cloves, minced
* 1 tablespoon minced fresh ginger root
* 1 teaspoon chili powder
* 2 tablespoons cornstarch
* ¼ cup water
* 1 teaspoon sesame seeds

Directions
* **Step 1**

Turn on a multi-functional pressure cooker (such as Instant Pot) and select Saute function. Heat olive oil and add chicken cubes; cook until golden, stirring constantly, about 3 minutes. Stir in chicken broth, brown sugar, soy sauce, carrot, garlic, ginger, and chili powder. Close and lock the lid. Select high pressure according to manufacturer's instructions; set timer for 7 minutes. Allow 10 to 15 minutes for pressure to build.

* **Step 2**

Release pressure using the natural-release method according to manufacturer's instructions, about 10 minutes. Complete releasing pressure carefully using the quick-release method according to manufacturer's instructions, about 5 minutes. Unlock and remove the lid. Reselect Saute function.

* **Step 3**

Whisk cornstarch in 1/4 cup water until fully dissolved. Pour into the pot and stir to combine. Cook until sauce thickens, stirring gently, about 4 minutes. Sprinkle with sesame seeds before serving.

Nutrition Facts
Per Serving:
218.5 calories; protein 16.5g 33% DV; carbohydrates 23.4g 8% DV; fat 6.5g 10% DV; cholesterol 40mg 13% DV; sodium 1439.2mg 58% DV

Instant Pot Keto Thai Chicken Soup (Tom Kha Gai)

Prep: 10 mins Cook: 40 mins Additional: 15 mins Total: 1 hr 5 mins

Servings: 6

Ingredients

* 4 eaches boneless chicken breasts, diced
* 2 ½ cups chicken broth
* 2 ½ cups water
* 1 (14 ounce) can coconut cream
* 2 tablespoons Thai garlic chile paste
* 2 tablespoons coconut aminos
* 1 tablespoon lime juice
* 1 teaspoon salt
* 1 teaspoon ground ginger
* 1 teaspoon finely chopped Thai basil
* 1 tablespoon fresh cilantro

Directions
* **Step 1**

Combine chicken, chicken broth, water, coconut cream, garlic chile paste, coconut aminos, lime juice, salt, ginger, and basil in a multi-functional pressure cooker (such as Instant Pot). Close and lock the lid. Select Soup/Broth function according to manufacturer's instructions; set timer for 30 minutes. Allow 10 to 15 minutes for pressure to build.
- **Step 2**

Release pressure carefully using the slow-release method according to manufacturer's instructions, about 10 minutes. Release remaining pressure using the quick-release method, about 5 minutes. Unlock and remove the lid. Serve soup in bowls and sprinkle with fresh cilantro.

Nutrition Facts
Per Serving:
320.8 calories; protein 17.6g 35% DV; carbohydrates 9.2g 3% DV; fat 25.4g 39% DV; cholesterol 41.5mg 14% DV; sodium 1043.7mg 42% DV

Instant Pot Ground Chicken Chili

Prep: 15 mins Cook: 45 mins Additional: 10 mins Total: 1 hr 10 mins

Servings: 8

Ingredients

- 2 tablespoons olive oil
- 1 onion, diced
- 2 pounds air-chilled ground chicken breast (such as Smart Chicken)
- 1 large sweet potato, diced
- 1 (8 ounce) package sliced baby bella mushrooms
- 3 stalks celery, diced
- 2 (14.5 ounce) cans no-salt-added diced tomatoes
- 2 (14.5 ounce) cans no-salt-added tomato sauce
- 1 (14 ounce) can no-salt-added beef broth
- 2 tablespoons chili powder
- 1 tablespoon ground cumin
- ½ tablespoon mustard seeds
- 1 pinch garlic powder, or to taste
- 1 pinch salt and ground black pepper to taste
- 4 peppers whole jalapeno peppers

Directions
- **Step 1**

Turn on a multi-functional pressure cooker (such as Instant Pot) and select Saute function. Pour oil into the pot. Add onion and cook until softened and translucent, about 5 minutes. Add chicken; cook and stir until nearly browned, 3 to 5 minutes.
- **Step 2**

Stir in sweet potato, mushrooms, and celery, followed by tomatoes, tomato sauce, broth, chili powder, cumin, mustard seeds, garlic powder, salt, and pepper. Add whole jalapeno peppers. Close and lock the lid. Select low pressure according to manufacturer's instructions; set timer for 25 minutes. Allow 10 to 15 minutes for pressure to build.
- **Step 3**

Release pressure using the natural-release method according to manufacturer's instructions, 10 to 40 minutes.

Cook's Note:
Use no-salt-added chicken broth if preferred.

Nutrition Facts
Per Serving:
300.9 calories; protein 30.8g 62% DV; carbohydrates 28.1g 9% DV; fat 8.2g 13% DV; cholesterol 69.2mg 23% DV; sodium 198.6mg 8% DV.

Instant Pot Coconut Chicken Curry with Sweet Potato

Prep: 10 mins Cook: 25 mins Additional: 5 mins Total: 40 mins

Servings: 6

Ingredients

- 2 tablespoons grapeseed oil, divided
- 1 pound chicken tenders
- 1 teaspoon salt, divided
- 1 pinch ground black pepper
- ½ cup coarsely chopped onion
- ½ cup diced red bell pepper
- ½ cup diced green bell pepper
- 2 ½ teaspoons curry powder
- 1 (14 ounce) can coconut milk
- 1 medium sweet potato, peeled and diced
- ½ cup peeled and chopped carrots
- 1 tablespoon peanut butter

Directions
- **Step 1**

Turn on a multi-functional pressure cooker (such as Instant Pot) and select Saute function. Once the pot is hot, add 1 tablespoon oil. Season chicken with 1/2 teaspoon salt and pepper. Add chicken to the pot and cook until no longer pink in the center, 5 to 7 minutes. Remove chicken and cover to keep warm. Add remaining 1 tablespoon oil to the pot and cook onion and bell peppers until softened, 3 to 5 minutes. Season with curry powder and remaining salt. Mix in coconut milk, sweet potatoes, and carrots. Bring to a boil.
- **Step 2**

Hit cancel on Saute function. Close and lock the lid. Select high pressure according to manufacturer's instructions; set timer for 3 minutes. Allow 10 to 15 minutes for pressure to build.
- **Step 3**

Dice cooked chicken while vegetables are cooking.
- **Step 4**

Release pressure carefully using the quick-release method according to manufacturer's instructions, about 5 minutes. Unlock and remove the lid. Mix in chicken and peanut butter and serve.

Nutrition Facts
Per Serving:

320.2 calories; protein 18.9g 38% DV; carbohydrates 14.2g 5% DV; fat 21.9g 34% DV; cholesterol 43.1mg 14% DV; sodium 476.1mg 19% DV.

Instant Pot Kalua Pig (Quick Hawaiian Pulled Pork)

Prep: 20 mins Cook: 2 hrs 10 mins Additional: 15 mins Total: 2 hrs 45 mins

Servings: 12

Ingredients

- 1 (5 pound) boneless pork loin roast
- 1 ½ tablespoons Hawaiian sea salt
- 1 tablespoon liquid smoke flavoring

Directions
- **Step 1**
Set roast in a multi-functional pressure cooker (such as Instant Pot). Rub liberally with Hawaiian sea salt and pierce the meat all over with a large fork or narrow knife. Drizzle with liquid smoke. Close and lock the lid. Select high pressure according to manufacturer's instructions; set timer for 120 minutes. Allow 15 to 30 minutes for pressure to build.
- **Step 2**
Release pressure using the natural-release method according to manufacturer's instructions, about 15 minutes. Unlock and remove the lid. Transfer roast to a plate.
- **Step 3**
Separate the fat off the meat (if you like) and shred the meat lightly into a serving bowl with 2 forks.
- **Step 4**
Remove the fat from the cooking liquid with a fat separator and drizzle the strained liquid over the meat.

Cook's Note:
You can use a pork loin roast or pork shoulder for this recipe with a weight between 4 and 6 lbs.

Nutrition Facts
Per Serving:
168.7 calories; protein 21.9g 44% DV; carbohydratesg; fat 8.4g 13% DV; cholesterol 66.1mg 22% DV; sodium 901.2mg 36% DV

Instant Pot Quinoa

Prep: 5 mins Cook: 15 mins Additional: 5 mins Total: 25 mins

Servings: 2

Ingredients

- 1 cup water
- 1 cup quinoa, rinsed and drained

Directions
- **Step 1**

Combine water and quinoa in a multi-functional pressure cooker (such as Instant Pot); mix well. Close and lock the lid; set the pressure release valve to the sealing position. Press Steam button twice and set timer for 5 minutes. Allow 10 to 15 minutes for pressure to build.
- **Step 2**

Release pressure carefully using the quick-release method according to manufacturer's instructions, about 5 minutes. Unlock and remove the lid.

Nutrition Facts
Per Serving:
312.8 calories; protein 12g 24% DV; carbohydrates 54.5g 18% DV; fat 5.2g 8% DV; cholesterolmg; sodium 7.8mg

Instant Pot Salt and Vinegar Boiled Peanuts

Prep: 5 mins Cook: 2 hrs 10 mins Additional: 8 hrs 20 mins Total: 10 hrs 35 mins

Servings: 16

Ingredients

- 2 cups distilled white vinegar
- 2 cups water
- ⅓ cup sea salt
- 1 pound raw Virginia peanuts in shells

Directions
- **Step 1**

Whisk vinegar, water, and salt in a large bowl. Add peanuts and stir to coat. Transfer mixture to a gallon-sized plastic zip-top bag and let sit for 8 hours or overnight.
- **Step 2**

Pour bag of peanuts and liquid into a multi-functional pressure cooker (such as Instant Pot). Close and lock the lid. Select high pressure according to manufacturer's instructions; set timer for 120 minutes. Allow 10 to 15 minutes for pressure to build.
- **Step 3**

Release pressure using the natural-release method according to manufacturer's instructions, about 20 minutes. Unlock and remove the lid.

Cook's Note:
Refrigerate leftovers in a covered bowl with the liquid.
Editor's Note:
Nutrition data for this recipe includes the full amount of salt. The actual amount of salt consumed will vary.

Nutrition Facts
Per Serving:
161.5 calories; protein 7.3g 15% DV; carbohydrates 4.6g 2% DV; fat 14g 22% DV; cholesterolmg; sodium 1766mg 71% DV.

Instant Pot Live Crawfish Boil for Four

Prep: 10 mins Cook: 35 mins Additional: 35 mins Total: 1 hr 20 mins

Servings: 4

Ingredients

- Crawfish:
- 4 cups water
- 2 tablespoons concentrated liquid shrimp and crab boil (such as Zatarain's)
- 2 tablespoons seafood seasoning (such as Old Bay)
- 2 pounds live crawfish, rinsed
- Potatoes, Corn, and Sausage:
- 1 pound bite-sized red potatoes (such as Ruby Sensations)
- 3 ears corn, shucked and cut into thirds, or more to taste
- 1 (12 ounce) package andouille sausage, sliced
- 1 tablespoon seafood seasoning (such as Old Bay)
- 2 cups water

Directions

- **Step 1**

Combine water, dry crab boil, and seafood seasoning in a multi-functional pressure cooker (such as Instant Pot). Add live crawfish. Close and lock the lid. Select high pressure according to manufacturer's instructions; set timer for 0 minutes. Allow 15 minutes for pressure to build.

- **Step 2**

Release pressure carefully using the quick-release method according to manufacturer's instructions, about 2 minutes. Carefully pour crawfish and the liquid into a large bowl and let sit for 30 minutes to soak while you prepare the rest of the meal.

- **Step 3**

Add potatoes, corn, andouille sausage, and 1 tablespoon seafood seasoning to the pot. Pour in water and stir until evenly combined. Close and lock the lid.

- **Step 4**

Select high pressure according to manufacturer's instructions; set timer for 5 minutes. Allow 15 minutes for pressure to build.

- **Step 5**

Release pressure carefully using the quick-release method according to manufacturer's instructions, about 2 minutes. Divide the mixture between 4 plates and serve with crawfish.

Cook's Note:
Have plenty of napkins ready and extra plates for discarding shells.

Nutrition Facts
Per Serving:

570.5 calories; protein 45.8g 92% DV; carbohydrates 34.4g 11% DV; fat 27.7g 43% DV; cholesterol 291.6mg 97% DV; sodium 5130.6mg 205% DV

Instant Pot Cheddar Cheese Sauce

Prep: 5 mins Cook: 10 mins Total: 15 mins

Servings: 6

Ingredients

- ¼ cup butter
- 1 teaspoon salt
- 1 teaspoon ground black pepper
- 1 teaspoon onion powder
- 2 tablespoons tapioca starch
- 1 ¼ cups whole milk
- 1 ½ cups sharp Cheddar cheese, grated

Directions

- **Step 1**

Turn on a multi-functional pressure cooker (such as Instant Pot) and select the Saute function. Add butter and let it melt. Season with salt, pepper, and onion powder and stir. Sprinkle with tapioca starch and stir roux until blended; it will be thick.
- **Step 2**

Pour in milk gradually, 1/4 cup at a time, stirring each addition until well combined. Keep stirring to remove clumps. Sauce should be creamy and just under boiling temperature. If it starts to boil, turn Instant Pot off and set to Keep Warm.
- **Step 3**

Add Cheddar cheese and stir continuously until cheese has melted and is well combined into the sauce.

Nutrition Facts
Per Serving:
223.4 calories; protein 8.8g 18% DV; carbohydrates 5.4g 2% DV; fat 18.7g 29% DV; cholesterol 55.1mg 18% DV; sodium 638.3mg 26% DV.

Instant Pot Asparagus Risotto

Prep: 10 mins Cook: 30 mins Additional: 10 mins Total: 50 mins

Servings: 4

Ingredients

- 3 tablespoons unsalted butter
- 2 eaches shallots, finely chopped
- 2 cloves garlic, minced
- 1 pound asparagus spears, trimmed and cut into 1-inch pieces
- ½ cup dry white wine

* 1 ½ cups Arborio rice
* 3 ½ cups chicken broth
* ½ cup heavy cream
* ½ teaspoon salt
* ¼ teaspoon ground black pepper
* ¼ teaspoon dried thyme
* ½ cup shredded Parmesan cheese
* 2 tablespoons lemon juice

Directions
* **Step 1**

Turn on a multi-functional pressure cooker (such as Instant Pot) and select Saute function. Add butter and melt. Stir in shallots and garlic; cook for 2 minutes. Remove shallots and garlic with a slotted spoon and set aside. Add asparagus and saute in butter for 2 minutes; remove and set aside on a plate.
* **Step 2**

Return shallots and garlic to the Instant Pot and pour in wine. Stir well, scraping the bottom of the pot with a wooden or plastic spoon, for 30 seconds. Stir in rice and saute in the wine mixture for 2 1/2 minutes, stirring constantly and scraping the bottom of the pot to loosen any brown bits. Stir in chicken broth, cream, salt, pepper, and thyme. Cancel Saute function.
* **Step 3**

Close and lock the lid. Select high pressure according to manufacturer's instructions; set timer for 6 minutes. Allow 10 to 15 minutes for pressure to build.
* **Step 4**

Release pressure carefully using the quick-release method according to manufacturer's instructions, about 5 minutes. Unlock and remove the lid. Gradually stir in Parmesan cheese and lemon juice, stirring until cheese is melted. Stir in reserved asparagus pieces. Allow risotto to thicken in the pot, uncovered, for 3 to 4 minutes before serving.

Nutrition Facts
Per Serving:
611.4 calories; protein 14.5g 29% DV; carbohydrates 81.3g 26% DV; fat 23.1g 36% DV; cholesterol 76.2mg 25% DV; sodium 1498.2mg 60% DV.

Instant Pot Chilorio

Prep: 25 mins Cook: 30 mins Additional: 25 mins Total: 1 hr 20 mins

Servings: 10
Ingredients

* 2 ½ pounds pork shoulder, trimmed and cut into 1-inch cubes
* 4 eaches oranges, juiced
* 1 (14.25 ounce) can low-sodium chicken broth
* 1 onion, sliced and separated into rings
* 1 teaspoon dried oregano
* 3 peppers dried ancho chiles (poblanos), stemmed and torn into small pieces
* 2 cups boiling water
* ¼ cup apple cider vinegar
* 1 jalapeno, seeded and chopped
* 2 garlic clove (blank)s garlic cloves
* 2 tablespoons chopped cilantro
* ¼ teaspoon ground cumin

Directions
* **Step 1**

Combine pork, orange juice, broth, onion, and oregano in the inner pot of an electric pressure cooker (such as Instant Pot). Close and lock the lid. Select high pressure according to manufacturer's instructions; set timer for 20 minutes. Allow 10 to 15 minutes for pressure to build.
* **Step 2**

Release pressure using the natural-release method according to manufacturer's instructions, 10 to 40 minutes. Unlock and remove lid.
* **Step 3**

Remove pork from the pot and drain. Transfer to a serving dish.
* **Step 4**

Place ancho chiles in a heat-proof bowl. Pour boiling water over chiles and soak for 15 minutes. Drain chiles, reserving soaking water.
* **Step 5**

Combine 1/2 cup chile soaking water, soaked ancho chiles, apple cider vinegar, jalapeno pepper, garlic, cilantro, and cumin in a blender. Blend to form a thick sauce. Pour sauce over pork and mix well.

Note book :

You can get a second wind out of your Instant Pot Chilorio with these Torta Sandwiches by user Betty Soup:
Stir together 1 thinly sliced red onion, 3 tablespoons cider vinegar, and 1 teaspoon sugar in a small bowl. Let stand at least 1 hour. Drain. Reheat 1 1/3 cups pork and sauce, covered, in a 2-quart saucepan over medium heat, 5 to 7 minutes. Mash 1 avocado and spread over the bottom half of 4 toasted buns. Top each bun with 1/3 cup pork and sauce and red onion mixture.

Nutrition Facts

Per Serving:
309.1 calories; protein 16.6g 33% DV; carbohydrates 14.9g 5% DV; fat 20.7g 32% DV; cholesterol 65.5mg 22% DV; sodium 1339.7mg 54% DV.

Instant Pot Egg Bites

Prep: 15 mins Cook: 13 mins Additional: 10 mins Total: 38 mins

Servings: 6
Ingredients

* 12 eaches eggs
* 1 teaspoon granulated garlic
* 1 ½ teaspoons salt, or to taste
* 1 ½ teaspoons ground black pepper, or to taste

* 1 cup chopped spinach
* ¾ cup shredded Muenster cheese
* ½ cup chopped onion

Directions
* **Step 1**

Beat eggs in a medium bowl until yellow and frothy. Add garlic, salt, and pepper.
* **Step 2**

Toss spinach, Muenster cheese, and onion together in a small bowl. Divide evenly among the cavities of a silicone egg mold. Pour beaten eggs into each cavity, filling each 3/4 full. Cover mold with aluminum foil.
* **Step 3**

Pour 1/2 cup water into a multi-functional pressure cooker (such as Instant Pot). Place egg mold inside. Close and lock the lid, sealing the vent. Select Steam function; set timer for 13 minutes.
* **Step 4**

Release pressure naturally according to manufacturer's instructions, 10 to 40 minutes.

Nutrition Facts
Per Serving:
187.1 calories; protein 14.8g 30% DV; carbohydrates 3g 1% DV; fat 13g 20% DV; cholesterol 340.9mg 114% DV; sodium 798.1mg 32% DV.

Instant Pot Pork Loin in Cranberry-Dijon Sauce

Prep: 10 mins Cook: 25 mins Additional: 20 mins Total: 55 mins

Servings: 4

Ingredients

* 1 pound boneless pork loin roast
* 1 pinch salt and pepper to taste
* 1 tablespoon butter
* 1 (14 ounce) can whole cranberry sauce
* ½ yellow onion, sliced
* 2 tablespoons Dijon mustard
* 2 tablespoons chopped fresh tarragon
* 1 packet dry onion soup mix
* 1 tablespoon cornstarch

Directions
* **Step 1**

Pat pork loin dry and season on all sides with salt and pepper.
* **Step 2**

Turn on a multi-functional pressure cooker (such as Instant Pot) and select Saute function. Add butter and let melt. Add pork loin and cook on all sides until just a little bit of color shows, about 1 minute per side. Turn off Saute function and add cranberry sauce, sliced onion, Dijon mustard, tarragon, and dry onion mix. Gently combine and spoon some of the sauce over the pork loin.
* **Step 3**

Close and lock the lid. Select high pressure according to manufacturers' instructions; set timer for 9 minutes. Allow 10 to 15 minutes for pressure to build.
* **Step 4**

Release pressure using the natural-release method according to manufacturer's instructions, about 10 minutes. Check internal temperature of the pork loin; an instant-read thermometer inserted into the center should read at least 180 degrees F (82 degrees C). Temperature will continue to rise slightly after the pork loin is removed from pot.
* **Step 5**

Place on a cutting board to allow to rest for 8 to 10 minutes before cutting into thin slices.
* **Step 6**

While pork loin is resting, select Saute function again and stir cornstarch into sauce. Whisk until sauce thickens, 2 to 5 minutes. Serve pork loin with cranberry-Dijon sauce.

Cook's Note:
I made this recently and did not have tarragon on hand. I substituted 1 to 2 teaspoons of dried marjoram and it was great.

Nutrition Facts

Per Serving:
384.5 calories; protein 19.5g 39% DV; carbohydrates 49.3g 16% DV; fat 12.2g 19% DV; cholesterol 61.2mg 20% DV; sodium 1091.3mg 44% DV

Instant Pot Chicken Noodle Soup

Prep: 25 mins Cook: 40 mins Additional: 15 mins Total: 1 hr 20 mins

Servings: 6

Ingredients

- 2 tablespoons salted butter
- 3 eaches carrots, or more to taste, peeled and sliced
- 3 stalks celery, or more to taste, chopped
- 1 medium onion, chopped
- 1 teaspoon ground thyme
- 1 teaspoon dried oregano
- 1 teaspoon salt, or to taste
- ½ teaspoon ground black pepper, or to taste
- 4 cups chicken broth
- 4 cups water
- 4 cubes chicken bouillon
- 2 eaches bay leaves
- 1 pound frozen skinless, boneless chicken breast halves
- 1 (8 ounce) package thin egg noodles
- 1 tablespoon dried parsley

Directions
- **Step 1**

Turn on a multi-functional pressure cooker (such as Instant Pot), select Saute function, and add butter. Add carrots, celery, and onion to the melted butter; saute until soft, 3 to 5 minutes. Stir in thyme, oregano, salt, and pepper. Cancel Saute function.
- **Step 2**

Stir in chicken broth, water, bouillon cubes, and bay leaves. Add frozen chicken breasts. Close and lock the lid. Select high pressure according to manufacturer's instructions; set timer for 12 minutes. Allow 10 to 15 minutes for pressure to build.
- **Step 3**

Release pressure using the natural-release method according to manufacturer's instructions, 10 minutes. Switch to the quick-release method according to manufacturer's instructions, about 5 minutes. Unlock and remove the lid.
- **Step 4**

Remove chicken from the pot. Carefully chop or shred the meat, and add back to the pot.
- **Step 5**

Select Saute function and add egg noodles. Cook until noodles are tender yet firm to the bite, 8 to 10 minutes. Stir in dried parsley and serve.

Cook's Note:

If using unfrozen chicken, you could reduce the time from 12 to 10 minutes

Nutrition Facts
Per Serving:
300.2 calories; protein 22.1g 44% DV; carbohydrates 34.5g 11% DV; fat 7.8g 12% DV; cholesterol 85mg 28% DV; sodium 2046mg 82% DV.

Instant Pot Pineapple Chicken (Frozen Chicken Method)

Prep: 10 mins Cook: 30 mins Additional: 10 mins Total: 50 mins

Servings: 4

Ingredients

- 1 (19 ounce) can unsweetened pineapple chunks
- 3 tablespoons low-sodium soy sauce (such as Bragg)
- 2 tablespoons light-colored honey
- ½ teaspoon salt
- 4 (7 ounce) frozen skinless, boneless chicken breast halves
- 1 red bell pepper, seeded and cut into 1-inch pieces
- 2 tablespoons cornstarch
- ¼ teaspoon ground ginger
- ½ teaspoon red pepper flakes

Directions
- **Step 1**

Drain pineapple chunks and pour the juice into the bottom of a multi-functional pressure cooker (such as Instant Pot), reserving 2 tablespoons of the juice. Add soy sauce, honey, and salt; stir to combine. Place frozen chicken breasts into the pot, making sure that they are not touching.
- **Step 2**

Close and lock the lid. Select Poultry setting according to manufacturer's instructions; set timer for 10 minutes. Allow 10 to 15 minutes for pressure to build.
- **Step 3**

Release pressure using the natural-release method according to manufacturer's instructions, for 5 minutes, then release remaining pressure carefully using the quick-release method according to manufacturer's instructions, about 5 minutes. Unlock and remove the lid. Transfer chicken to a warm plate, cover, and let rest for 5 minutes.
- **Step 4**

Meanwhile, select Saute function on Instant Pot and select high temperature. Add bell pepper and saute for 5 minutes. Mix reserved 2 tablespoons pineapple juice with cornstarch and add slowly to the pot. Stir until mixture thickens. Mix in ginger.
- **Step 5**

Cut the chicken into 1 inch pieces and add to the pot along with the pineapple chunks. Heat through and serve.

Cook's Note:
I find that honey that is lighter in color is less sweet.

Nutrition Facts

Per Serving:
364.1 calories; protein 42.8g 86% DV; carbohydrates 36.4g 12% DV; fat 5g 8% DV; cholesterol 112.8mg 38% DV; sodium 790.7mg 32% DV.

Instant Pot Lemon-Garlic Chicken Thighs with Rice

Prep: 10 mins Cook: 25 mins Additional: 20 mins Total: 55 mins

Servings: 4

Ingredients

- 1 teaspoon cantanzaro herbs (from Savory Spice Shop)
- ½ teaspoon supreme shallot salt (from Savory Spice Shop)
- ½ teaspoon Mt. Olympus Greek seasoning (from Savory Spice Shop)
- ¼ teaspoon garlic powder
- 1 ½ pounds boneless, skinless chicken thighs

- 1 tablespoon grapeseed oil
- 2 cloves minced garlic
- 2 cups chicken broth, divided
- 1 ¾ cups uncooked white rice
- ¼ cup heavy cream
- 1 small lemon, juiced
- 1 tablespoon cornstarch

Directions
- **Step 1**

Turn on a multi-functional pressure cooker (such as Instant Pot) and select Saute function. Add oil once the Instant Pot is hot.
- **Step 2**

Combine cantanzaro herbs, shallot salt, Greek seasoning, and garlic powder in a small bowl. Sprinkle mixture over chicken thighs; sear until chicken can easily come unstuck from the bottom of the pot, 2 to 3 minutes per side. Transfer chicken to a plate. Add minced garlic to Instant Pot and cook for 1 minute. Pour in 1/2 cup chicken broth and scrape off any
 brown bits off the bottom.

- **Step 3**

Turn off Instant Pot . Return chicken thighs to the pot. Add an elevated rack.
- **Step 4**

Combine rice and remaining chicken broth in a small bowl. Set bowl on top of the elevated rack. Close and lock the lid. Select high pressure according to manufacturer's instructions; set timer for 10 minutes. Allow 10 to 15 minutes for pressure to build.
- **Step 5**

Release pressure using the natural-release method according to manufacturer's instructions, about 15 minutes. Release remaining pressure carefully using the quick-release method according to manufacturer's instructions, about 5 minutes. Unlock and remove the lid. Remove cooked rice and transfer chicken to a plate.
- **Step 6**

Whisk together cream, lemon juice, and cornstarch in a small bowl. Stir into the remaining liquid in the Instant Pot and turn on Saute function. Whisk and simmer until sauce has thickened. Serve chicken thighs with sauce.

Nutrition Facts
Per Serving:
696.2 calories; protein 35.6g 71% DV; carbohydrates 73.9g 24% DV; fat 27.5g 42% DV; cholesterol 129.4mg 43% DV; sodium 971.1mg 39% DV.

Instant Pot Midwest Goulash

Prep: 15 mins Cook: 10 mins Additional: 15 mins Total: 40 mins

Servings: 4

Ingredients

- 1 tablespoon olive oil
- 1 pound ground turkey
- 2 small carrots, grated
- ½ onion, diced
- ½ green bell pepper, diced
- 1 tablespoon Italian seasoning, or to taste
- 1 teaspoon garlic powder, or to taste
- 1 teaspoon seasoned salt (such as Lawry's), or to taste
- 1 teaspoon ground black pepper, or to taste
- 1 ½ cups water
- 1 tablespoon Worcestershire sauce
- 1 ½ teaspoons beef bouillon granules
- 2 cups elbow macaroni
- 1 teaspoon paprika
- 1 (15 ounce) can petite diced tomatoes
- 1 (8 ounce) can tomato sauce

Directions
- **Step 1**

Turn on a multi-functional pressure cooker (such as Instant Pot) and select Saute function. Add olive oil and turkey; cook until halfway browned and crumbly, 3 to 4 minutes. Add carrots, onion, bell pepper, Italian seasoning, garlic powder, seasoned salt, and black pepper.
- **Step 2**

Mix water with Worcestershire sauce and bouillon granules in a small bowl. Pour into meat mixture and mix well. Bring to a simmer. Add macaroni and paprika and stir. Add tomatoes and tomato sauce, making sure not to stir after this addition. Close and lock the lid. Set timer for 4 minutes. Allow about 10 minutes for pressure to build.
- **Step 3**

Release pressure carefully using the quick-release method according to manufacturer's instructions to prevent sauce from mixing with the steam, about 5 minutes. Unlock and remove the lid. Mix well.

Cook's Note:
You can also use Italian-seasoned diced tomatoes or stewed tomatoes instead of regular diced.

Nutrition Facts
Per Serving:
460.4 calories; protein 32.1g 64% DV; carbohydrates 53.1g 17% DV; fat 13.2g 20% DV; cholesterol 83.7mg 28% DV; sodium 1414.5mg 57% DV.

Instant Pot Mongolian Chicken

Prep: 10 mins Cook: 20 mins Additional: 15 mins Total: 45 mins

Servings: 6

Ingredients

- 2 tablespoons olive oil
- 4 eaches boneless chicken breast, cut into cubes
- 1 cup chicken broth
- ½ cup brown sugar
- ½ cup soy sauce
- 1 carrot, chopped
- 4 eaches garlic cloves, minced
- 1 tablespoon minced fresh ginger root
- 1 teaspoon chili powder
- 2 tablespoons cornstarch
- ¼ cup water
- 1 teaspoon sesame seeds

Directions
- **Step 1**

Turn on a multi-functional pressure cooker (such as Instant Pot) and select Saute function. Heat olive oil and add chicken cubes; cook until golden, stirring constantly, about 3 minutes. Stir in chicken broth, brown sugar, soy sauce, carrot, garlic, ginger, and chili powder. Close and lock the lid. Select high pressure according to manufacturer's instructions; set timer for 7 minutes. Allow 10 to 15 minutes for pressure to build.
- **Step 2**

Release pressure using the natural-release method according to manufacturer's instructions, about 10 minutes. Complete releasing pressure carefully using the quick-release method according to manufacturer's instructions, about 5 minutes. Unlock and remove the lid. Reselect Saute function.
- **Step 3**

Whisk cornstarch in 1/4 cup water until fully dissolved. Pour into the pot and stir to combine. Cook until sauce thickens, stirring gently, about 4 minutes. Sprinkle with sesame seeds before serving.

Nutrition Facts
Per Serving:
218.5 calories; protein 16.5g 33% DV; carbohydrates 23.4g 8% DV; fat 6.5g 10% DV; cholesterol 40mg 13% DV; sodium 1439.2mg 58% DV.

Instant Pot Colorado Chile Verde

Prep: 15 mins Cook: 50 mins Additional: 15 mins Total: 1 hr 20 mins

Servings: 8

Ingredients

- 1 tablespoon olive oil
- 1 pound chicken breasts, cubed, or more to taste

- ½ large onion, diced
- 2 eaches roasted Hatch chile peppers - seeded, de-veined, and diced, or more to taste
- 3 cloves garlic, minced
- 1 tablespoon ground cumin
- ½ teaspoon salt
- ½ teaspoon freshly ground black pepper
- 2 cups chicken broth
- 1 (16 ounce) jar salsa verde (green salsa)
- 1 (15.5 ounce) can white beans, drained and rinsed
- 2 ears corn, kernels cut from cob
- ¼ cup minced cilantro
- ¼ cup all-purpose flour
- 1 tablespoon potato starch
- 2 tablespoons cold water
- 1 lime, cut into wedges

Directions
- **Step 1**

Turn on a multi-functional pressure cooker (such as Instant Pot), select Saute function, and add olive oil. Add chicken breast, onion, chile peppers, garlic, cumin, salt, and pepper to hot oil. Saute until chicken is browned and onions are soft and translucent, about 5 minutes. Add chicken broth, salsa verde, white beans, corn kernels, and cilantro; mix well. Turn off Saute mode.
- **Step 2**

Close and lock the lid. Select high pressure according to manufacturer's instructions; set timer for 30 minutes. Allow 10 to 15 minutes for pressure to build.
- **Step 3**

Release pressure using the natural-release method according to manufacturer's instructions, about 15 minutes. Unlock and remove the lid. Select Saute function. Stir in flour and cook chile until it thickens, 1 to 2 minutes. If you like a thicker consistency, mix potato starch and water in a small bowl and stir into chile with the flour. Serve with lime wedges.

Nutrition Facts
Per Serving:
337.2 calories; protein 26.8g 54% DV; carbohydrates 48.6g 16% DV; fat 4.2g 6% DV; cholesterol 33.8mg 11% DV; sodium 666.4mg 27% DV.

Instant Pot Chicken and Farro Soup

Prep:15 mins Cook: 30 mins Additional: 15 mins Total: 1 hr

Servings: 6

Ingredients

- 2 tablespoons avocado oil
- 2 cups carrots that have been sliced lengthwise and cut into 3/4-inch slices
- 1 cup sliced celery with leaves
- 1 leek, halved lengthwise and sliced
- 1 ½ teaspoons minced garlic
- 2 tablespoons tomato paste
- 1 teaspoon ground thyme
- 1 teaspoon dried oregano
- 1 teaspoon dried parsley
- 1 teaspoon salt
- ½ teaspoon ground black pepper
- 5 cups low-sodium chicken broth
- 1 cup farro, rinsed
- 1 pound skinless, boneless chicken breasts, trimmed

Directions
- **Step 1**

Turn on a multi-functional pressure cooker (such as Instant Pot) and select Saute function. Heat oil in the hot pot and add carrots, celery, and leek. Cook, stirring frequently, until vegetables start to soften, 3 to 4 minutes. Add garlic and cook until just fragrant, about 30 seconds. Add tomato paste and cook for 1 minute. Stir in thyme, oregano, parsley, salt, and pepper. Pour broth into the pot, add farro, and stir. Push chicken breasts down into the liquid. Close and lock the lid.
- **Step 2**

Select high pressure according to manufacturer's instructions; set timer for 12 minutes. Allow 10 to 15 minutes for pressure to build.
- **Step 3**

Release pressure using the natural-release method according to manufacturer's instructions for 10 minutes. Release remaining pressure carefully using the quick-release method according to manufacturer's instructions, about 5 minutes. Unlock and remove the lid. Transfer chicken to a clean work surface and roughly chop; return to the pot and stir. Taste and salt. Serve.

Nutrition Facts
Per Serving:
279.2 calories; protein 22.9g 46% DV; carbohydrates 32g 10% DV; fat 7.9g 12% DV; cholesterol 46.4mg 16% DV; sodium 613.6mg 25% DV

Instant Pot Vegan Steel-Cut Oats with Apple and Cinnamon

Prep: 5 mins Cook: 20 mins Additional: 10 mins Total: 35 mins

Servings: 6

Ingredients

- 2 cups water
- 1 cup almond milk
- 1 cup steel-cut oats
- 2 tablespoons maple syrup
- 2 tablespoons flaxseed meal
- 1 apple, diced
- 1 teaspoon ground cinnamon
- 1 tablespoon chopped almonds, or more to taste

Directions
- **Step 1**

Combine water, almond milk, oats, maple syrup, flax seed meal, apple, cinnamon, and almonds in a multi-functional pressure cooker (such as Instant Pot). Close and lock the lid. Select high pressure according to manufacturer's instructions; set timer for 10 minutes. Allow 10 minutes for pressure to build.
- **Step 2**

Release pressure using the natural-release method according to manufacturer's instructions, 10 to 15 minutes. Unlock and remove the lid. Stir oatmeal thoroughly and serve immediately.

Cook's Notes:
You can use any non-dairy milk of your choice.

Instead of almonds you can also use chopped pecans, walnuts, or any choice of nuts.

Nutrition Facts
Per Serving:
110.4 calories; protein 2.7g 5% DV; carbohydrates 19.4g 6% DV; fat 2.9g 4% DV; cholesterolmg; sodium 31.4mg 1% DV.

Instant Pot Butter Chicken from Frozen

Prep: 10 mins Cook: 45 mins Additional: 20 mins Total: 1 hr 15 mins

Servings: 3

Ingredients

- 6 tablespoons salted butter, divided
- 3 cloves garlic, minced
- ⅓ cup diced onion
- 9 ounces frozen cubed chicken
- 1 (8 ounce) can tomato sauce
- ¼ cup heavy whipping cream
- 1 tablespoon tandoori seasoning
- 2 teaspoons garam masala
- 1 pinch cayenne pepper
- ¼ cup chopped fresh cilantro, or to taste

Directions
- **Step 1**
Turn on a multi-functional pressure cooker (such as Instant Pot), select Saute function, and add butter. Add onion and garlic to melted butter; saute until fragrant, 3 to 5 minutes. Add frozen chicken, then pour tomato sauce on top. Hit Cancel.
- **Step 2**
Close and lock the lid. Select high pressure according to manufacturer's instructions; set timer for 30 minutes. Allow 10 to 15 minutes for pressure to build.
- **Step 3**
Release pressure using the natural-release method according to manufacturer's instructions, for 15 minutes. Then use the quick-release method to release remaining pressure, about 5 minutes. Unlock and remove the lid.
- **Step 4**
Add whipping cream, tandoori seasoning, garam masala, and cayenne pepper; stir to combine. Serve immediately garnished with cilantro.

Nutrition Facts
Per Serving:
400.3 calories; protein 18.8g 38% DV; carbohydrates 9.6g 3% DV; fat 33g 51% DV; cholesterol 132.1mg 44% DV; sodium 610mg 24% DV

Instant Pot Vegan Chili

Prep: 15 mins Cook: 35 mins Additional: 5 mins Total: 55 mins

Servings: 8

Ingredients

- 1 large onion, diced
- 1 red bell pepper, diced
- 1 ½ cups water
- 4 tablespoons miso powder
- 4 tablespoons chili powder
- 2 tablespoons coconut milk powder
- 2 teaspoons ground cumin
- 1 teaspoon paprika
- ½ teaspoon oregano
- 4 tablespoons vegetable broth powder (such as Seitenbacher Vegetarian Vegetable Broth and Seasoning)
- 2 (16 ounce) cans 3-bean mix, drained and rinsed
- 1 (15 ounce) can black beans, drained and rinsed
- 1 (15 ounce) can pinto beans, drained and rinsed
- 1 (15 ounce) can whole kernel corn, drained
- 1 (10 ounce) can diced tomatoes
- 1 (8 ounce) can tomato sauce
- 1 (6 ounce) can chopped green chilies
- 4 cloves garlic, minced

Directions

- **Step 1**

Turn on a multi-functional pressure cooker (such as Instant Pot) and select Saute function. Add onion and bell pepper and saute for 5 minutes.

- **Step 2**

Combine water, miso powder, chili powder, coconut milk powder, cumin, paprika, and oregano in a bowl and whisk until blended. Pour into the pot with the onion and add vegetable broth powder. Add 3-bean mix, black beans, pinto beans, corn, diced tomatoes, tomato sauce, green chiles, and garlic to the pot and simmer 5 minutes.

- **Step 3**

Close and lock the lid. Select high pressure according to manufacturer's instructions; set timer for 15 minutes. Allow 10 to 15 minutes for pressure to build.

- **Step 4**

Release pressure carefully using the quick-release method according to manufacturer's instructions, about 5 minutes. Unlock and remove the lid.

Cook's Notes:
Use any color bell pepper you prefer.
Feel free to wait for a natural release for the pressure cooker if you have the time.

Nutrition Facts
Per Serving:
327 calories; protein 15.8g 32% DV; carbohydrates 53.4g 17% DV; fat 6.7g 10% DV; cholesterolmg; sodium 1668.4mg 67% DV.

Instant Pot Bahn Flan (Vietnamese Flan)

Prep: 15 mins Cook: 35 mins Additional: 4 hrs 10 mins Total: 5 hrs

Servings: 3

Ingredients

- 2 cups milk
- 1 ⅔ cups white sugar, divided

- 4 large eggs
- 1 large egg yolk

- 1 teaspoon vanilla extract

Directions
- **Step 1**

Warm milk in a saucepan over medium heat. Add 2/3 cup sugar and stir to dissolve, about 3 minutes. Make sure milk does not boil; turn off heat if necessary.
- **Step 2**

Whisk eggs and egg yolk by hand; do not overmix. Pour slowly into the warm milk-sugar mixture and stir continuously over low heat for 1 1/2 minutes.
- **Step 3**

Strain through a tightly woven mesh strainer into a bowl to remove any solids that may have formed. Add vanilla extract to the bowl; mix until well combined. Set aside.
- **Step 4**

Pour 1 cup sugar into a wide skillet over medium heat. Stir occasionally with a wooden spoon until sugar has evenly melted and turned a golden caramel color, about 5 minutes. Immediately remove from heat and pour into a pressure cooker-safe cake pan, coating the bottom with liquid sugar. Pour in custard. Cover tightly with aluminum foil.
- **Step 5**

Place a trivet in the bottom of a multi-functional pressure cooker (such as Instant Pot) and add 1 cup water. Place the cake pan onto the trivet and close and lock the lid. Seal the valve and select high pressure according to manufacturer's instructions; set timer for 9 minutes. Allow 10 to 15 minutes for pressure to build.
- **Step 6**

Release pressure using the natural-release method according to manufacturer's instructions, for 10 minutes, then turn the valve to Venting to release remaining pressure. Unlock and remove the lid. Remove the trivet and pan.
- **Step 7**

Allow to cool for 1 hour, then chill for at least 3 to 4 hours, or overnight. Slide knife carefully around the edges and hold the bottom securely as you invert onto a large serving dish; the caramel should drip over the flan and onto the plate.

Cook's Note:
You can also make 3 individual flans in ramekins. Set cook time to 6 minutes if using ramekins.

Nutrition Facts
Per Serving:
628.4 calories; protein 14.6g 29% DV; carbohydrates 119.6g 39% DV; fat 11.3g 17% DV; cholesterol 329.3mg 110% DV; sodium 162.8mg 7% DV.

Instant Pot Mexican Lentil Soup

Prep: 10 mins Cook: 20 mins Additional: 10 mins Total: 40 mins

Servings: 8

Ingredients

- 1 tablespoon olive oil
- 1 large carrot, peeled and sliced
- 1 small onion, chopped

- 1 yellow bell pepper, chopped
- 1 fresh jalapeño chile pepper, seeded and chopped

- 2 cloves garlic, minced
- 5 cups low-sodium chicken broth
- 1 (16 ounce) jar picante sauce
- 1 ¼ cups dry lentils
- 1 tablespoon taco seasoning
- 1 teaspoon cumin
- ½ cup chopped fresh cilantro
- 1 tablespoon lime juice

Directions
- **Step 1**

Turn on a multi-functional pressure cooker (such as Instant Pot) and select Saute function. Add olive oil and let heat for 1 minute. Add carrot, onion, bell pepper, and jalapeno; saute for 2 minutes. Add garlic and saute for 30 seconds. Hit Cancel.
- **Step 2**

Add broth, picante sauce, lentils, taco seasoning, and cumin. Stir to combine. Close and lock the lid. Select high pressure according to manufacturer's instructions; set timer for 6 minutes. Allow 10 minutes for pressure to build.
- **Step 3**

Release pressure using the natural-release method according to manufacturer's instructions, about 10 minutes. Remove the lid and stir in cilantro and lime juice. Ladle into bowls and serve immediately.

Nutrition Facts
Per Serving:
173.1 calories; protein 11.3g 23% DV; carbohydrates 26.3g 9% DV; fat 2.6g 4% DV; cholesterol 2.5mg 1% DV; sodium 526.3mg 21% DV.

Instant Pot Live Crawfish Boil for Four

Prep :10 mins Cook: 35 mins Additional: 35 mins Total: 1 hr 20 mins

Servings: 4

Ingredients
Crawfish:
4 cups water
2 tablespoons concentrated liquid
shrimp and crab boil (such as Zatarain's
)
2 tablespoons seafood seasoning (such
as Old Bay)
2 pounds live crawfish, rinsed
Potatoes, Corn, and Sausage:

1 pound bite-sized red potatoes (such as
Ruby Sensations)
3 ears corn, shucked and cut into thirds,
or more to taste
1 (12 ounce) package andouille
sausage, sliced
1 tablespoon seafood seasoning (such
as Old Bay)
2 cups water

Directions
- **Step 1**

Combine water, dry crab boil, and seafood seasoning in a multi-functional pressure cooker (such as Instant Pot). Add live crawfish. Close and lock the lid. Select high pressure according to manufacturer's instructions; set timer for 0 minutes. Allow 15 minutes for pressure to build.
- **Step 2**

Release pressure carefully using the quick-release method according to manufacturer's instructions, about 2 minutes. Carefully pour crawfish and the liquid into a large bowl and let sit for 30 minutes to soak while you prepare the rest of the meal.
* **Step 3**

Add potatoes, corn, andouille sausage, and 1 tablespoon seafood seasoning to the pot. Pour in water and stir until evenly combined. Close and lock the lid.
* **Step 4**

Select high pressure according to manufacturer's instructions; set timer for 5 minutes. Allow 15 minutes for pressure to build.
* **Step 5**

Release pressure carefully using the quick-release method according to manufacturer's instructions, about 2 minutes. Divide the mixture between 4 plates and serve with crawfish.

Cook's Note:
Have plenty of napkins ready and extra plates for discarding shells.

Nutrition Facts
Per Serving:
570.5 calories; protein 45.8g 92% DV; carbohydrates 34.4g 11% DV; fat 27.7g 43% DV; cholesterol 291.6mg 97% DV; sodium 5130.6mg 205% DV

Instant Pot Wheat Berries

Prep: 5 mins Cook: 40 mins Additional: 10 mins Total: 55 mins

Servings: 10

Ingredients

* 6 eaches water
* 2 cups wheat berries

* ½ teaspoon kosher salt, or to taste

Directions
* **Step 1**

Turn on a multi-functional pressure cooker (such as Instant Pot). Add water and wheat berries; stir once. Close and lock the lid. Select Manual pressure according to manufacturer's instructions and set timer for 27 minutes. Allow 10 to 15 minutes for pressure to build.
* **Step 2**

Release pressure using the natural-release method according to manufacturer's instructions, about 10 minutes. Release remaining pressure carefully using the quick-release method according to manufacturer's instructions, about 5 minutes. Unlock and remove the lid.
* **Step 3**

Drain wheat berries and mix in salt.

Cook's Note:
Place a thin hand towel over the Instant Pot(R) vent before flicking it open. I like setting my Instant Pot(R) on a cool stove with the overhead vent on to pull the steam out of the house.

Nutrition Facts
Per Serving:
125.6 calories; protein 4.8g 10% DV; carbohydrates 27.3g 9% DV; fat 0.6g 1% DV; cholesterolmg; sodium 102.4mg 4% DV.

Instant Pot Beef Pho

Prep: 20 mins Cook: 53 mins Additional: 35 mins Total: 1 hr 48 mins

Servings: 6

Ingredients

- 3 pounds beef soup bones
- 3 eaches whole cloves
- 3 eaches whole star anise pods
- 1 (1/2 inch) piece cinnamon stick
- 1 teaspoon olive oil
- 1 large onion, chopped
- 1 (2 inch) piece ginger, peeled
- ½ pound chuck roast
- 2 tablespoons fish sauce
- 1 tablespoon raw sugar
- 2 teaspoons kosher salt
- 9 cups water
- ½ pound top round beef
- 12 ounces dry rice stick noodles
- ¼ cup chopped cilantro
- 2 medium (4-1/8" long)s green onions, chopped

Directions
- **Step 1**

Set an electric pressure cooker (such as Instant Pot) on "Saute" mode. Add beef bones with water to cover; bring to a boil. Boil vigorously for 3 minutes; drain. Transfer bones to a plate. Dry out the pot and return it to the pressure cooker.
- **Step 2**

Set cooker on "Saute" mode. Add cloves, star anise, and cinnamon stick to the bottom of the pot. Toast, turning once to avoid burning, until aromatic, about 5 minutes. Transfer to a bowl.
- **Step 3**

Pour olive oil into the hot pot. Add chopped onion and ginger; cook and stir until softened and starting to brown, about 10 minutes.
- **Step 4**

Place the beef bones, toasted spices, chuck roast, fish sauce, sugar, and salt in the pot. Pour in 9 cups of water, filling the pot 3/4 full. Seal pressure cooker and bring to high pressure according to manufacturer's instructions; cook for 30 minutes. Release pressure through natural-release method for 20 minutes.

- **Step 5**

Remove the chuck roast from the pot. Pour the stock through a sieve into another pot. Discard the bones and spices. Put the pot on the stove, cover, and keep hot over low heat.
- **Step 6**

Place top round into the freezer for 15 minutes. Place rice noodles in a bowl with warm water to cover; soak until pliable, about 15 minutes. Drain the noodles.
- **Step 7**

Remove the top round from the freezer and slice it as thinly as possible, cutting against the grain for best results. Slice the chuck roast.

- **Step 8**

Put a small pile of rice noodles in the middle of a soup bowl. Top with cilantro and green onions. Arrange slices of raw top round and chuck roast around the noodles. Pour in the hot stock, carefully, until the bowl is full. Repeat for additional servings.

Editor's Note:

Consuming raw beef may increase your risk of foodborne illness, especially if you have certain medical conditions.

Nutrition data for this recipe includes the full amount of beef bones and aromatics. The actual amount consumed will vary.

Nutrition Facts

Per Serving:

366.8 calories; protein 17.5g 35% DV; carbohydrates 52.1g 17% DV; fat 8.7g 14% DV; cholesterol 40.2mg 13% DV; sodium 1050.1mg 42% DV.

Instant Pot Keto Thai Chicken Soup (Tom Kha Gai)

Prep: 10 mins Cook: 40 mins Additional: 15 mins Total: 1 hr 5 mins

Servings: 6

Ingredients

- 4 eaches boneless chicken breasts, diced
- 2 ½ cups chicken broth
- 2 ½ cups water
- 1 (14 ounce) can coconut cream
- 2 tablespoons Thai garlic chile paste
- 2 tablespoons coconut aminos
- 1 tablespoon lime juice
- 1 teaspoon salt
- 1 teaspoon ground ginger
- 1 teaspoon finely chopped Thai basil
- 1 tablespoon fresh cilantro

Directions

- **Step 1**

Combine chicken, chicken broth, water, coconut cream, garlic chile paste, coconut aminos, lime juice, salt, ginger, and basil in a multi-functional pressure cooker (such as Instant Pot). Close and lock the lid. Select Soup/Broth function according to manufacturer's instructions; set timer for 30 minutes. Allow 10 to 15 minutes for pressure to build.

- **Step 2**

Release pressure carefully using the slow-release method according to manufacturer's instructions, about 10 minutes. Release remaining pressure using the quick-release method, about 5 minutes. Unlock and remove the lid. Serve soup in bowls and sprinkle with fresh cilantro.

Nutrition Facts

Per Serving:

320.8 calories; protein 17.6g 35% DV; carbohydrates 9.2g 3% DV; fat 25.4g 39% DV; cholesterol 41.5mg 14% DV; sodium 1043.7mg 42% DV.

Instant Pot Coconut Chicken Curry with Sweet Potato

Prep: 10 mins Cook: 25 mins Additional: 5 mins Total: 40 mins

Servings: 6

Ingredients

- 2 tablespoons grapeseed oil, divided
- 1 pound chicken tenders
- 1 teaspoon salt, divided
- 1 pinch ground black pepper
- ½ cup coarsely chopped onion
- ½ cup diced red bell pepper
- ½ cup diced green bell pepper
- 2 ½ teaspoons curry powder
- 1 (14 ounce) can coconut milk
- 1 medium sweet potato, peeled and diced
- ½ cup peeled and chopped carrots
- 1 tablespoon peanut butter

Directions
- **Step 1**

Turn on a multi-functional pressure cooker (such as Instant Pot) and select Saute function. Once the pot is hot, add 1 tablespoon oil. Season chicken with 1/2 teaspoon salt and pepper. Add chicken to the pot and cook until no longer pink in the center, 5 to 7 minutes. Remove chicken and cover to keep warm. Add remaining 1 tablespoon oil to the pot and cook onion and bell peppers until softened, 3 to 5 minutes. Season with curry powder and remaining salt. Mix in coconut milk, sweet potatoes, and carrots. Bring to a boil.

- **Step 2**

Hit cancel on Saute function. Close and lock the lid. Select high pressure according to manufacturer's instructions; set timer for 3 minutes. Allow 10 to 15 minutes for pressure to build.

- **Step 3**

Dice cooked chicken while vegetables are cooking.

- **Step 4**

Release pressure carefully using the quick-release method according to manufacturer's instructions, about 5 minutes. Unlock and remove the lid. Mix in chicken and peanut butter and serve.

Nutrition Facts
Per Serving:
320.2 calories; protein 18.9g 38% DV; carbohydrates 14.2g 5% DV; fat 21.9g 34% DV; cholesterol 43.1mg 14% DV; sodium 476.1mg 19% DV

Instant Pot Beef and Vegetable Soup

Prep: 30 mins Cook: 50 mins Additional: 10 mins Total: 1 hr 30 mins

Servings: 8

Ingredients

- 1 tablespoon olive oil
- 2 pounds boneless beef chuck roast, cut into cubes, or to taste
- 5 large carrots, chopped
- 1 large yellow onion, chopped
- 2 stalks celery, chopped
- 6 cups water
- 3 large turnips, peeled and diced
- 1 pound fresh green beans, trimmed and sliced
- 2 tablespoons tomato paste
- 2 tablespoons salt, or more to taste
- 2 tablespoons garlic powder, or more to taste
- 1 tablespoon onion powder, or more to taste
- 1 tablespoon celery seed
- 2 leaf (blank)s bay leaves
- 1 pinch ground black pepper to taste

Directions

Step 1

Heat olive oil in a multi-functional pressure cooker (such as Instant Pot) and select Saute function. Cook beef cubes until brown on all sides, 5 to 10 minutes. Transfer to a plate. Cook carrots, onion, and celery until translucent, about 5 minutes. Return beef to the pot; add water, turnips, green beans, tomato paste, salt, garlic powder, onion powder, celery seed, and bay leaves.

Step 2

Close and lock the lid. Select high pressure according to manufacturer's instructions; set timer for 30 minutes. Allow 10 to 15 minutes for pressure to build.

Step 3

Release pressure using the natural-release method according to manufacturer's instructions, 10 to 40 minutes. Unlock and remove the lid. Taste the soup; add more salt, garlic, onion, and pepper, if needed.

Cook's Note:
Sometimes we mix 1 tablespoon xanthan gum with some water to thicken it up.

Nutrition Facts
Per Serving:
264.8 calories; protein 16.4g 33% DV; carbohydrates 18.2g 6% DV; fat 14.7g 23% DV; cholesterol 51.5mg 17% DV; sodium 1905.2mg 76% DV.

Instant Pot Kung Pao Broccoli

Prep: 10 mins Cook: 10 mins Additional: 5 mins Total: 25 mins

Servings: 4

Ingredients

- 6 tablespoons soy sauce
- 3 tablespoons rice vinegar
- 2 tablespoons toasted sesame oil
- 2 tablespoons sambal oelek (chile paste)
- 1 tablespoon dry sherry
- 1 teaspoon minced garlic
- 6 cups broccoli florets
- 2 tablespoons chopped roasted peanuts
- 2 medium (4-1/8" long)s green onions, chopped

Directions
- **Step 1**

Whisk soy sauce, rice vinegar, sesame oil, sambal oelek, sherry, and garlic together in a bowl. Pour sauce into a multi-functional pressure cooker (such as Instant Pot). Set a steamer basket on top of the sauce and place broccoli inside the basket. Close and lock the lid. Select high pressure according to manufacturer's instructions; set timer for 0 minutes. Allow 10 to 15 minutes for pressure to build.
- **Step 2**

Release pressure carefully using the quick-release method according to manufacturer's instructions, about 5 minutes. Lift the steamer basket out and dump broccoli into the sauce below. Stir to coat.
- **Step 3**

Divide broccoli between serving plates and garnish with peanuts and green onions.

Nutrition Facts
Per Serving:
171.3 calories; protein 6.5g 13% DV; carbohydrates 17.2g 6% DV; fat 10.7g 17% DV; cholesterolmg; sodium 1485.9mg 59% DV.

Instant Pot Cheesy Mexican Lentils and Rice

Prep: 10 mins Cook:20 mins Additional: 15 mins Total: 45 mins

Servings: 6

Ingredients

- 3 cups chicken broth
- 1 (10 ounce) can diced tomatoes with green chile peppers
- ¾ cup brown lentils
- ¾ cup brown rice
- 1 small onion, chopped
- 2 eaches jalapeno peppers, seeded and chopped
- 2 cloves garlic, minced
- 1 tablespoon taco seasoning
- 1 teaspoon dried Mexican oregano
- 1 teaspoon ground cumin
- 2 cups shredded Mexican cheese blend
- 1 tablespoon chopped fresh cilantro, or to taste

Directions
- **Step 1**

Combine chicken broth, tomatoes, lentils, rice, onion, jalapeno peppers, garlic, taco seasoning, oregano, and cumin in a multi-functional pressure cooker (such as Instant Pot). Close and lock the lid. Select high pressure according to manufacturer's instructions; set timer for 8 minutes. Allow 10 to 15 minutes for pressure to build.

- **Step 2**

Release pressure using the natural-release method according to manufacturer's instructions, about 10 minutes.
- **Step 3**

Open the lid and stir in 1/2 of the Mexican cheese blend. Sprinkle remaining cheese over the top. Put the lid back on top and let sit for 4 minutes. Garnish with cilantro.

Cook's Note:
You can also use green lentils, if preferred.

Nutrition Facts
Per Serving:
338.5 calories; protein 17.5g 35% DV; carbohydrates 39.8g 13% DV; fat 12g 19% DV;
cholesterol 36.4mg 12% DV; sodium 1108.8mg 44% DV

Instant Pot Potato and Bacon Soup

Prep: 10 mins Cook: 40 mins Additional: 10 mins Total: 1 hr

Servings: 6

Ingredients

- 1 tablespoon olive oil
- 6 slices bacon, chopped
- 1 large onion, chopped
- 2 ribs celery, sliced
- 1 tablespoon minced garlic
- 1 teaspoon ground thyme
- 2 ½ pounds red potatoes, diced
- 4 cups chicken broth
- 2 tablespoons milk
- 2 tablespoons cornstarch
- 1 cup milk
- 1 pinch salt and ground black pepper to taste

Directions
- **Step 1**

Turn on a multi-functional pressure cooker (such as Instant Pot) and select Saute
function. Add olive oil and let heat for 1 minute. Add bacon and cook until bacon is
crispy and fat has rendered out, about 8 minutes. Transfer bacon to a paper towel-lined
plate using a slotted spoon.
- **Step 2**

Add onion and celery to the bacon drippings and cook for 2 minutes. Add garlic and
thyme and cook for 1 minute. Cancel Saute mode. Add potatoes and broth. Close and
lock the lid. Select high pressure according to manufacturer's instructions; set timer for 8
minutes. Allow 10 minutes for pressure to build.
- **Step 3**

Release pressure using the natural-release method according to manufacturer's
instructions, about 10 minutes.
- **Step 4**

Whisk together 2 tablespoons of milk and cornstarch in a small bowl to make a slurry.
Open the pot and stir in cornstarch slurry and 1 cup of milk. Season with salt and pepper.
Let soup sit, stirring several times, until thickened, about 10 minutes. Ladle into bowls
and sprinkle with bacon.

Nutrition Facts
Per Serving:
263.3 calories; protein 9.8g 20% DV; carbohydrates 39.2g 13% DV; fat 7.7g 12% DV;
cholesterol 17.8mg 6% DV; sodium 1062.2mg 43% DV.

Instant Pot Spicy Macaroni Salad

Prep: 15 mins Cook: 15 mins Additional: 1 hr 10 mins Total: 1 hr 40 mins

Servings: 4

Ingredients

- ½ (8 ounce) package elbow macaroni
- 1 ½ cups water
- 1 large egg
- ⅓ cup diced red bell pepper
- ⅓ cup cubed pepper Jack cheese
- ¼ cup diced jalapeno pepper, or to taste
- ¼ cup sliced celery
- 2 tablespoons diced onion
- ½ cup mayonnaise
- ½ tablespoon apple cider vinegar
- 2 teaspoons chile-garlic sauce (such as Sriracha)
- ½ teaspoon salt
- ¼ teaspoon garlic powder
- ⅛ teaspoon cayenne pepper
- 1 pinch freshly ground black pepper to taste

Directions
- **Step 1**

Place macaroni into the bottom of a multi-functional pressure cooker (such as Instant Pot) and pour in water. Add a trivet on top of that, so that it sits above the the water, and place the egg on it. Close and lock the lid; turn the valve to Sealing. Select high pressure according to manufacturer's instructions; set timer for 5 minutes. Allow 10 to 15 minutes for pressure to build.
- **Step 2**

Release pressure carefully using the quick-release method according to manufacturer's instructions, about 5 minutes. Unlock and remove the lid. Remove the egg and place into a bowl of ice water for 5 minutes; remove the trivet.
- **Step 3**

Leave the macaroni in the liner, but remove it from the Instant Pot to avoid additional residual cooking. Add several ice cubes and cold water to the liner, stirring macaroni, which will stop the cooking process.
- **Step 4**

Pour macaroni into a colander; drain very well to avoid a watery macaroni salad. Dry out the inside of the liner and return the macaroni to the liner.
- **Step 5**

Peel the egg and dice. Add egg, red bell pepper, pepper Jack cheese, jalapeno, celery, and onion to the pot and stir.
- **Step 6**

Whisk mayonnaise, vinegar, Sriracha, salt, garlic powder, cayenne, and black pepper together in a small bowl. Add dressing to the macaroni mixture, stir until well incorporated. Transfer the salad to a bowl and refrigerate for at least 1 hour, allowing time for the flavors to meld.

Cook's Note:
If your preference is salad dressing (such as Miracle Whip(R)) rather than mayonnaise, please feel free to sub it.

Nutrition Facts
Per Serving:

374.3 calories; protein 8.2g 16% DV; carbohydrates 24.6g 8% DV; fat 27.1g 42% DV; cholesterol 68.7mg 23% DV; sodium 655.9mg 26% DV.

Instant Pot Lentil Chicken Noodle Soup

Prep: 10 mins Cook: 20 mins Additional: 20 mins Total: 50 mins

Servings: 6

Ingredients

- 2 tablespoons butter
- 1 medium onion, chopped
- 10 medium (blank)s baby carrots, sliced
- 2 stalks celery, sliced
- 1 tablespoon all-purpose flour
- 6 cups chicken broth
- 1 pound cubed, cooked chicken
- 1 cup lentils
- 1 teaspoon dried parsley flakes
- 1 teaspoon paprika
- 1 teaspoon dried dill
- ½ teaspoon thyme
- 1 cup egg noodles (such as No Yolks)
- 1 tablespoon lemon juice
- 1 pinch salt and ground black pepper to taste

Directions
- **Step 1**

Turn on a multi-functional pressure cooker (such as Instant Pot) and select Saute function. Melt butter and add onion, carrots, and celery. Saute for 2 minutes. Sprinkle flour over the vegetables, stir, and hit cancel.
- **Step 2**

Add broth, chicken, lentils, parsley, paprika, dill, and thyme. Close and lock the lid. Select high pressure according to manufacturer's instructions; set timer for 8 minutes. Allow 10 minutes for pressure to build.
- **Step 3**

Release pressure using the quick release method according to manufacturer's instructions, about 5 minutes. Turn the pot off and remove the lid. Stir in noodles and lemon juice. Let sit for 15 minutes or until noodles are cooked. Ladle into bowls and salt and pepper to taste.

Nutrition Facts
Per Serving:
292.9 calories; protein 23.4g 47% DV; carbohydrates 30.1g 10% DV; fat 8.4g 13% DV; cholesterol 59.4mg 20% DV; sodium 1281.9mg 51% DV.

Instant Pot Spicy Orange Chicken

Prep: 15 mins Cook: 25 mins Additional: 10 mins Total: 50 mins

Servings: 4

Ingredients

- 1 tablespoon hot chili sesame oil

- 1 medium sweet onion, coarsely chopped
- 1 cup chopped broccoli
- 2 tablespoons finely chopped garlic
- 1 tablespoon red pepper flakes
- 1 teaspoon garlic salt
- 1 teaspoon ground ginger
- ¼ teaspoon grated orange zest
- ¾ cup orange juice
- ½ cup reduced-sodium tamari
- ¼ cup spicy chili sauce (such as Maggi Masala)
- ¼ cup honey
- 1 pound chicken breasts, cut into 1-inch pieces
- 3 tablespoons cornstarch
- ½ cup chicken broth, warmed
- 2 tablespoons aji mirin sweet rice cooking wine (such as Kikkoman)

Directions
- **Step 1**

Turn on a multi-functional pressure cooker (such as Instant Pot) and select Saute function. Heat sesame oil in the pot and add onion. Saute, stirring occasionally, until translucent, about 2 minutes.
- **Step 2**

Add broccoli, garlic, red pepper flakes, garlic salt, ginger, and orange zest. Cook and stir until fragrant, about 1 minute. Pour in orange juice, tamari, chili sauce, and honey. Stir in chicken. Select high pressure according to manufacturer's instructions; set timer for 5 minutes. Allow 10 to 15 minutes for pressure to build.
- **Step 3**

Release pressure using the natural-release method according to manufacturer's instructions, 10 to 40 minutes. Meanwhile, whisk cornstarch with chicken broth until dissolved.
- **Step 4**

Pull chicken and vegetables out of the sauce using a large slotted spoon. Place pressure cooker back on Saute mode. Cook until sauce starts bubbling; add cornstarch mixture. Let sit for 1 minute, stir, and turn pressure cooker off.
- **Step 5**

Stir aji mirin into the sauce. Add chicken and vegetables back in.

Cook's Note:
Use any cuts of chicken you prefer.

Nutrition Facts
Per Serving:
339.7 calories; protein 28g 56% DV; carbohydrates 40g 13% DV; fat 6.4g 10% DV; cholesterol 59.3mg 20% DV; sodium 2692.6mg 108% DV.

Instant Pot Beef Paprika

Prep: 15 mins Cook: 50 mins Additional: 10 mins Total: 1 hr 15 mins

Servings: 8

Ingredients

- 2 tablespoons olive oil
- 2 pounds cubed beef stew meat
- 1 pinch salt and ground black pepper to taste

- 2 cloves garlic, minced
- 1 cup diced onion
- Sauce:
- 1 ½ cups water, divided
- ¾ cup ketchup
- 2 tablespoons Worcestershire sauce
- 1 tablespoon brown sugar
- 2 teaspoons salt
- 2 teaspoons smoked paprika
- ½ teaspoon dry mustard
- ⅛ teaspoon cayenne pepper
- 1 dash hot pepper sauce (such as Tabasco)
- 2 tablespoons all-purpose flour

Directions
- **Step 1**

Turn on a 6- or 8-quart multi-functional pressure cooker (such as Instant Pot) and select Saute function. Add olive oil and meat, season with salt and pepper, and saute in batches until browned, 5 to 7 minutes per batch. Remove meat to a plate. Add onion and garlic to the pot and cook until tender and fragrant, about 5 minutes.
- **Step 2**

Return meat to the pot and stir in 1 1/4 cups water, ketchup, Worcestershire sauce, brown sugar, salt, paprika, dry mustard, cayenne pepper, and hot pepper sauce. Cancel Saute function.
- **Step 3**

Close and lock the lid. Select high pressure according to manufacturer's instructions; set timer for 15 minutes. Allow 10 to 15 minutes for pressure to build.
- **Step 4**

Release pressure using the natural-release method according to manufacturer's instructions, about 10 minutes.
- **Step 5**

Blend remaining 1/4 cup water with flour in a small bowl. Gradually stir into the meat mixture and select Saute function. Heat until thickened, about 5 minutes.

Cook's Note:
For the adventurous folks, turn it into stew by adding chopped carrots, green beans, chopped potatoes, and chopped celery.

Nutrition Facts
Per Serving:
297.2 calories; protein 19.5g 39% DV; carbohydrates 12.1g 4% DV; fat 19g 29% DV; cholesterol 62.6mg 21% DV; sodium 941mg 38% DV.

Instant Pot Savory Sriracha Oatmeal

Prep: 10 mins Cook: 15 mins Additional: 5 mins Total: 30 mins

Servings:2

Ingredients

- 1 cup chicken broth
- 1 cup water
- 1 cup old-fashioned rolled oats
- 1 tablespoon low-sodium soy sauce
- 1 tablespoon Sriracha sauce
- 2 teaspoons minced fresh rosemary
- 1 clove garlic, minced
- 1 teaspoon butter

- 2 eaches eggs
- 1 teaspoon Sriracha sauce, or to taste

Directions
- **Step 1**

Combine chicken broth, water, oats, soy sauce, 1 tablespoon Sriracha, rosemary, and garlic in a multi-functional pressure cooker (such as Instant Pot). Stir well. Close and lock the lid.
- **Step 2**

Select High pressure according to manufacturer's instructions; set timer for 5 minutes. Allow 10 to 15 minutes for pressure to build.
- **Step 3**

Release pressure carefully using the quick-release method according to manufacturer's instructions, about 5 minutes. Unlock and remove the lid.
- **Step 4**

While oatmeal is cooking, melt butter in a nonstick skillet over medium heat. Add eggs to the skillet and cook until outer edges become opaque, about 1 minute. Cover, reduce heat to low, and cook until whites are completely set, about 4 minutes.
- **Step 5**

Spoon the oatmeal mixture into 2 bowls, top each with a fried egg and remaining Sriracha sauce.

Cook's Note:
You can poach the eggs instead of frying them.

Nutrition Facts
Per Serving:
254.6 calories; protein 12g 24% DV; carbohydrates 30.4g 10% DV; fat 9.4g 15% DV; cholesterol 172.1mg 57% DV; sodium 1308.9mg 52% DV.

Instant Pot Egg Roll in a Bowl

Prep:15 mins Cook:30 mins Total: 45 mins

Servings: 4

Ingredients

- 2 tablespoons olive oil
- ½ cup diced sweet onion
- ½ cup grated carrot
- 1 teaspoon minced garlic
- ½ pound ground chicken
- ½ cup bulk pork sausage
- 4 ½ cups sliced cabbage
- ½ cup water
- 2 tablespoons tamari
- 1 tablespoon honey
- ½ teaspoon ground ginger
- ½ teaspoon freshly ground black pepper
- ¼ teaspoon salt
- 1 teaspoon sesame oil

Directions
- **Step 1**

Turn on a multi-functional pressure cooker (such as Instant Pot) and select Saute function. Add olive oil, followed by onion, carrot, and garlic; cook until onion is translucent, 5 to 7 minutes. Add ground chicken and ground sausage and cook until browned, 5 to 10 minutes.

- **Step 2**

Stir in cabbage, water, tamari, honey, ginger, pepper, and salt. Close and lock the lid. Select high pressure according to manufacturer's instructions; set timer for 10 minutes. Allow 10 to 15 minutes for pressure to build.
- **Step 3**

Release pressure using the natural-release method according to manufacturer's instructions, 10 to 15 minutes. Stir and add sesame oil.

Cook's Note:
You can use brown sugar instead of honey if you like.

Nutrition Facts
Per Serving:
231.6 calories; protein 17.7g 35% DV; carbohydrates 14.6g 5% DV; fat 11.9g 18% DV; cholesterol 41mg 14% DV; sodium 841mg 34% DV

Instant Pot Ham and Bean Soup

Prep: 15 mins Cook: 35 mins Additional: 10 mins Total: 1 hr

Servings: 8

Ingredients

- 2 tablespoons butter
- 2 medium carrots, sliced
- 2 stalk (blank)s celery ribs, chopped
- ½ cup chopped onion
- 4 (15.5 ounce) cans great northern beans, rinsed and drained
- 4 cups chicken broth
- 2 cups cubed fully cooked ham
- 1 teaspoon chili powder
- ½ teaspoon minced garlic
- ¼ teaspoon ground black pepper
- 1 bay leaf

Directions
- **Step 1**

Turn on a multi-functional pressure cooker (such as Instant Pot) and select Saute function. Melt butter in the pot; add carrots, celery, and onion. Saute until vegetables are tender, 5 to 7 minutes.
- **Step 2**

Add beans, broth, ham, chili powder, garlic, pepper, and bay leaf to the pot. Close and lock the lid. Select Soup setting according to manufacturers' instructions. Cook until flavors meld, about 30 minutes.
- **Step 3**

Release pressure using the natural-release method according to manufacturer's instructions, 10 to 40 minutes.

Cook's Notes:
Substitute margarine for the butter if desired.
You can use one 48-ounce jar of mixed beans plus 1 can Northern beans instead of the 4 cans of Northern beans.

Nutrition Facts

Per Serving:
383.5 calories; protein 23.5g 47% DV; carbohydrates 50.2g 16% DV; fat 10.4g 16% DV; cholesterol 29.6mg 10% DV; sodium 1075.5mg 43% DV.

Instant Pot Make-Ahead Breakfast Burritos

Prep: 20 mins Cook: 40 mins Additional: 20 mins Total: 1 hr 20 mins

Servings: 12

Ingredients

- 3 silicone ice cube trays for water bottles
- 1 serving cooking spray
- 12 slices bacon, cooked and crumbled
- ¾ cup shredded Cheddar cheese
- ½ cup chopped green bell pepper
- 3 medium (4-1/8" long)s green onions, chopped
- 12 large eggs
- ¼ cup half-and-half
- 1 pinch salt and ground black pepper to taste
- 3 sheets aluminum foil
- 12 (8 inch) flour tortillas

Directions
- **Step 1**

Spray ice cube trays with nonstick cooking spray. Divide bacon, Cheddar cheese, bell pepper, and green onions among the molds.
- **Step 2**

Whisk eggs, half-and-half, salt, and pepper together in a measuring glass with a pour spout. Slowly pour egg mixture into the molds until they are full but not overflowing. Spray foil sheets with cooking spray and seal each mold individually.
- **Step 3**

Pour 1 1/4 cups water into the bottom of a multi-functional pressure cooker (such as Instant Pot) and place a trivet inside. Carefully stack all 3 molds on top of the trivet.
- **Step 4**

Close and lock the lid. Select high pressure according to manufacturer's instructions; set timer for 30 minutes. Allow 10 minutes for pressure to build.
- **Step 5**

Release pressure using the natural-release method according to manufacturer's instructions, about 15 minutes. Unlock and remove the lid. Transfer molds to a clean work surface, remove foil, and let sit for 5 minutes.
- **Step 6**

Turn molds over to release the cooked filling. Place one in the center of each flour tortilla and roll into burritos. Let burritos cool. Wrap in parchment paper, place in a large resealable plastic bag, and freeze.

Cook's Notes:
Feel free to substitute the burrito filling with the **Ingredients** of your choice. Just keep in mind that you need 4 eggs per mold (1 per slot).
I recommend wrapping them in parchment paper instead of foil so you can go straight from the freezer to the microwave.

Nutrition Facts

Per Serving:
333.3 calories; protein 17g 34% DV; carbohydrates 28.7g 9% DV; fat 16.4g 25% DV; cholesterol 208.5mg 70% DV; sodium 641.1mg 26% DV.

Instant Pot Strawberries and Cream Oatmeal

Prep: 5 mins Cook:15 mins Additional: 5 mins Total: 25 mins

Servings: 1

Ingredients

- ½ cup water
- ⅔ cup 1% milk
- ½ cup rolled oats
- 2 tablespoons dried strawberries
- 1 tablespoon heavy whipping cream
- 1 teaspoon cinnamon sugar
- 1 dash salt
- 2 eaches fresh strawberries, sliced

Directions
- **Step 1**

Pour water into a multi-functional pressure cooker (such as Instant Pot). Set elevated trivet inside of the pot.
- **Step 2**

Mix milk, oats, freeze-dried strawberries, cream, cinnamon sugar, and salt together in a small glass bowl. Set bowl on top of the trivet. Close and lock the lid. Select Porridge function; set timer for 5 minutes. Allow 10 to 15 minutes for pressure to build.
- **Step 3**

Release pressure carefully using the quick-release method according to manufacturer's instructions, about 5 minutes. Unlock and remove the lid. Garnish oatmeal with fresh strawberries.

Cook's Note:
You can also release pressure naturally for 15 minutes and then quick-release the remaining pressure.

Nutrition Facts
Per Serving:
341.6 calories; protein 11.6g 23% DV; carbohydrates 52.6g 17% DV; fat 9.9g 15% DV; cholesterol 28.5mg 10% DV; sodium 471.2mg 19% DV.

Instant Pot Spanish Rice with Ground Beef

Prep: 10 mins Cook: 30 mins Additional: 10 mins Total: 50 mins

Servings: 6

Ingredients

- 1 pound ground beef
- 2 (14 ounce) cans petite diced tomatoes
- 1 cup long-grain rice
- 1 cup chopped green bell pepper
- 1 cup chopped onion
- ¼ cup beef broth

- 2 cloves garlic, minced
- 2 teaspoons chili powder
- 1 teaspoon browning and seasoning sauce (such as Kitchen Bouquet)
- 1 teaspoon dried thyme

Directions
- **Step 1**

Turn on a multi-functional pressure cooker (such as Instant Pot) and select Saute function. Cook and stir until browned and crumbly, 5 to 7 minutes. Drain if necessary.
- **Step 2**

Stir tomatoes, rice, bell pepper, onion, beef broth, garlic, chili powder, seasoning sauce, and thyme into the pot. Close and lock the lid. Select low pressure according to manufacturer's instructions; set timer for 12 minutes. Allow 10 to 15 minutes for pressure to build.
- **Step 3**

Release pressure using the natural-release method according to manufacturer's instructions for 10 minutes. Unlock and remove the lid.

Nutrition Facts
Per Serving:
300.9 calories; protein 16.9g 34% DV; carbohydrates 34.2g 11% DV; fat 9.6g 15% DV; cholesterol 47.3mg 16% DV; sodium 298.4mg 12% DV

Instant Pot Jamaican Chicken Curry

Prep: 15 mins Cook: 20 mins Additional: 15 mins Total: 50 mins

Servings: 6

Ingredients

- 2 tablespoons ghee
- 1 medium onion, chopped
- 1 tablespoon minced garlic
- 1 tablespoon minced fresh ginger
- 2 tablespoons Jamaican curry powder
- 1 fresh jalapeno pepper, seeded and sliced
- ¼ teaspoon ground thyme
- 1 pinch salt and ground black pepper to taste
- 2 cups chicken broth
- 1 ½ pounds boneless, skinless chicken thighs, cut into 3 pieces each
- 2 medium potatoes, peeled and cubed
- 1 pound baby carrots
- 3 cups steamed basmati rice

Directions
- **Step 1**

Turn on a multi-functional pressure cooker (such as Instant Pot) and select Saute function. Heat ghee. Add onion and cook until starting to turn clear, 2 to 3 minutes. Add garlic and ginger and cook, stirring, until garlic is fragrant, about 1 minute. Stir in Jamaican curry powder, jalapeno, thyme, salt, and pepper until well combined.
- **Step 2**

Pour in 1/4 cup of chicken broth, scraping off the browned bits from the bottom of the inner pot. Add chicken pieces, potatoes, and carrots; stir until well coated with the spices and seasonings. Pour in remaining chicken broth. Close and lock the lid.
- **Step 3**

Select high pressure according to manufacturer's instructions; set timer for 6 minutes. Allow 10 to 15 minutes for pressure to build.
- **Step 4**

Release pressure using the natural-release method according to manufacturer's instructions for 10 minutes. Release pressure carefully using the quick-release method, about 5 minutes. Unlock and remove the lid. Serve over steamed rice.

Cook's Note:
Curry from the island adds heat in the pepper selected for the dish. We like mild-flavored curry, so I used a sliced, seeded jalapeno. If you have a more adventurous palate, choose a serrano pepper or even a Scotch Bonnet, for the truly brave!

Nutrition Facts
Per Serving:
329.8 calories; protein 22g 44% DV; carbohydrates 22.7g 7% DV; fat 16.7g 26% DV; cholesterol 83.6mg 28% DV; sodium 542.4mg 22% DV.

Instant Pot Chicken in Milk

Prep: 15 mins Cook: 45 mins Additional: 10 mins Total: 1 hr 10 mins

Servings: 6

Ingredients

- 1 tablespoon olive oil
- 1 whole chicken
- 1 pinch salt and ground black pepper to taste
- 1 cup milk
- 2 eaches lemons, zested
- 10 cloves garlic, unpeeled
- 1 bunch fresh sage
- 1 teaspoon salt
- ½ cinnamon stick

Directions
- **Step 1**

Turn on a multi-cooker (such as Instant Pot) and the select Saute function. Add olive oil to coat the bottom of the pot. Season both sides of the chicken with salt and pepper; place in pot breast side-down. Cook until browned, 5 to 7 minutes. Turn and cook until other side is browned, about 5 minutes more. Turn off Saute function.
- **Step 2**

Pour milk into the pot with the chicken. Add lemon zest, garlic, sage, salt, and cinnamon. Close and lock the lid. Select high pressure according to manufacturer's instructions; set timer for 25 minutes. Allow 10 to 15 minutes for pressure to build.
- **Step 3**

Let chicken rest for 5 to 10 minutes. Release pressure carefully using the quick-release method according to manufacturer's instructions, about 5 minutes. Unlock and remove lid. Remove chicken from the sauce; take chicken meat off the bone and cut into bite-size pieces. Place meat back into the sauce; stir to combine.

Cook's Notes:
You can substitute fresh thyme or 1 teaspoon dried sage or thyme for the sage.

If you have a lot of caked-on browning, it could possibly interfere with browning. Rather than cleaning out the pot I would recommend deglazing. To deglaze, take chicken out of the pot and set aside. Add a small amount of milk (or water or chicken stock) to the pot on Saute function. Scrape the browned bits off the bottom of the pot with a wooden spoon. Add more liquid, a small amount at a time until you've released all the browning. Turn off Saute function, add the chicken back to the pot, and proceed normally.

Nutrition Facts
Per Serving:
524.8 calories; protein 21.7g 44% DV; carbohydrates 8.5g 3% DV; fat 45.6g 70% DV; cholesterol 83.7mg 28% DV; sodium 503.8mg 20% DV.

Instant Pot Green Bean Casserole

Prep: 15 mins Cook: 20 mins Additional: 10 mins Total: 45 mins

Servings: 6

Ingredients

- 1 cup cold half-and-half
- ¾ cup chicken broth, divided
- 2 tablespoons cornstarch
- 1 teaspoon Worcestershire sauce
- ½ teaspoon salt
- ½ teaspoon ground black pepper
- 1 tablespoon olive oil
- 1 tablespoon unsalted butter
- ½ cup chopped onions
- 1 (8 ounce) package sliced button mushrooms
- 1 pound fresh green beans, trimmed
- 1 (6 ounce) can crispy fried onions, divided

Directions
- **Step 1**

Whisk half-and-half, 1/4 cup broth, cornstarch, Worcestershire sauce, salt, and pepper together in a bowl. Set soup mixture aside.
- **Step 2**

Turn on a multi-functional pressure cooker (such as Instant Pot) and select Saute function. Add oil, butter, and onions. Cook for 2 minutes. Add mushrooms and 1/4 cup broth; cook 3 minutes more. Turn pot off.
- **Step 3**

Add soup mixture, green beans, 1/2 cup crispy onions, and remaining 1/4 cup broth. Stir to combine. Close and lock the lid, select manual and set timer for 1 minute. Allow 10 minutes for pressure to build.
- **Step 4**

Release pressure using the natural-release method according to manufacturer's instructions, about 5 minutes. Carefully release remaining pressure manually. Remove lid and transfer green bean mixture to a serving dish. Let sit to thicken, about 5 minutes. Top with remaining crispy onions.

Nutrition Facts
Per Serving:
320.2 calories; protein 4.1g 8% DV; carbohydrates 24.5g 8% DV; fat 23.1g 36% DV; cholesterol 20.8mg 7% DV; sodium 612.6mg 25% DV

Instant Pot Sausage Dressing

Prep: 10 mins Cook: 25 mins Additional: 5 mins Total: 40 mins

Servings: 8

Ingredients

- 1 cup chicken broth, divided
- 1 large egg
- ½ pound sweet Italian sausage
- 2 tablespoons unsalted butter
- 1 small onion, chopped
- 2 ribs celery, chopped
- 1 (8 ounce) can diced water chestnuts, drained

- ¼ cup chopped fresh flat-leaf parsley
- 1 teaspoon salt
- ½ teaspoon dried thyme
- ½ teaspoon dried sage
- ½ teaspoon ground black pepper
- 5 cups plain stuffing bread cubes

Directions

- **Step 1**

Whisk 1/2 cup broth and egg together in a mixing bowl. Set aside.

- **Step 2**

Turn on a multi-functional pressure cooker (such as Instant Pot) and select Saute function. Add sausage and cook, breaking up with a spoon, for 3 minutes. Add butter, onion, celery, and water chestnuts. Cook 4 minutes more and turn pot off. Add parsley, salt, thyme, sage, and black pepper. Stir to combine. Add bread cubes to pot and pour egg mixture on top. Toss to combine.

- **Step 3**

Close and lock the lid. Select manual and set the timer for 6 minutes; allow 2 minutes for pressure to build. There will be no pressure to release in this step; when timer is up, carefully remove the lid and add remaining broth.

- **Step 4**

Close and lock the lid again. Select manual and set the timer for 5 minutes; allow 2 minutes for pressure to build. Release pressure carefully using the quick-release method according to manufacturer's instructions, about 5 minutes. Unlock and remove the lid.

- **Step 5**

Remove the lid and transfer dressing to a serving dish.

Cook's Notes:

Due to the way the bread absorbs the liquid, it is important that you cook this in two steps as noted.

If store-bought stuffing bread cubes are not available, you can easily make your own. Cube 8 slices of bread and place on a baking sheet. Cook for 15 to 20 minutes in an oven set to 300 degrees F (200 degrees C).

Nutrition Facts

Per Serving:

607.7 calories; protein 19g 38% DV; carbohydrates 101.3g 33% DV; fat 13.2g 20% DV; cholesterol 44mg 15% DV; sodium 2684.7mg 107% DV

Instant Pot Taco Bowls

Prep:10 mins Cook: 50 mins Additional:40 mins Total: 1 hr 40 mins

Servings: 6

Ingredients

- 2 tablespoons olive oil
- 2 pounds beef stew meat
- ½ onion, sliced
- ⅓ cup taco seasoning mix (such as Savory Spice)
- ¼ cup water
- 2 teaspoons garlic salt
- 2 ½ cups water

- 1 (10 ounce) bag yellow rice (such as Vigo)
- 1 (15.25 ounce) can black beans, drained, or to taste
- 1 (15.25 ounce) can corn kernels, drained, or to taste
- 1 (8 ounce) package shredded Cheddar cheese, or to taste

Directions
- **Step 1**

Turn on a multi-functional pressure cooker (such as Instant Pot) and select Saute function. Heat oil. Add beef and cook until browned, about 3 minutes per side. Add onion, taco seasoning, 1/4 cup water, and garlic salt. Stir to combine.
- **Step 2**

Close and lock the lid. Select high pressure according to manufacturer's instructions; set timer for 30 minutes. Allow 10 to 15 minutes for pressure to build.
- **Step 3**

Meanwhile, bring 2 1/2 cups water to a boil in a large saucepan. Add rice and stir for 1 minute. Cover saucepan tightly. Reduce heat to a simmer and cook until rice is tender, 20 to 25 minutes. Remove from heat and let cool completely.
- **Step 4**

Release pressure naturally according to manufacturer's instructions, 10 to 40 minutes. Let cool completely.
- **Step 5**

Divide beef and rice among 6 reusable containers. Top with equal amounts of black beans, corn, and Cheddar cheese. Cover and refrigerate.

Nutrition Facts
Per Serving:
792.4 calories; protein 44.4g 89% DV; carbohydrates 68g 22% DV; fat 38.2g 59% DV; cholesterol 122.7mg 41% DV; sodium 2577.5mg 103% DV.

Instant Pot Vegan Lentil Soup

Prep: 10 mins Cook: 25 mins Additional: 10 mins Total: 45 mins

Servings: 6
Ingredients

- 2 tablespoons olive oil

- 1 yellow onion, chopped

- 2 eaches carrots, chopped
- 2 stalks celery, chopped
- 1 ½ cups red lentils
- 1 (28 ounce) can diced tomatoes
- 4 cups vegetable broth
- 4 cloves garlic, minced
- 1 teaspoon dried thyme
- 1 teaspoon kosher salt
- ¾ teaspoon smoked paprika
- ½ teaspoon black pepper
- 1 tablespoon chopped fresh parsley

Directions
- **Step 1**

Turn on a multi-functional pressure cooker (such as Instant Pot) and select Saute function. Heat olive oil; cook and stir until the onion has softened and turned translucent, about 5 minutes. Add carrots and celery and cook until tender, about 3 minutes. Combine lentils, diced tomatoes, vegetable broth, garlic, thyme, salt, paprika, and black pepper in the pot. Close and lock the lid. Select high pressure according to manufacturer's instructions; set timer for 15 minutes. Allow 10 to 15 minutes for pressure to build.

- **Step 2**

Release pressure using the natural-release method according to manufacturer's instructions, 10 to 40 minutes. Serve in bowls and sprinkle with parsley.

Nutrition Facts
Per Serving:
278.6 calories; protein 14.9g 30% DV; carbohydrates 41.5g 13% DV; fat 5.5g 8% DV; cholesterolmg; sodium 848mg 34% DV.

Instant Pot Sausage Queso

Prep: 10 mins Cook: 25 mins Additional: 5 mins Total: 40 mins

Servings: 8

Ingredients

- 1 pound bulk country sausage
- 1 tablespoon olive oil
- 1 small onion, chopped
- 1 large jalapeno pepper, seeded and diced
- 1 teaspoon chili powder
- ½ teaspoon ground cumin
- 1 (12 fluid ounce) can or bottle light beer
- 1 (10 ounce) can diced tomatoes with green chiles
- 2 cups shredded sharp Cheddar cheese
- 2 cups shredded Monterey Jack cheese

Directions
- **Step 1**

Crumble sausage in a large skillet and cook over medium-high heat until no longer pink, about 5 minutes. Drain excess grease.

- **Step 2**

Turn on a multi-functional pressure cooker (such as Instant Pot) and select Saute function. Add olive oil, onion, and jalapeno; cook for 3 minutes. Add chili powder and cumin and cook for 2 minutes more. Stir in sausage, beer, and tomatoes. Close and lock the lid. Select Manual; set timer for 5 minutes. Allow 10 to 15 minutes for pressure to build.

- **Step 3**

Release pressure using the natural-release method according to manufacturer's instructions, about 5 minutes. Carefully release remain pressure manually. Remove the lid. Add Cheddar and Monterey Jack cheeses; whisk vigorously until melted. Serve immediately.

Cook's Note:

If you are not serving immediately, you can use the Keep Warm setting, but you will need to stir every 20 minutes to keep the cheese from clumping.

Nutrition Facts

Per Serving:

412.9 calories; protein 28.4g 57% DV; carbohydrates 3.8g 1% DV; fat 31.1g 48% DV; cholesterol 107.3mg 36% DV; sodium 893.6mg 36% DV.

Instant Pot Pudina Pulao (Mint Rice)

Prep: 15 mins Cook: 25 mins Additional: 10 mins Total: 50 mins

Servings: 4

Ingredients

- 1 (4 ounce) can chopped green chiles
- 3 tablespoons finely chopped fresh mint leaves
- 3 cloves garlic, finely minced
- 2 ½ tablespoons water
- 2 tablespoons unsweetened shredded coconut
- 1 tablespoon finely chopped fresh cilantro
- 1 teaspoon cumin seeds
- ½ teaspoon ground ginger
- 2 tablespoons olive oil
- 2 eaches whole cloves
- 2 eaches cardamom pod
- 1 star anise
- ½ teaspoon ground cinnamon
- 1 small bay leaf, torn into pieces
- 1 onion, diced
- ¼ teaspoon ground turmeric
- ¼ teaspoon red chile powder
- 4 small Yukon Gold potatoes, sliced into rounds, then halved (skin on)
- 1 tomato, diced
- ½ cup frozen peas
- 1 cup basmati rice
- 1 ¼ cups water
- ¼ teaspoon salt

Directions

- **Step 1**

Combine green chiles, mint leaves, garlic, 2 1/2 tablespoons water, shredded coconut, cilantro, cumin seeds, and ginger in a mortar; grind with a pestle into a paste.

- **Step 2**

Turn on a multi-functional pressure cooker (such as Instant Pot) and select Saute function. Add olive oil and heat until warm. Add cloves, cardamom pods, star anise, bay leaf, and cinnamon. Saute until spices are fragrant, 4 to 5 minutes. Add mint paste, onion, turmeric, and red chile powder and cook for 2 minutes longer.

- **Step 3**

Mix in potatoes, tomatoes, and peas. Stir in basmati rice and saute for 1 minute longer. Pour in 1 1/4 cups water and salt. Scrape up any browned bits on the bottom of the pot and let warm 1 minute longer.
* **Step 4**

Turn off Saute mode. Close and lock the lid. Select high pressure according to manufacturer's instructions; set timer for 6 minutes. Allow 10 to 15 minutes for pressure to build.
* **Step 5**

Release pressure using the natural-release method according to manufacturer's instructions, 10 to 40 minutes.

Cook's Note:

Flat-leaf parsley may be used in place of cilantro, and long-grain rice may be used instead of basmati, if preferred.

Nutrition Facts

Per Serving:

353.2 calories; protein 7g 14% DV; carbohydrates 61.9g 20% DV; fat 9.7g 15% DV; cholesterolmg; sodium 489mg 20% DV.

Instant Pot Goulash

Prep: 15 mins Cook: 20 mins Additional: 5 mins Total: 40 mins

Servings: 6

Ingredients

* 1 pound ground beef
* 1 pint sliced mushrooms
* ½ onion, chopped
* 3 cloves garlic
* 1 pinch salt and ground black pepper to taste
* 2 (15 ounce) cans tomato sauce
* 2 (15 ounce) cans diced tomatoes
* 2 ½ cups water
* 2 cups noodles
* 3 tablespoons soy sauce
* 2 tablespoons Italian seasoning
* 3 leaf (blank)s bay leaves

Directions
* **Step 1**

Turn on a multi-functional pressure cooker (such as Instant Pot) and select Saute function. Add beef, mushrooms, onion, garlic, salt, and pepper. Cook and stir until browned and crumbly, 5 to 7 minutes. Drain and discard fat.
* **Step 2**

Add tomato sauce, diced tomatoes, water, dry noodles, soy sauce, Italian seasoning, and bay leaves. Close and lock the lid. Select high pressure according to manufacturer's instructions; set timer for 4 minutes. Allow 10 to 15 minutes for pressure to build.
* **Step 3**

Release pressure carefully using the quick-release method according to manufacturer's instructions, about 5 minutes. Unlock and remove the lid. Remove bay leaves before serving.

Cook's Notes:
Use any kind of noodle/pasta you prefer.

Nutrition Facts
Per Serving:
278.1 calories; protein 20.1g 40% DV; carbohydrates 26.8g 9% DV; fat 10.3g 16% DV; cholesterol 57.9mg 19% DV; sodium 1485.9mg 59% DV.

Instant Pot Eggs and Soldiers

Prep: 5 mins Cook: 10 mins Additional: 5 mins Total: 20 mins

Servings: 4

Ingredients

- 4 large eggs
- 1 pinch salt and ground black pepper to taste
- 4 slices bread
- 4 teaspoons unsalted butter

Directions
- **Step 1**

Turn on a multi-functional pressure cooker (such as Instant Pot), and pour 1 cup of water into the pot. Add a trivet or egg rack, and place the eggs on it. Close and lock the lid. Set the pressure valve to Sealing. Select high pressure according to manufacturer's instructions; set timer for 3 minutes. Allow 5 to 10 minutes for pressure to build.
- **Step 2**

Cover the valve loosely with a kitchen towel. Use a wooden spoon or tongs to move the valve from Sealing to Venting to release pressure immediately. Unlock and remove the lid. Remove the eggs to a bowl of ice water for 2 minutes to stop cooking.
- **Step 3**

Toast bread and spread with butter. Cut into strips.
- **Step 4**

Drain the eggs and tap the tops with a spoon to crack the upper shell. Remove the tops. Season with salt and pepper, and serve with the toast sticks for dipping.

Cook's Notes:
The pressure must be released immediately when timer stops. If you don't do this, the eggs will continue to cook from the residual heat in the pot, and they will not be perfectly cooked with runny yolks and firm egg whites. I just throw a kitchen towel on top of the valve when first releasing the pressure to keep the steam from going everywhere.

Nutrition Facts
Per Serving:
171.7 calories; protein 8.2g 17% DV; carbohydrates 13g 4% DV; fat 9.6g 15% DV; cholesterol 196.1mg 65% DV; sodium 279.5mg 11% DV.

Instant Pot Sweet Acorn Squash

Prep: 5 mins Cook: 15 mins Additional: 7 mins Total: 27 mins

Servings: 2

Ingredients

- 2 tablespoons brown sugar
- 2 tablespoons maple syrup
- 1 tablespoon butter
- ½ teaspoon ground cinnamon
- 1 medium acorn squash, halved and seeded

Directions
- **Step 1**

Divide sugar, maple syrup, butter, and cinnamon between both halves of acorn squash.
- **Step 2**

Add 1 cup of water into an electric pressure cooker (such as Instant Pot) and place trivet inside. Carefully place squash halves on top of trivet. Lock lid and close pressure valve.
- **Step 3**

Select High pressure according to manufacturer's instructions; set timer for 5 minutes. Allow 10 to 15 minutes for pressure to build.

- **Step 4**

Release pressure using the natural-release method, about 7 minutes. Release any remaining pressure according to manufacturer's instructions. Unlock lid, carefully remove squash, and serve.

Nutrition Facts
Per Serving:
242.3 calories; protein 1.8g 4% DV; carbohydrates 49.6g 16% DV; fat 6g 9% DV; cholesterol 15.3mg 5% DV; sodium 53mg 2% DV.

Instant Pot Swiss Steak

Prep: 15 mins Cook: 1 hr Additional: 10 mins Total: 1 hr 25 mins

Servings: 4

Ingredients

- 1 ½ pounds bottom round steak, 1 inch thick and trimmed of fat
- 1 pinch salt and freshly ground black pepper to taste
- ¼ cup all-purpose flour
- 2 tablespoons avocado oil, divided, or as needed
- 1 medium onion, chopped
- ½ cup carrot, chopped
- ½ cup chopped celery
- 1 green bell pepper, chopped
- 2 cloves garlic, finely chopped
- ¼ cup Merlot wine
- 2 ¾ cups canned chopped Italian-style tomatoes in juice
- 1 tablespoon Worcestershire sauce
- 1 teaspoon salt
- 1 teaspoon oregano
- 1 teaspoon paprika

Directions
- **Step 1**

Dry steak well with paper towels and cut into four 4-inch pieces. Season with salt and pepper.
- **Step 2**

Place flour into a shallow bowl. Dredge steak pieces in flour, shaking off excess.
- **Step 3**

Turn on a multi-functional pressure cooker (such as Instant Pot) and select Saute function. Once the pot is hot, add 1 tablespoon avocado oil. Brown the steak in batches, so you don't crowd the pot, 2 minutes per side. Transfer browned meat to a warm plate and set aside.
- **Step 5**

Add 1 tablespoon of avocado oil to the pot and cook onion, carrot, celery, and bell pepperzuntil onions are soft and translucent, 3 to 4 minutes. Stir in garlic and cook until fragrant, about 1 minute. Deglaze the pot with Merlot. Mix in tomatoes, Worcestershire sauce, 1 teaspoon salt, oregano, and paprika. Return steak to the pot and push down into the tomato mixture.
- **Step 5**

Close and lock the lid. Select manual pressure according to manufacturer's instructions; set timer for 30 minutes. Allow 10 to 15 minutes for pressure to build.

- **Step 6**

Allow pressure to release naturally according to manufacturer's instructions for 5 minutes. Carefully open the valve to release the remaining pressure, about 5 minutes more. Unlock and remove the lid.

Nutrition Facts
Per Serving:
337 calories; protein 28.1g 56% DV; carbohydrates 19.7g 6% DV; fat 13.9g 21% DV; cholesterol 73.5mg 25% DV; sodium 982mg 39% DV.

Instant Pot Au Gratin Potatoes

Prep: 5 mins Cook: 15 mins Additional: 15 mins Total: 35 mins

Servings: 6

Ingredients

- 2 pounds russet potatoes, peeled
- 1 cup chicken broth
- ¼ cup diced onion
- 1 tablespoon parsley flakes
- ½ teaspoon garlic powder
- ½ teaspoon paprika
- ½ teaspoon salt
- ¼ teaspoon pepper
- ½ cup evaporated milk
- 1 cup shredded Cheddar cheese
- ½ cup shredded Monterey Jack cheese

Directions

- **Step 1**

Slice potatoes into 1/4-inch thick slices using a mandolin. Rinse under cold water to remove excess starch.

- **Step 2**

Turn on a multi-functional pressure cooker (such as Instant Pot). Add potatoes, chicken broth, onion, parsley, garlic powder, paprika, salt, and pepper. Close and lock the lid. Select high pressure according to manufacturer's instructions; set timer for 1 minute. Allow 10 minutes for pressure to build.

- **Step 3**

Release pressure carefully using the quick-release method according to manufacturer's instructions, about 5 minutes. Unlock and remove the lid.

- **Step 4**

Add evaporated milk, Cheddar cheese, and Monterey Jack cheese to the pot. Gently stir until cheese is melted. Transfer potatoes to an oven-safe baking dish.

- **Step 5**

Set an oven rack about 6 inches from the heat source and preheat the oven's broiler to low. Broil for 4 minutes or until top is brown and bubbly. Remove potatoes from the oven and let rest for 10 minutes to thicken.

Nutrition Facts

Per Serving:
264.7 calories; protein 12g 24% DV; carbohydrates 30.3g 10% DV; fat 11g 17% DV; cholesterol 35.3mg 12% DV; sodium 589.6mg 24% DV.

Instant Pot Pulled Pork

Prep: 30 mins Cook: 1 hr 45 mins Additional: 8 hrs 5 mins Total: 10 hrs 20 mins

Servings: 16

Ingredients

Dry Rub:
- ¼ cup brown sugar
- 1 tablespoon chili powder
- 1 tablespoon paprika
- 2 teaspoons garlic powder
- oast, trimmed, or more as desired
- 2 teaspoons kosher salt
- 1 teaspoon ground black pepper
- 1 teaspoon cayenne pepper
- 1 (4 pound) pork shoulder r

Sauce:

- 2 teaspoons olive oil
- 1 cup chicken stock
- 2 cups water
- ⅓ cup apple cider vinegar
- 2 tablespoons brown sugar
- 1 (6 ounce) can tomato paste, divided
- 1 large sweet onion, quartered, or more to taste
- ½ cup ketchup, divided
- ½ cup brown sugar

Directions
- **Step 1**

Combine brown sugar, chili powder, paprika, garlic powder, kosher salt, black pepper, and cayenne pepper in a small bowl. Rub the dry rub mixture all over the trimmed shoulder roast. Pierce roast with a fork to help seasoning penetrate meat. Wrap with plastic wrap and refrigerate, 8 hours to overnight.
- **Step 2**

Turn on a multi-functional pressure cooker (such as Instant Pot) and select Saute function. Add olive oil. Cut pork into 4 to 6 pieces and add to the hot oil. Cook a few pieces at a time until browned, about 5 minutes. Transfer cooked meat to a plate.
- **Step 3**

Add chicken broth to the pot and deglaze the browned bits from the bottom by stirring constantly with a whisk until smooth. Turn Instant Pot off.
- **Step 4**

Add water, apple cider vinegar, 2 tablespoons brown sugar, 2 tablespoons tomato paste, onion, and 2 tablespoons ketchup. Top with browned pork. Close and lock the lid, making sure the vent is closed. Select high pressure according to manufacturer's instructions; set timer for 60 minutes. Allow 10 to 15 minutes for pressure to build.
- **Step 5**

Release pressure carefully using the quick-release method according to manufacturer's instructions, about 5 minutes. Unlock and remove the lid. Remove meat and onions and cover to keep warm.
- **Step 6**

Set Instant Pot to saute and add remaining tomato paste, remaining ketchup, and 1/2 cup brown sugar. Use a ladle to skim excess fat from the top of the liquid and discard it. Cook until sauce is reduced in volume by about 1/2, about 15 minutes.
- **Step 7**

Meanwhile, use 2 forks to shred cooked pork into small chunks. Serve meat as desired, topped with the thickened sauce.

Nutrition Facts
Per Serving:
316.3 calories; protein 15.6g 31% DV; carbohydrates 17.8g 6% DV; fat 20.9g 32% DV; cholesterol 64.9mg 22% DV; sodium 1777.4mg 71% DV.

Instant Pot Apple Pie Steel Cut Oats

Prep: 5 mins Cook: 15 mins Additional: 10 mins Total: 30 mins

Servings: 4

Ingredients

- 3 cups water
- 1 cup steel-cut oats
- 1 apple, or more to taste, chopped
- 1 ½ teaspoons ground cinnamon
- ½ teaspoon salt
- ¼ teaspoon ground nutmeg

Directions
- **Step 1**

Combine water, oats, apple, cinnamon, salt, and nutmeg in a multi-functional pressure cooker (such as Instant Pot). Close and lock the lid. Seal vent. Select Manual function; set timer for 5 minutes. Allow 10 to 15 minutes for pressure to build.
- **Step 2**

Release pressure using the natural-release method according to manufacturer's instructions, about 10 minutes. Release remaining pressure naturally. Stir and remove pot carefully with oven mitts.

Nutrition Facts
Per Serving:
171.1 calories; protein 5.1g 10% DV; carbohydrates 32.6g 11% DV; fat 2.6g 4% DV; cholesterolmg; sodium 296.5mg 12% DV.

Instant Pot Hard-Boiled Eggs

Prep: 5 mins Cook: 15 mins Additional: 10 mins Total: 30 mins

Servings: 16

Ingredients
- 1 cup water
- 16 eaches eggs

Directions
- **Step 1**

Insert a wire rack in the bottom of a multi-functional pressure cooker (such as Instant Pot). Pour in water. Carefully place raw eggs onto the rack, fitting them in tightly. Close and lock the lid.
- **Step 2**

Select high pressure according to manufacturer's instructions; set timer for 4 minutes. Allow 10 to 15 minutes for pressure to build.
- **Step 3**

As soon as the timer goes off, hit cancel and release the pressure using the quick-release method according to manufacturer's instructions, about 5 minutes. Unlock and remove the lid, as leaving eggs in longer will result in overcooked eggs.
- **Step 4**

Transfer eggs to a large bowl using a serving spoon and cover with cold water. Let cool for 5 minutes. Peel while still warm and rinse off any shell pieces. Use immediately or store in the fridge.

Nutrition Facts
Per Serving:
62.9 calories; protein 5.5g 11% DV; carbohydrates 0.3g; fat 4.4g 7% DV; cholesterol 163.7mg 55% DV; sodium 62mg 3% DV.

Instant Pot Chicken Tortilla Soup

Prep: 25 mins Cook: 30 mins Additional: 10 mins Total: 1 hr 5 mins

Servings: 8

Ingredients

- 2 medium (blank)s zucchini, chopped, or to taste
- 4 eaches shallots, chopped
- 2 large (5" long)s poblano peppers, seeded and chopped, or more to taste
- 2 medium (blank)s carrots, peeled and diced
- 2 teaspoons ground cumin
- 1 teaspoon kosher salt
- 1 teaspoon chili powder
- 1 teaspoon dried oregano
- ¼ teaspoon cayenne pepper
- 1 tablespoon grapeseed oil
- 1 (14.5 ounce) can fire-roasted diced tomatoes
- 4 large bone-in, skin-on chicken thighs
- 6 cups chicken stock
- 2 eaches bay leaves, or more to taste
- 1 (15 ounce) can black beans, drained and rinsed
- 1 lime, juiced

Directions
- **Step 1**

Place zucchini, shallots, poblano peppers, and carrots in a multi-cooker (such as Instant Pot). Add cumin, salt, chili powder, oregano, and cayenne pepper; stir well to combine. Add oil. Turn on cooker and select Saute function. Cook and stir until just slightly softened, about 5 minutes. Pour in tomatoes. Nestle chicken thighs into the mixture. Add stock and bay leaves.
- **Step 2**

Close and lock the lid. Select high pressure according to manufacturer's instructions; set timer for 15 minutes. Allow 10 to 15 minutes for pressure to build.
- **Step 3**

Release pressure using the natural-release method according to manufacturer's instructions, 10 to 40 minutes. Unlock and remove lid. Transfer chicken thighs to a plate and remove skin, bones, and any cartilage. Shred into bite-sized pieces. Add shredded chicken back to the pot. Stir in black beans and lime juice.

Cook's Notes:
You can use an onion in place of the shallots.
You can use olive or avocado oil in place of the grapeseed oil.
If using frozen chicken thighs, set cook time to 20 minutes.

Nutrition Facts

Per Serving:
243.7 calories; protein 20.3g 41% DV; carbohydrates 21.8g 7% DV; fat 8.8g 14% DV; cholesterol 53mg 18% DV; sodium 1169.9mg 47% DV.

Instant Pot Collard Greens

Prep: 10 mins Cook: 20 mins Additional: 25 mins Total: 55 mins

Servings: 6

Ingredients

- 1 bunch collard greens
- 4 thick slices bacon, cut into 1-inch pieces
- 4 cups water
- 2 tablespoons white vinegar
- 4 cups chicken broth
- 1 pinch salt to taste

Directions
- **Step 1**

Rinse collard greens; remove and discard thick parts of stems. Chop greens to desired size.
- **Step 2**

Turn on a multi-functional pressure cooker (such as Instant Pot) and select Saute function. Cook bacon until brown and crisp, about 5 minutes. Turn off Saute function. Pour in water and vinegar. Scrape the bottom of the pot to release stuck bits of bacon. Add collard greens and stir to coat. Pour in chicken broth and season with salt. Close and lock the lid.
- **Step 3**

Select high pressure according to manufacturer's instructions; set timer for 5 minutes. Allow 10 to 15 minutes for pressure to build.
- **Step 4**

Release pressure using the natural-release method according to manufacturer's instructions for 20 minutes. Quick-release remaining steam, according to manufacturer's instructions, about 5 minutes. Unlock and remove the lid. Season with more salt if necessary.

Cook's Notes:
Add chopped onions and cook either with the bacon or after the bacon, and cook until soft and translucent. You can add other spices to your liking in addition to salt.

Nutrition Facts
Per Serving:
67.9 calories; protein 4.3g 9% DV; carbohydrates 3.5g 1% DV; fat 4.2g 6% DV; cholesterol 13mg 4% DV; sodium 988.3mg 40% DV.

Instant Pot Mississippi Roast

Prep: 5 mins Cook: 1 hr 50 mins Additional: 10 mins Total: 2 hrs 5 mins

Servings: 10
Ingredients

- 1 (14 ounce) can beef broth
- 3 ½ pounds beef chuck roast, cut into 3 or 4 chunks
- 1 stick butter
- ½ (16 ounce) jar pepperoncini peppers and juice
- 1 (1 ounce) package ranch dressing mix
- 1 (1 ounce) package dry onion soup mix

Directions
- **Step 1**

Pour broth into a multi-functional pressure cooker (such as Instant Pot). Place beef in the pot and sprinkle with ranch dressing mix and onion soup mix. Place butter on top. Add pepperoncinis and juice.
- **Step 2**

Close and lock the pressure cooker lid. Select high pressure according to manufacturer's instructions; set timer for 110 minutes. Allow 10 to 15 minutes for pressure to build.
- **Step 3**

Release pressure using the natural-release method according to manufacturer's instructions, 10 to 40 minutes.

Nutrition Facts
Per Serving:
342.8 calories; protein 19.4g 39% DV; carbohydrates 3.9g 1% DV; fat 27.3g 42% DV; cholesterol 96.6mg 32% DV; sodium 1155.2mg 46% DV.

Instant Pot Keto Chicken Thighs in Lemon-Garlic Cream Sauce

Prep: 5 mins Cook: 40 mins Additional: 15 mins Total: 1 hr

Servings: 4

Ingredients

- 2 tablespoons vegetable oil
- 4 eaches bone-in, skin-on chicken thighs
- 1 pinch salt and pepper to taste
- ½ medium onion, thinly sliced
- 4 garlic clove (blank)s garlic cloves, minced
- ½ cup dry white wine
- 1 cup chicken broth
- 3 tablespoons fresh lemon juice
- 2 tablespoons butter or margarine
- ½ cup heavy cream
- ½ teaspoon thyme leaves
- ⅛ teaspoon salt

Directions
- **Step 1**

Turn on a multi-functional pressure cooker (such as Instant Pot) and select Saute function. Heat vegetable oil.
- **Step 2**

Season chicken thighs with salt and pepper on both sides; add to Instant Pot. Cook one side at a time until both sides of the chicken are a golden brown, 3 to 4 minutes per side. Remove chicken from the pot and set aside.
- **Step 3**

Add onion and sauté for 1 minute. Add garlic and cook for 1 more minute. Pour in white wine and stir to scrape brown bits from the bottom of the pot. Stir in chicken broth and lemon juice; bring to a boil and cook until broth has reduced slightly, 2 to 3 minutes. Turn off the Sauté function.
- **Step 4**

Return chicken Instant Pot. Close and lock the lid. Select High pressure according to manufacturer's instructions; set timer for 10 minutes. Allow 10 to 15 minutes for pressure to build.
- **Step 5**

Release pressure using the natural-release method according to manufacturer's instructions, for 10 minutes. Release remaining pressure carefully using the quick-release method, about 5 minutes. Unlock and remove the lid.
- **Step 6**

Remove chicken from the pot and set aside. Select the Sauté mode and bring sauce to a boil. Whisk in butter or margarine, heavy cream, salt, and thyme. Cook until sauce has thickened slightly, 2 to 3 minutes. Serve chicken drizzled with the sauce.

Nutrition Facts
Per Serving:
445.2 calories; protein 20.5g 41% DV; carbohydrates 5.2g 2% DV; fat 35.6g 55% DV; cholesterol 128.5mg 43% DV; sodium 521.3mg 21% DV.

Instant Pot Double Bean and Ham Soup

Prep: 25 mins Cook: 45 mins Total: 1 hr 10 mins

Servings: 6

Ingredients

- 2 cups dry navy beans
- 2 cups chicken broth
- 2 cups water
- 1 (14.5 ounce) can diced tomatoes, undrained
- 2 eaches carrots, chopped
- 1 onion, chopped
- 2 stalks celery, chopped
- 1 (16 ounce) can pork and beans, undrained
- 1 cup chopped ham

- 1 pinch salt and ground black pepper to taste

Directions
- **Step 1**

Put navy beans, chicken broth, water, tomatoes, carrots, onion, and celery into an electric pressure cooker (such as Instant Pot). Seal pressure cooker and turn the venting knob to point at "Sealed." Press the "Manual" button for high pressure and set timer for 45 minutes. When countdown is complete, release pressure naturally according to manufacturer's instructions.
- **Step 2**

Remove lid, stir in pork and beans and ham. Season with salt and pepper.

Nutrition Facts
Per Serving:
398.4 calories; protein 24.2g 49% DV; carbohydrates 67.6g 22% DV; fat 4.4g 7% DV; cholesterol 18.4mg 6% DV; sodium 1055.3mg 42% DV.

Instant Pot General Tso's Chicken

Prep: 15 mins Cook: 30 mins Additional: 5 mins Total: 50 mins

Servings: 2

Ingredients

Sauce:
- 2 tablespoons reduced-sodium soy sauce
- 2 tablespoons rice vinegar
- 1 tablespoon honey
- 1 tablespoon dark brown sugar

Chicken:
1 (16 ounce) package chicken breast tenderloins, cut into bite-size pieces
- 1 egg, beaten
- ½ cup cornstarch
- 1 tablespoon olive oil

- 1 tablespoon tomato paste
- 2 teaspoons sesame oil
- 1 teaspoon red pepper flakes

- 1 tablespoon sesame seeds
- 1 clove garlic, minced
- ½ teaspoon ginger paste
- ¼ cup chicken broth

Directions
- **Step 1**

Whisk together soy sauce, rice vinegar, honey, brown sugar, tomato paste, sesame oil, and red pepper flakes in a bowl. Set sauce aside.
- **Step 2**

Place egg in a shallow bowl. Place cornstarch in a second shallow bowl. Dip chicken pieces in egg, coat in cornstarch, then place on a plate.
- **Step 3**

Turn on a multi-functional pressure cooker (such as Instant Pot) and select Saute function. Add olive oil and heat for about 1 minute. Add chicken in a single layer and cook until crisp, about 2 minutes per side. Transfer chicken to a plate.
- **Step 4**

Stir sesame seeds, garlic, and ginger paste into the pot. Whisk in chicken broth and the reserved sauce until combined; cook for 2 minutes. Press Cancel button. Add chicken to the pot and stir to coat.
- **Step 5**

Close and lock the lid. Select high pressure according to manufacturer's instructions; set timer for 5 minutes. Allow 10 minutes for pressure to build.
- **Step 6**

Release pressure using the quick release method according to manufacturer's instructions, about 5 minutes. Stir the chicken.
- **Step 7**

Select Saute function again and cook until sauce has thickened, about 3 minutes.

Cook's Notes:
You can find ginger paste in the produce section.

Nutrition Facts
Per Serving:
652.9 calories; protein 56g 112% DV; carbohydrates 51.9g 17% DV; fat 23.8g 37% DV; cholesterol 230.3mg 77% DV; sodium 901.2mg 36% DV.

Instant Pot Pepper Chicken

Prep: 15 mins Cook: 25 mins Total: 40 mins

Servings: 6

Ingredients

- 6 thigh, bone removeds chicken thighs
- 2 medium (blank)s green bell peppers, chopped
- 1 large yellow onion, chopped
- ½ cup soy sauce
- ¼ cup brown sugar
- 2 tablespoons honey
- 3 cloves garlic, peeled
- 1 pinch ground black pepper to taste

Directions
- **Step 1**

Place chicken in the Instant Pot and cook for 10 minutes on the 'Manual' setting. Release pressure naturally according to manufacturer's instructions.

- **Step 2**

Set the pot to 'Saute' and add green bell peppers, yellow onion, soy sauce, brown sugar, honey, garlic, and black pepper. Cook until most liquid is evaporated, vegetables are soft, and chicken is no longer pink in the center, about 15 minutes. An instant-read thermometer inserted into the center should read at least 165 degrees F (74 degrees C).

Cook's Notes:
If using frozen chicken thighs, cook for 25 minutes in **Step 1**

Nutrition Facts
Per Serving:
233.8 calories; protein 16.7g 33% DV; carbohydrates 21.2g 7% DV; fat 9.4g 14% DV; cholesterol 52.8mg 18% DV; sodium 1252.5mg 50% DV.

Instant Pot Pork Adobo

Prep:10 mins Cook:40 mins Additional:10 mins Total:1 hr

Servings: 4

Ingredients

- 2 tablespoons olive oil
- 1 pound boneless pork roast, cubed
- 1 medium onion, sliced
- 4 cloves garlic, minced
- 1 cup water
- ½ cup reduced-sodium soy sauce
- ½ cup white vinegar
- 1 tablespoon sugar
- 1 teaspoon salt
- 1 teaspoon ground black pepper
- 1 bay leaf
- 1 tablespoon tapioca starch

Directions
- **Step 1**

Turn on a multi-functional pressure cooker (such as Instant Pot) and select Saute function. Once hot, add oil and pork pieces. Cook until meat is browned, about 5 minutes. Add onion and cook until soft and translucent, 3 to 5 minutes. Mix in garlic and cook until fragrant, about 30 seconds. Add water, soy sauce, vinegar, sugar, salt, pepper, and bay leaf; mix to combine. Turn off Saute mode.
- **Step 2**

Close and lock the lid. Select high pressure according to manufacturer's instructions; set timer for 15 minutes. Allow 10 to 15 minutes for pressure to build.
- **Step 3**

Release pressure using the natural-release method according to manufacturer's instructions, 10 to 40 minutes. Remove pork to a medium bowl and keep hot. Pour out half of the liquid and reserve.
- **Step 4**

Turn on Saute mode again. Stir tapioca starch into remaining hot liquid in the pot to create a slurry. Cook until sauce thickens, about 5 minutes. Add in reserved liquid if sauce is too thick, 2 tablespoons at a time, or until desired consistency is achieved.

Nutrition Facts
Per Serving:

208.1 calories; protein 15.3g 31% DV; carbohydrates 11.5g 4% DV; fat 11.2g 17% DV; cholesterol 39.6mg 13% DV; sodium 1670.4mg 67% DV.

Instant Pot Kielbasa, Sauerkraut, and Potato

Prep:15 mins Cook: 40 mins Additional: 15 mins Total: 1 hr 10 mins

Servings: 6

Ingredients

- 2 slices bacon
- 2 pounds fresh kielbasa, sliced into 2-inch pieces
- 1 medium sweet onion, diced
- ¼ cup dark brown sugar
- 3 large yellow potatoes, chopped
- 2 (16 ounce) packages sauerkraut, drained
- 1 ½ cups chicken broth
- 1 apple - peeled, cored, and diced
- ½ cup beer
- ½ teaspoon sea salt

Directions
- **Step 1**

Turn on a multi-functional pressure cooker (such as Instant Pot) and select Saute function. Add bacon; cook until crispy, 8 to 10 minutes. Pull bacon out with tongs and set in a bowl. Add kielbasa to the pot; lightly brown on all sides, 5 to 7 minutes. Remove with tongs and place in the bowl with the bacon.

- **Step 2**

Saute onions in the pot until soft, 2 to 3 minutes. Crumble the bacon and add to the pot. Stir in brown sugar. Add potatoes, sauerkraut, chicken broth, apple, beer, and salt. Mix gently.
- **Step 3**

Close and lock the lid. Select high pressure according to manufacturer's instructions; set timer for 12 minutes. Allow 10 to 15 minutes for pressure to build.
- **Step 5**

Release pressure using the natural-release method for 10 minutes according to manufacturer's instructions. Release remaining pressure carefully using the quick-release method. Unlock and remove the lid.

Cook's Notes:
You can use yellow or russet potatoes. If you'd like to substitute liquid smoke for the bacon, melt 3 tablespoons butter in the pot before adding kielbasa. Stir in 3 drops liquid smoke before adding the broth. I suggest adding the drops to a teaspoon to avoid accidental overuse of smoke.
Nutrition Facts
Per Serving:
767.1 calories; protein 25.5g 51% DV; carbohydrates 56.4g 18% DV; fat 47.8g 74% DV; cholesterol 112.8mg 38% DV; sodium 2758.6mg 110% DV.

Instant Pot Red Beans and Rice

Prep: 10 mins Cook: 40 mins Additional: 2 hrs Total: 2 hrs 50 mins

Servings: 8

Ingredients

- 1 (16 ounce) package dry kidney beans
- 1 tablespoon olive oil
- 1 link smoked beef sausage, sliced
- 6 ounces frozen onion, green bell pepper, and celery mix
- 4 cloves garlic, minced
- 1 (32 ounce) carton chicken broth
- 2 teaspoons Cajun seasoning (such as Tony Chachere's)
- ¼ teaspoon ground thyme
- 2 eaches bay leaves
- 4 cups cooked rice

Directions

- **Step 1**

Place kidney beans into a large container and cover with several inches of cool water; let soak for 2 hours.
- **Step 2**

Turn pot on "Saute" mode; add olive oil and sausage. Cook and stir until sausage is browned, about 5 minutes. Add onion mix and garlic; cook and stir until onion mix is soft, 5 to 10 minutes. Turn off pot.
- **Step 3**

Drain beans and add to pot; stir in chicken broth, Cajun seasoning, thyme, and bay leaves.
- **Step 4**

Place lid on pot, turn valve to "Sealing" and push "Bean" button, about 30 minutes. When pot beeps, use the natural pressure release until the pin goes down. Remove lid.
- **Step 5**

Serve beans over rice.

Nutrition Facts
Per Serving:
341.8 calories; protein 16.5g 33% DV; carbohydrates 59.4g 19% DV; fat 4.3g 7% DV; cholesterol 6.4mg 2% DV; sodium 725.8mg 29% DV.

Instant Pot Canned Tomato Salsa

Prep: 10 mins Cook: 30 mins Additional: 10 mins Total: 50 mins

Servings: 8

Ingredients

- 1 (28 ounce) can crushed tomatoes
- 1 small onion, diced
- 2 medium (blank)s jalapeno peppers, seeded and diced
- ¼ cup white distilled vinegar
- ¼ cup water
- 2 teaspoons sea salt
- 2 teaspoons minced garlic
- ½ teaspoon ground cumin
- ½ cup chopped fresh cilantro
- 1 tablespoon lime juice

Directions
- **Step 1**

Combine tomatoes, onion, jalapeno peppers, vinegar, water, sea salt, garlic, and cumin in a multi-functional pressure cooker (such as Instant Pot). Close and lock the lid. Select high pressure according to manufacturer's instructions; set timer for 15 minutes. Allow 15 minutes for pressure to build.
- **Step 2**

Release pressure carefully using the quick-release method according to manufacturer's instructions, about 1 minute. Unlock and remove the lid.
- **Step 3**

Pull the pot out and let cool for 5 minutes. Stir in cilantro and lime juice.

Nutrition Facts
Per Serving:
38.7 calories; protein 1.9g 4% DV; carbohydrates 8.7g 3% DV; fat 0.4g 1% DV; cholesterolmg; sodium 571.7mg 23% DV.

Instant Pot Chicken Fried Rice

Prep: 15 mins Cook: 30 mins Additional: 20 mins Total: 1 hr 5 mins

Servings: 6

Ingredients

- 1 egg, separated, divided
- 1 tablespoon cornstarch
- 1 tablespoon rice vinegar
- 1 pound skinless, boneless chicken breast, cubed
- 2 cups long-grain brown rice
- 3 tablespoons peanut oil
- 1 cup diced fresh mushrooms
- 2 eaches green onions, sliced
- 1 clove garlic, minced
- 2 ½ cups low-sodium vegetable broth
- 1 (12 ounce) package frozen peas and carrots
- 1 (8 ounce) package fresh snow peas
- 1 (8 ounce) can diced water chestnuts, drained
- 1 cup chopped fresh broccoli
- 2 teaspoons ground white pepper
- 2 teaspoons sesame oil
- 2 large eggs eggs

- 1 cup fresh bean sprouts

- 3 tablespoons soy sauce, or more to taste

Directions
- **Step 1**

Whisk egg white in a large bowl. Whisk in cornstarch and rice vinegar. Add chicken and stir until completely coated. Allow to sit for 10 minutes, then remove chicken and pat dry with a paper towel.
- **Step 2**

Meanwhile, rinse rice under cool running water until water runs clear. Set aside to drain.
- **Step 3**

Turn on a multi-functional pressure cooker (such as Instant Pot) and select Saute function. Add peanut oil and chicken; saute for 2 to 3 minutes. Add mushrooms, green onions, and garlic; saute until fragrant and mushrooms have softened, 6 to 7 minutes. Turn off Saute function.
- **Step 4**

Add vegetable broth, rice, frozen peas and carrots, snow peas, water chestnuts, and broccoli. Stir in pepper. Select Rice function and close and lock the lid. Set timer for 15 minutes.
- **Step 5**

Release pressure using the natural-release method according to manufacturer's instructions, for 8 minutes. Release any remaining pressure carefully using the quick-release method according to manufacturer's instructions. Unlock and remove the lid.
- **Step 6**

Fluff rice with a rice spatula, add sesame oil, and turn on Saute function. Whisk together remaining egg yolk and 2 eggs in a small bowl and stir into rice mixture, working slowly and in a circular fashion until eggs are distributed throughout the rice and are fully cooked, 3 to 5 minutes. Turn off Saute function and fold in bean sprouts and soy sauce. Serve immediately.

Cook's Notes:
This timing is for brown rice. If you use white rice, set timer for 12 minutes instead of 15 minutes.

Nutrition Facts
Per Serving:
518.9 calories; protein 28.9g 58% DV; carbohydrates 68.5g 22% DV; fat 15g 23% DV; cholesterol 136.1mg 45% DV; sodium 668.1mg 27% DV.

Instant Pot Indian Chicken Curry

Prep: 10 mins Cook: 35 mins Additional: 10 mins Total: 55 mins

Servings: 6

Ingredients

- 3 tablespoons butter

- 1 yellow onion, chopped

- 1 tablespoon minced garlic
- 1 tablespoon minced fresh ginger root
- 1 pound boneless, skinless chicken breast, trimmed and cut into 1-inch pieces
- 2 tablespoons tomato sauce
- 1 ½ tablespoons ground coriander
- ¾ tablespoon Indian chili powder
- 1 ½ teaspoons salt
- 1 teaspoon garam masala
- ¾ teaspoon ground turmeric
- ¾ teaspoon ground black pepper
- ¼ teaspoon cumin
- 1 bay leaf

Directions
- **Step 1**

Turn on a multi-functional pressure cooker (such as Instant Pot) and select Saute function. Melt butter and cook onion until soft and translucent, about 3 minutes. Add garlic and ginger; cook until tender, about 1 minute. Add chicken; cook until golden, about 5 minutes. Add tomato sauce, coriander, chili powder, salt, garam masala, turmeric, pepper, cumin, and bay leaf. Close and lock the lid. Select poultry according to manufacturer's instructions; set timer for 15 minutes. Allow 10 to 15 minutes for pressure to build.
- **Step 2**

Release pressure using the natural-release method according to manufacturer's instructions, 10 to 40 minutes.

Nutrition Facts
Per Serving:
159.6 calories; protein 15.8g 32% DV; carbohydrates 6.4g 2% DV; fat 7.9g 12% DV; cholesterol 54.3mg 18% DV; sodium 694.6mg 28% DV

Instant Pot White Beans

Prep: 5 mins Cook: 40 mins Additional: 10 mins Total: 55 mins

Servings: 10

Ingredients

- 2 cups dry great Northern beans

Directions
- **Step 1**

Pour beans into a multi-functional pressure cooker (such as Instant Pot). Cover with a few inches of cool water. Close and lock the lid. Select Manual; set timer for 28 minutes on high pressure according to manufacturer's instructions. Allow 10 to 15 minutes for pressure to build.
- **Step 2**

Release pressure using the natural-release method according to manufacturer's instructions, 10 to 40 minutes. Unlock and remove the lid. Drain beans and let cool.

Cook's Notes:

Cook beans 2 to 3 minutes less if they're going into a soup, because they will continue cooking.
Cooked beans freeze well! Pour cooled beans into an airtight container with some of the cooking liquid. Leave room at the top for expansion; cover with the lid and freeze. Or pour into a heavy-duty zip-top bag with some of the cooking liquid. Seal and place on a plate to freeze flat. Once frozen, the flat bags are easier to store.

Nutrition Facts
Per Serving:
124.1 calories; protein 8g 16% DV; carbohydrates 22.8g 7% DV; fat 0.4g 1% DV; cholesterolmg; sodium 5.1mg.

Instant Pot Peel-and-Eat Shrimp

Prep: 5 mins Cook: 15 mins Additional: 5 mins Total: 25 mins

Servings: 4

Ingredients

- 1 cup beer
- 1 pound large raw shell-on shrimp, frozen
- 2 tablespoons unsalted butter
- 1 tablespoon seafood seasoning (such as Old Bay)
- ¼ cup chopped fresh parsley
- ¼ cup cocktail sauce, or to taste

Directions
- **Step 1**
Pour beer into a multi-functional pressure cooker (such as Instant Pot). Stir in shrimp, butter, and seafood seasoning. Close and lock the lid. Select high pressure according to manufacturer's instructions; set timer for 2 minutes. Allow 10 minutes for pressure to build.
- **Step 2**
Release pressure carefully using the quick-release method according to manufacturer's instructions, about 5 minutes. Unlock and remove the lid. Stir in parsley.
- **Step 3**
Transfer shrimp to serving plates and serve with cocktail sauce for dipping.

Cook's Notes:
It is important to use frozen shrimp or you will end up with overcooked shrimp.

Nutrition Facts
Per Serving:
186.2 calories; protein 19.4g 39% DV; carbohydrates 6.4g 2% DV; fat 7g 11% DV; cholesterol 187.8mg 63% DV; sodium 824.7mg 33% DV.

Instant Pot Pork Tenderloin

Prep: 5 mins Cook: 25 mins Additional: 15 mins Total: 45 mins

Servings: 8

Ingredients

- 2 teaspoons olive oil
- 1 (2 pound) pork tenderloin, or to taste
- 1 teaspoon Greek seasoning
- 1 pinch salt and ground black pepper to taste
- 1 cup apple juice
- 1 tablespoon cornstarch

Directions
- **Step 1**

Turn on a multi-functional pressure cooker (such as Instant Pot) and select Saute function. Heat olive oil until shimmering, 3 to 5 minutes.
- **Step 2**

Season pork tenderloin with Greek seasoning, salt, and pepper. Add to the preheated pot and cook until browned, about 3 minutes per side. Transfer to a plate. Pour apple juice into the pot; scrape up any pork bits left on the bottom. Set rack inside the pot and place tenderloin on the rack.
- **Step 3**

Close and lock the lid. Select high pressure according to manufacturer's instructions; set timer for 10 minutes. Allow 10 to 15 minutes for pressure to build.
- **Step 4**

Release pressure using the natural-release method for 10 minutes according to manufacturer's instructions. Quick-release any remaining pressure. Unlock and remove the lid. Lift out tenderloin and set aside to rest for 5 minutes.
- **Step 5**

Meanwhile, remove 1/4 cup of the liquid from the pot and mix with cornstarch to make a slurry. Pour slurry back into the pot. Select Saute function and simmer sauce until thickened, about 5 minutes. Slice pork and drizzle sauce on top.

Cook's Notes:
Substitute chicken stock or root beer for the apple juice if preferred.

Nutrition Facts
Per Serving:
164.9 calories; protein 20.1g 40% DV; carbohydrates 4.7g 2% DV; fat 6.7g 10% DV; cholesterol 63.2mg 21% DV; sodium 122.7mg 5% DV.

Instant Pot Frozen Turkey Breast

Prep: 15 mins Cook: 1 hr 10 mins Additional: 10 mins Total: 1 hr 35 mins

Servings: 6

Ingredients

- 2 tablespoons butter
- 1 onion, quartered
- 1 apple, cut into chunks

Spice Rub:
- 2 teaspoons kosher salt
- 2 teaspoons dried thyme
- 2 teaspoons dried rosemary
- 1 teaspoon ground black pepper
- 1 teaspoon dried sage
- ½ teaspoon garlic powder

- 3 stalks celery, chopped
- 2 cups chicken broth
- 1 (.87 ounce) package turkey gravy mix

- 1 (3 pound) frozen boneless turkey breast (such as Butterball)
- 1 cup water
- ½ cup quick-mixing flour (such as Wondra)

Directions

- **Step 1**

Turn on a multi-cooker (such as Instant Pot) and the select Saute function. Melt butter in the pot. Saute onion, apple, and celery until onion and celery are slightly translucent, about 5 minutes. Add broth; scrape off bits from the bottom of the pot. Add gravy mix; stir until dissolved.

- **Step 2**

Combine kosher salt, thyme, rosemary, black pepper, sage, and garlic powder in a small bowl. Rub onto the turkey breast.

- **Step 3**

Lower a trivet into the pot; place seasoned turkey on top. Close and lock the lid. Select high pressure according to manufacturer's instructions; set timer for 50 minutes. Allow 10 to 15 minutes for pressure to build.

- **Step 4**

Release pressure using the natural-release method according to manufacturer's instructions, 10 to 40 minutes.

- **Step 5**

Mix water and quick-mixing flour together slowly in a bowl until slurry is smooth.

- **Step 6**

Unlock the lid and open the pot; transfer turkey to a plate. Strain the liquid from the pot; return it to the pot and select Saute function. Bring to a boil. Stir in the slurry slowly until gravy is thickened to your satisfaction. Slice turkey and serve with gravy.

Cook's Notes:

After the turkey is done cooking, you can set it under the broiler until skin is crisped to your liking.

Nutrition Facts

Per Serving:
496.3 calories; protein 59.3g 119% DV; carbohydrates 19.3g 6% DV; fat 19.2g 30% DV; cholesterol 158.8mg 53% DV; sodium 1338.5mg 54% DV.

Instant Pot Teriyaki Chicken Thighs

Prep: 10 mins Cook: 35 mins Additional: 10 mins Total: 55 mins

Servings: 4

Ingredients

- 1 tablespoon olive oil
- 4 eaches skinless, boneless chicken thighs
- ½ cup brown sugar
- ½ cup soy sauce
- ¼ cup honey
- ¼ cup apple cider vinegar
- 1 (1/2 inch) piece fresh ginger, grated
- 2 cloves garlic, minced
- 2 tablespoons cold water
- 1 tablespoon cornstarch

Directions
- **Step 1**

Turn on a multi-functional pressure cooker (such as Instant Pot) and select Saute function. Pour in olive oil and warm until hot. Add chicken thighs and brown on both sides, 3 to 5 minutes per side.
- **Step 2**

Meanwhile, combine brown sugar, soy sauce, honey, apple cider vinegar, ginger, and garlic in a bowl for the marinade. Pour marinade over chicken thighs in the pot and bring to a simmer; cook for 2 minutes and scrape browned bits off bottom of pot. Turn off Saute mode. Close and lock the lid.
- **Step 3**

Select high pressure according to manufacturer's instructions; set timer for 10 minutes. Allow 10 to 15 minutes for pressure to build.
- **Step 4**

Release pressure using the natural-release method according to manufacturer's instructions, 10 to 40 minutes. Unlock and remove the lid.
- **Step 5**

Stir cold water and cornstarch together in a small bowl. Remove chicken thighs from Instant Pot and transfer to a plate.
- **Step 6**

Select Saute function. Pour cornstarch mixture into the remaining sauce in the pot. Cook until sauce has thickened, 2 to 3 minutes. Turn off Saute mode. Pour some of the sauce over teriyaki thighs and serve.

Nutrition Facts
Per Serving:
383.8 calories; protein 21.5g 43% DV; carbohydrates 40.3g 13% DV; fat 15.3g 24% DV; cholesterol 71.6mg 24% DV; sodium 1876mg 75% DV.

Instant Pot Borracho Cranberry Beans

Prep: 10 mins Cook: 1 hr Additional: 10 mins Total: 1 hr 20 mins

Servings: 8

Ingredients

- 1 teaspoon olive oil
- 1 small onion, chopped
- 1 pound dried cranberry beans
- 4 cups chicken broth
- 1 (12 fluid ounce) can or bottle beer
- 1 cup picante sauce
- ½ cup chopped cilantro
- ¼ cup pickled jalapeno peppers
- 1 tablespoon minced garlic
- 2 teaspoons Mexican oregano
- 1 teaspoon cumin
- 1 pinch salt and ground black pepper to taste

Directions
- **Step 1**

Turn on a multi-functional pressure cooker (such as Instant Pot) and select Saute function. Add oil and let heat about 1 minute. Add onion and cook for 2 minutes. Turn Saute function off.
- **Step 2**

Add cranberry beans, chicken broth, beer, picante sauce, cilantro, jalapeno peppers, garlic, oregano, and cumin; stir to combine. Close and lock the lid. Select high pressure according to manufacturer's instructions; set timer for 45 minutes. Allow 10 to 15 minutes for pressure to build.
- **Step 3**

Release pressure using the natural-release method according to manufacturer's instructions, 10 to 15 minutes. Season with salt and pepper.

Nutrition Facts
Per Serving:
244.5 calories; protein 14.6g 29% DV; carbohydrates 40.5g 13% DV; fat 1.8g 3% DV; cholesterol 3mg 1% DV; sodium 891.9mg 36% DV.

Instant Pot Rice Pudding

Prep:10 mins Cook: 30 mins Additional: 15 mins Total: 55 mins

Servings: 6

Ingredients

- 1 cup long-grain rice
- 2 cups 2% milk
- 1 ½ cups water
- 1 teaspoon vanilla extract
- 1 teaspoon ground cinnamon
- 1 pinch salt
- 8 ounces sweetened condensed milk
- ¾ cup raisins

Directions

- **Step 1**

Rinse rice until water runs clear. Strain out most of the water and add rice to a multi-functional pressure cooker (such as Instant Pot). Add milk, water, vanilla extract, cinnamon, and salt and stir well. Close and lock the lid. Select the porridge function according to manufacturer's instructions; set timer for 20 minutes. Allow 10 to 15 minutes for pressure to build.

- **Step 2**

Release pressure using the natural-release method according to manufacturer's instructions for 10 minutes. Release remaining pressure carefully using the quick-release method according to manufacturer's instructions, about 5 minutes. Unlock and remove the lid.

- **Step 3**

Stir sweetened condensed milk into the rice pudding until combined. Stir in raisins and serve immediately.

Nutrition Facts

Per Serving:

331.8 calories; protein 8.4g 17% DV; carbohydrates 63.8g 21% DV; fat 5.2g 8% DV; cholesterol 19.4mg 7% DV; sodium 112.6mg 5% DV.

Instant Pot Spicy Beef Curry Stew

Prep: 20 mins Cook: 55 mins Additional: 15 mins Total:1 hr 30 mins

Servings: 8

Ingredients

- 2 tablespoons olive oil
- 2 pounds cubed beef stew meat
- 1 pinch salt and ground black pepper to taste
- 2 eaches jalapeno peppers, chopped
- 4 cloves garlic, minced
- 1 tablespoon minced fresh ginger root
- 4 tablespoons curry powder
- 2 cups beef broth
- 1 (28 ounce) can fire-roasted diced tomatoes
- 1 pound Yukon Gold potatoes
- 3 eaches carrots, sliced
- 1 large onion, sliced

Directions

- **Step 1**

Turn on a multi-functional pressure cooker (such as Instant Pot) and select Saute function. Pour in olive oil and heat until sizzling; add meat and season with salt and pepper. Cook until browned, 5 to 7 minutes per side.

- **Step 2**

Transfer meat to a plate, reserving juices in the pot. Add jalapenos, garlic, and ginger to the pot. Cook and stir until tender, about 2 minutes. Season with curry powder.

- **Step 3**

Pour 1/2 of the beef broth into the pot; scrape brown bits from the bottom of the pot using a wooden spoon. Return meat to the pot with remaining beef broth, tomatoes, potatoes, carrots, and onion. Close and lock the lid.
- **Step 4**

Select high pressure according to manufacturer's instructions and set timer for 35 minutes. Allow 10 to 15 minutes for pressure to build.
- **Step 5**

Release pressure using the natural-release method according to manufacturer's instructions for 10 minutes. Release remaining pressure carefully using the quick-release method according to manufacturer's instructions, about 5 minutes more. Unlock and remove the lid.

Nutrition Facts
Per Serving:
356.4 calories; protein 22.1g 44% DV; carbohydrates 22.8g 7% DV; fat 19.4g 30% DV; cholesterol 62.6mg 21% DV; sodium 548.5mg 22% DV.

Instant Pot Spicy Butternut Squash Soup

Prep: 20 mins Cook:35 mins Additional: 5 mins Total: 1 hr

Servings: 6

Ingredients

- 1 tablespoon olive oil
- 1 onion, diced
- 2 cloves garlic
- 1 pound butternut squash - peeled, seeded, and cut into 1-inch pieces
- 5 cups vegetable broth
- 1 tablespoon brown sugar
- 1 teaspoon salt
- ½ teaspoon ground black pepper
- ½ teaspoon ground ginger
- ½ teaspoon curry powder
- 1 cup heavy whipping cream

Directions
- **Step 1**

Turn on a multi-functional pressure cooker (such as Instant Pot) and select Saute function. Heat olive oil and add onion; cook until translucent, about 7 minutes. Add garlic and cook for 1 minute more.
- **Step 2**

Combine butternut squash, vegetable broth, brown sugar, salt, ground black pepper, ginger, and curry powder in the pot. Close and lock the lid. Select high pressure according to manufacturer's instructions; set timer for 10 minutes. Allow 10 to 15 minutes for pressure to build.
- **Step 3**

Release pressure carefully using the quick-release method according to manufacturer's instructions, about 5 minutes. Unlock and remove lid. Blend with an immersion blender until creamy.

- **Step 5**

Stir in heavy whipping cream.

Nutrition Facts

Per Serving:

234.7 calories; protein 2.7g 6% DV; carbohydrates 18.7g 6% DV; fat 17.5g 27% DV; cholesterol 54.3mg 18% DV; sodium 790.8mg 32% DV.

Instant Pot Steamed Artichokes

Prep: 5 mins Cook: 20 mins Additional: 5 mins Total: 30 mins

Servings: 4

Ingredients

- 1 cup water
- 2 cloves garlic
- 1 bay leaf
- ½ teaspoon salt
- 4 eaches artichokes, trimmed and stemmed
- 2 tablespoons lemon juice

Directions

- **Step 1**

Combine water, garlic, bay leaf, and salt inside a multi-functional pressure cooker (such as Instant Pot). Place steamer in the pot. Add artichokes, trimmed top facing up; drizzle with lemon juice. Close and lock the lid. Select high pressure according to manufacturer's instructions; set timer for 10 minutes. Allow 10 to 15 minutes for pressure to build.

- **Step 2**

Release pressure carefully using the quick-release method according to manufacturer's instructions, about 5 minutes. Unlock and remove lid.

- **Step 3**

Cool until easily handled. Pull off outer petals one at a time. Pull through teeth to remove the soft portion of the petal. Discard remaining petal. Spoon out fuzzy center near the stem and discard. Eat the bottom whole or cut into pieces.

Cook's Notes:

Artichokes may be served hot or cold. They can be eaten by pulling off outer petals and dipping them in lemon juice, then pulling through teeth to remove soft, pulpy portion of petal. Discard remaining petal. You may also eat the heart of the artichoke, by removing the fuzzy center at the base.

Nutrition Facts

Per Serving:

64.4 calories; protein 4.3g 9% DV; carbohydrates 14.6g 5% DV; fat 0.2g; cholesterolmg; sodium 413.1mg 17% DV.

Instant Pot Taco Soup

Prep: 5 mins Cook: 20 mins Additional: 5 mins Total: 30 mins

Servings: 6

Ingredients

- 1 pound ground beef
- 1 small onion, diced
- 1 (15.5 ounce) can black beans, rinsed and drained
- 1 (15.25 ounce) can whole kernel corn, drained
- 1 (10 ounce) can diced tomatoes and green chiles (such as RO*TEL)
- 1 (8 ounce) can tomato sauce
- 1 cup beef broth
- 1 (1.25 ounce) package taco seasoning mix
- 2 eaches avocados, sliced
- ¼ cup shredded Oaxaca cheese, or to taste

Directions
- **Step 1**

Turn on a multi-functional pressure cooker (such as Instant Pot) and select Saute function to heat up the pot. Add ground beef and onion. Stir to break up ground beef into crumbles and cook until beef is browned, about 5 minutes. Drain as much excess grease as possible. Stir in black beans, corn, diced tomatoes and chiles, tomato sauce, beef broth, and taco seasoning. Mix until well combined. Cancel Saute mode.
- **Step 2**

Close and lock the lid. Select high pressure according to manufacturer's instructions; set timer for 3 minutes. Allow 10 to 15 minutes for pressure to build.
- **Step 3**

Release pressure carefully using the quick-release method according to manufacturer's instructions, about 5 minutes. Unlock and remove the lid. Serve soup with avocado slices and Oaxaca cheese.

Nutrition Facts
Per Serving:
428.4 calories; protein 22.8g 46% DV; carbohydrates 40.2g 13% DV; fat 21.3g 33% DV; cholesterol 52.2mg 17% DV; sodium 1518mg 61% DV.

Instant Pot Vegan Korma

Prep: 30 mins Cook: 15 mins Additional: 10 mins Total: 55 mins

Servings: 4

Ingredients

- 1 red onion, quartered, divided
- 1 green bird's eye chile pepper, stemmed
- ½ cup water, divided
- ¼ cup raw cashews
- 2 cloves garlic
- 2 tablespoons tomato paste
- 1 (1 inch) piece fresh ginger
- 5 eaches whole cloves
- 3 eaches green cardamom pods
- 1 black cardamom pod
- 1 bay leaf
- 1 teaspoon cumin seeds
- ¼ teaspoon whole black peppercorns
- ¼ teaspoon ground coriander
- ¼ inch cinnamon stick
- ¼ cup light vegetable oil
- 8 ¾ ounces cauliflower, cut into large pieces
- 5 ¼ ounces broccoli, cut into large pieces
- 2 eaches tomatoes, cut into large chunks
- 1 cup canned chickpeas (garbanzo beans), drained with liquid reserved
- 1 carrot, sliced
- 1 red bird's eye chile pepper, chopped
- ½ tablespoon garam masala
- ½ teaspoon ground turmeric
- ¼ teaspoon chili powder
- 1 cup baby spinach leaves
- 1 cup full-fat coconut milk
- ½ cup vegan yogurt
- 2 ounces roasted cashews, chopped
- ½ cup chopped fresh cilantro

Directions
- **Step 1**

Blend 1/4 of the onion, green chile pepper, 1/4 cup water, cashews, garlic, tomato paste, and ginger together in an electric blender, adding extra water if necessary, until paste is creamy and has the consistency of a pesto. Set aside.
- **Step 2**

Combine cloves, green and black cardamom pods, bay leaf, cumin seeds, peppercorns, coriander, and cinnamon in a mortar. Smash using a pestle to break open spices slightly, 3 to 4 times. Thinly slice remaining onion quarters.
- **Step 3**

Turn on a multi-functional pressure cooker (such as Instant Pot) and select Saute function. Add smashed spice mixture and toast until fragrant, about 30 seconds. Pour in oil followed by cashew pesto, onion slices, cauliflower, broccoli, tomatoes, chickpeas, carrot, red chile pepper, garam masala, turmeric, and chili powder. Stir. Cancel the Saute function. Close and lock the lid.
- **Step 4**

Select high pressure according to manufacturer's instructions; set timer for 5 minutes. Allow 10 minutes for pressure to build.
- **Step 5**

Release pressure using the natural-release method according to manufacturer's instructions, 10 to 40 minutes. Unlock and remove the lid. Stir in spinach and mix to help wilt. Stir in coconut milk and yogurt. Mix and serve with roasted cashews and cilantro on top.

Nutrition Facts
Per Serving:
544.4 calories; protein 12.9g 26% DV; carbohydrates 45g 15% DV; fat 38.7g 60% DV; cholesterolmg; sodium 449.1mg 18% DV.

Instant Pot Chicken Biryani

Prep: 30 mins Cook: 35 mins Additional: 35 mins Total: 1 hr 40 mins

Servings: 4

Ingredients

- 1 ½ cups basmati rice
- 2 cups water
- 7 ounces skinless, boneless chicken breast, cut into 1-inch cubes
- 7 ounces skinless, boneless chicken thighs, cut into 1-inch cubes
- 3 tablespoons Greek yogurt
- 1 ½ tablespoons fresh lemon juice
- ½ tablespoon grated fresh ginger
- ½ tablespoon minced fresh garlic
- 1 ½ teaspoons garam masala, divided
- 1 pinch salt and ground black pepper to taste
- 3 tablespoons ghee
- 2 eaches whole cloves
- 2 pods cardamom, crushed
- 1 bay leaf
- ½ cinnamon stick
- 1 teaspoon coriander seed
- 1 teaspoon brown mustard seed
- ¾ teaspoon cumin seeds
- 1 large red onion, cut in half and thinly sliced
- 1 ½ cups chicken stock
- ½ cup roughly chopped fresh cilantro
- ¼ cup roughly chopped fresh mint leaves
- ½ teaspoon ground turmeric
- ½ teaspoon paprika
- ½ teaspoon red chile powder

Directions
- **Step 1**

Thoroughly rinse basmati rice in a strainer until water runs clear. Transfer rice to a bowl, add fresh water to cover, and set aside for 30 minutes.
- **Step 2**

Place chicken breast and chicken thigh pieces in a large bowl. Add Greek yogurt, lemon juice, ginger, garlic, 1/2 teaspoon garam masala, salt, and pepper. Mix well to coat chicken. Cover and refrigerate for 30 minutes.
- **Step 3**

Drain rice and remove marinated chicken from the refrigerator. Turn on a multi-functional pressure cooker (such as Instant Pot), select Saute function, and add ghee. When ghee starts to bubble, add cloves, cardamom pods, bay leaf, cinnamon stick, coriander seed, mustard seed, and cumin seeds and saute until fragrant, 2 to 3 minutes. Add sliced onion and cook, stirring often, until tender and fragrant, about 5 minutes.
- **Step 4**

Add chicken and extra marinade to the cooker. Saute until browned on all sides, about 5 minutes. Turn off Saute function. Add rice, chicken stock, cilantro, mint, remaining 1 teaspoon garam masala, turmeric, paprika, and chili powder; stir until well mixed.
- **Step 5**

Close and lock the lid. Select high pressure according to manufacturer's instructions; set timer for 6 minutes. Allow 10 to 15 minutes for pressure to build.
- **Step 6**

Release pressure carefully using the quick-release method according to manufacturer's instructions, about 5 minutes. Unlock and remove the lid. Fluff with a fork and serve immediately.

Nutrition Facts
Per Serving:
499 calories; protein 25.4g 51% DV; carbohydrates 62.8g 20% DV; fat 16.6g 26% DV; cholesterol 84.3mg 28% DV; sodium 542.7mg 22% DV.

Instant Pot Chickpeas

Prep: 5 mins Cook: 50 mins Additional: 10 mins Total: 1 hr 5 mins

Servings: 5

Ingredients
1 cup dry chickpeas (garbanzo beans)

Directions
- **Step 1**

Pour chickpeas into a multi-functional pressure cooker (such as Instant Pot). Cover with a few inches of cool water. Close and lock the lid. Select Manual; set timer for 36 minutes on high pressure according to manufacturer's instructions. Allow 10 to 15 minutes for pressure to build.
- **Step 2**

Release pressure using the natural-release method according to manufacturer's instructions, 10 to 40 minutes. Unlock and remove the lid. Drain chickpeas and let cool.

Cook's Notes:
Cook time can range from 35 to 40 minutes. Choose the shorter time if the chickpeas will be going into soup (since they will keep cooking). Choose the longer time if the chickpeas are going into finished dishes like salads.
Cooked beans freeze well! Pour cooled beans into an airtight container with some of the cooking liquid. Leave room at the top for expansion; cover with the lid and freeze. Or pour into a heavy-duty zip-top bag with some of the cooking liquid. Seal and place on a plate to freeze flat. Once frozen, the flat bags are easier to store.

Nutrition Facts
Per Serving:
145.6 calories; protein 7.7g 15% DV; carbohydrates 24.3g 8% DV; fat 2.4g 4% DV; cholesterolmg; sodium 9.6mg.

Instant Pot Fresh Corn Risotto

Prep: 15 mins Cook: 25 mins Additional: 5 mins Total: 45 mins

Servings: 4

Ingredients

- 3 tablespoons butter, divided
- 3 tablespoons extra virgin olive oil, divided
- 2 ears fresh corn, kernels cut from cob
- ½ cup finely chopped red onion
- 2 cloves garlic, minced

- 1 ½ cups Arborio rice
- ½ cup white wine
- 4 cups chicken broth
- ½ cup grated Parmigiano-Reggiano cheese
- ½ teaspoon chopped fresh parsley

Directions
- **Step 1**

Turn on a multi-functional pressure cooker (such as Instant Pot) and select Saute function. Add 1 tablespoon butter and 1 tablespoon olive oil; stir until butter melts. Add corn kernels and cook, stirring occasionally, about 2 minutes. Remove corn to a bowl and set aside.
- **Step 2**

Pour remaining 2 tablespoons of olive oil in the pot. Add red onion and cook for 1 minute. Add garlic and rice and stir until each grain of rice is coated with the oil mixture. Cook until rice is slightly toasted, about 2 minutes. Pour in white wine and simmer for about 30 seconds. Stir in chicken broth.

- **Step 3**

Turn off Saute function. Close and lock the lid. Select high pressure according to manufacturer's instructions; set timer for 6 minutes. Allow 5 to 10 minutes for pressure to build.
- **Step 4**

Release pressure carefully using the quick-release method according to manufacturer's instructions, about 5 minutes. Unlock and remove the lid. Add corn and remaining 2 tablespoons butter; stir until risotto is creamy, about 1 minute. Stir in Parmigiano-Reggiano cheese until melted and well combined. Garnish with parsley.

Cook's Notes:

If you don't have a pressure cooker, this recipe can certainly be made on the stovetop by cooking over medium heat, adding hot broth 1 ladle at a time, and stirring between until the broth has been absorbed. You will need much more broth if making it on the stovetop, close to 6 to 7 cups, and it will take close to 45 minutes to reach "al dente".

Nutrition Facts
Per Serving:
607.7 calories; protein 12.6g 25% DV; carbohydrates 81.9g 26% DV; fat 22.8g 35% DV; cholesterol 37.8mg 13% DV; sodium 1387.4mg 56% DV.

Instant Pot Chicken Taco Soup

Prep: 15 mins Cook: 40 mins Additional: 10 mins Total: 1 hr 5 mins

Servings: 5

Ingredients

- 1 small onion, diced
- 2 tablespoons butter
- 1 clove garlic, minced
- 3 cups chicken broth
- 1 (4 ounce) boneless skinless chicken breast
- ½ cup uncooked white rice
- 1 (10 ounce) can roasted tomatoes with green chiles (such as Ro-Tel)
- ½ cup corn
- 2 tablespoons taco seasoning
- ½ teaspoon cumin
- 1 pinch salt and ground black pepper to taste
- ½ cup shredded Cheddar cheese

Directions

- **Step 1**

Turn on a multi-functional pressure cooker (such as Instant Pot) and select Saute function. Add onion and butter to the hot pot. Cook and stir until fragrant and onion has softened, about 3 minutes, adding garlic during the last 30 seconds. Remove onion mixture to a small bowl. Hit Cancel. Add chicken broth, chicken breast, and rice.

- **Step 2**

Close and lock the lid. Select high pressure according to manufacturer's instructions; set timer for 10 minutes. Allow 10 to 15 minutes for pressure to build.

- **Step 3**

Release pressure carefully using the quick-release method according to manufacturer's instructions, about 5 minutes. Unlock and remove the lid. Remove chicken breast, and shred.

- **Step 4**

Add tomatoes and corn to the pot, along with shredded chicken. Close and lock the lid. Select high pressure according to manufacturer's instructions; set timer for 3 minutes. Allow 10 to 15 minutes for pressure to build.

- **Step 5**

Release pressure carefully using the quick-release method according to manufacturer's instructions, about 5 minutes. Unlock and remove the lid. Stir in reserved onion mixture, taco seasoning, cumin, salt, and pepper. Add Cheddar cheese and stir until melted.

Cook's Notes:

If desired, ladle soup into a blender and blend on high until mixture is creamy.

Nutrition Facts

Per Serving:
230.9 calories; protein 10.7g 22% DV; carbohydrates 24.7g 8% DV; fat 9.7g 15% DV; cholesterol 40.6mg 14% DV; sodium 1334.5mg 53% DV.

Instant Pot Mac and Cheese

Prep: 5 mins Cook: 15 mins Additional: 20 mins Total: 40 mins

Servings: 10

Ingredients

- 1 (16 ounce) package elbow macaroni
- 1 quart chicken stock
- ½ teaspoon salt
- ½ teaspoon dry mustard
- ½ teaspoon liquid smoke flavoring
- ½ teaspoon paprika
- ½ teaspoon ground black pepper
- ½ teaspoon garlic powder
- 2 tablespoons butter
- 1 cup milk
- 8 ounces shredded Cheddar cheese
- 1 cup grated Parmesan cheese

Directions
- **Step 1**

Combine macaroni, chicken stock, salt, dry mustard, liquid smoke, paprika, pepper, and garlic powder in a multi-functional pressure cooker (such as Instant Pot). Close and lock the lid. Select high pressure according to manufacturer's instructions; set timer for 4 minutes. Allow 10 to 15 minutes for pressure to build.
- **Step 2**

Release pressure carefully using the quick-release method according to manufacturer's instructions, about 5 minutes. Unlock and remove the lid. Stir in butter, milk, Cheddar cheese, and Parmesan cheese until melted. Mixture will be soupy at first.
- **Step 3**

Select the "Keep Warm" setting on the Instant Pot and allow macaroni to sit, uncovered and stirring occasionally, until all liquid has been absorbed and consistency is smooth and creamy, about 15 minutes.

Nutrition Facts
Per Serving:
332.8 calories; protein 15.7g 32% DV; carbohydrates 35.9g 12% DV; fat 13.8g 21% DV; cholesterol 39.2mg 13% DV; sodium 681.1mg 27% DV.

Instant Pot Sauerkraut

Prep: 5 mins Cook: 25 mins Additional: 10 mins Total: 40 mins

Servings: 6

Ingredients

- 1 head cabbage, coarsely chopped
- 1 cup white vinegar
- ¼ cup water
- ¼ cup salt

Directions
- **Step 1**

Place cabbage in the pot of a multi-functional electric pressure cooker. Add vinegar, water, and salt. Stir and cover.

- **Step 2**

Lock the lid, close the vent, and select Chicken/Meat setting according to manufacturer's instructions. Set timer for 15 minutes. Allow 10 to 15 minutes for pressure to build.
* **Step 3**
Release pressure using the natural-release method according to manufacturer's instructions, 10 to 40 minutes.

Nutrition Facts
Per Serving:
50 calories; protein 2.5g 5% DV; carbohydrates 11.4g 4% DV; fat 0.2g; cholesterolmg; sodium 3927.6mg 157% DV.

Instant Pot Vegan Rice Pudding

Prep: 5 mins Cook: 30 mins Total: 35 mins

Servings: 6

Ingredients

* 3 cups almond milk
* ⅔ cup jasmine rice, rinsed
* ⅓ cup granulated sugar
* ½ teaspoon salt
* 1 ½ teaspoons vanilla extract

Directions
* **Step 1**
Combine almond milk, rice, sugar, and salt in a multi-functional pressure cooker (such as Instant Pot). Close and lock the lid. Select high pressure according to manufacturer's instructions; set timer for 18 minutes. Allow 10 to 15 minutes for pressure to build.
* **Step 2**
Release pressure using the natural-release method according to manufacturer's instructions, about 10 minutes. Unlock and remove the lid. Stir in vanilla extract. Serve warm or chilled. Rice pudding will thicken as it cools.

Nutrition Facts
Per Serving:
153.9 calories; protein 2g 4% DV; carbohydrates 32.6g 11% DV; fat 1.3g 2% DV; cholesterolmg; sodium 273.8mg 11% DV.

Instant Pot Lentil and Ham Soup

Prep: 20 mins Cook: 30 mins Additional: 10 mins Total: 1 hr

Servings: 10

Ingredients

- 1 tablespoon olive oil
- 1 cup chopped onion
- 1 cup chopped celery
- 1 cup carrots, 1/4-inch slices
- 2 cloves garlic, minced
- 1 ½ cups diced cooked ham
- 1 cup lentils
- ½ teaspoon dried basil leaves
- ½ teaspoon dried oregano
- ¼ teaspoon dried thyme
- 4 cups chicken broth
- 1 (8 ounce) can tomato sauce
- 1 cup water
- 1 small bay leaf
- 1 ¼ teaspoons kosher salt
- ½ teaspoon lemon juice
- ¼ teaspoon ground black pepper

Directions
- **Step 1**

Turn on a multi-functional pressure cooker (such as Instant Pot) and select Saute function. Add oil and warm for a few minutes. Add onion and celery; saute for 2 minutes. Add carrots; saute for 4 minutes. Add garlic and cook for 2 minutes. Stir in ham, lentils, basil, oregano, and thyme. Add chicken broth, tomato sauce, and water. Stir in bay leaf.
- **Step 2**

Close and lock the lid. Select high pressure according to manufacturer's instructions; set timer for 8 minutes. Allow 10 to 15 minutes for pressure to build.
- **Step 3**

Release pressure using the natural-release method according to manufacturer's instructions, 10 to 40 minutes. Remove lid carefully. Discard bay leaf. Stir salt, lemon juice, and pepper into the soup.

Cook's Notes:
Substitute Himalayan salt for the kosher salt if desired.

Nutrition Facts
Per Serving:
157.4 calories; protein 9.9g 20% DV; carbohydrates 16.7g 5% DV; fat 5.7g 9% DV; cholesterol 13.8mg 5% DV; sodium 1104mg 44% DV.

Instant Pot Yardbird Chili with White Beans

Prep: 15 mins Cook: 1 hr 5 mins Additional: 25 mins Total: 1 hr 45 mins

Servings: 8

Ingredients

- 2 tablespoons vegetable oil
- 1 ½ breast half, bone and skin removed (blank)s chicken breasts, cut into 1/2-inch cubes
- 1 medium onion, diced
- 4 cloves garlic, crushed
- 1 (28 ounce) can green enchilada sauce

* 2 cups dry great northern beans, sorted and rinsed
* 2 cups chicken broth

Garnish:
* 1 cup shredded Cheddar-Monterey Jack cheese blend, or to taste

* 2 (4 ounce) cans chopped green chiles (such as Hatch), undrained
* 1 tablespoon oregano
* 1 teaspoon cumin

* ½ cup chopped cilantro, or to taste

Directions
* **Step 1**

Turn on a multi-functional pressure cooker (such as Instant Pot) and select Saute function. Pour in oil. Add chicken pieces to the hot oil and saute until lightly browned, 5 to 7 minutes. Add onion and garlic and saute until soft and translucent, about 5 minutes more

* **Step 2**

Add enchilada sauce, dry beans, broth, green chiles, oregano, and cumin to the pot. Close and lock the lid. Select high pressure according to manufacturer's instructions; set timer for 45 minutes. Allow 10 to 15 minutes for pressure to build.

* **Step 3**

Release pressure using the natural-release method according to manufacturer's instructions, at least 25 minutes to allow beans to fully cook. Unlock and remove the lid. Garnish chili with shredded Cheddar-Monterey Jack cheese blend and cilantro.

Cook's Notes:
You can use chicken thighs in place of breasts, if you prefer.

Nutrition Facts
Per Serving:
330.1 calories; protein 20g 40% DV; carbohydrates 39.7g 13% DV; fat 10.7g 17% DV; cholesterol 26.6mg 9% DV; sodium 977.2mg 39% DV.

Instant Pot Creamy Chicken and Leek Alfredo

Prep: 15 mins Cook: 25 mins Additional: 15 mins Total: 55 mins

Servings: 6

Ingredients

* ½ tablespoon olive oil
* ½ tablespoon butter
* 1 pound chicken breast, cubed
* 1 cup diced leek (white and light green only)
* 2 eaches garlic, chopped, or more to taste
* 1 tablespoon Italian seasoning

* ¼ teaspoon salt
* ¼ teaspoon ground black pepper
* 1 pinch red pepper flakes
* 1 ½ cups chicken broth
* ¼ cup dry white wine
* ⅔ cup heavy whipping cream
* 1 egg yolk
* 8 ounces penne pasta

- 1 cup shredded Parmesan-Romano cheese blend
- 1 pinch cornstarch
- 1 ounce cream cheese, cubed
- ½ cup milk, or more as needed
- 1 pinch salt and freshly ground black pepper to taste

Directions
- **Step 1**

Turn on a multi-functional pressure cooker (such as Instant Pot) and select Saute function. Add oil and butter and heat until butter is melted. Add chicken and cook until lightly browned on all sides, 5 to 8 minutes. Add leek and garlic. Season with Italian seasoning, salt, black pepper, and red pepper flakes. Cook for 3 to 5 minutes.
- **Step 2**

Pour in chicken broth and wine to deglaze pot. Bring to a simmer, scraping browned bits off the bottom of the pot.
- **Step 3**

Stir cream and egg yolk together in a small bowl until well combined. Pour into the Instant Pot. Add pasta without mixing, letting it float on top, but making sure pasta does not stick together. You may push pasta slightly down into the liquid. Close and lock the lid and seal the vent. Select high pressure according to manufacturer's instructions; set timer for 1 minute. Allow 10 to 15 minutes for pressure to build.
- **Step 4**

Release pressure using the natural-release method according to manufacturer's instructions for 10 minutes. Release remaining pressure carefully using the quick-release method according to manufacturer's instructions, about 5 minutes.
- **Step 5**

Mix Parmesan-Romano cheese mixture and a pinch of cornstarch together in a bowl. Unlock and remove Instant Pot lid. Stir in cheese mixture and cream cheese. Slowly add enough milk until the sauce reaches desired creaminess. Mix well to create a smooth cream sauce.

Nutrition Facts
Per Serving:
494.6 calories; protein 25.4g 51% DV; carbohydrates 37.8g 12% DV; fat 26.3g 41% DV; cholesterol 136.1mg 45% DV; sodium 803.1mg 32% DV.

Instant Pot German Red Cabbage

Prep: 10 mins Cook: 20 mins Additional: 5 mins Total: 35 mins

Servings: 4

Ingredients
- 2 tablespoons butter
- 3 tablespoons cider vinegar
- ¼ cup brown sugar
- ½ teaspoon salt, or to taste
- ¼ cup onion, minced
- ½ cup grated peeled apple
- 2 pounds red cabbage, thinly sliced
- ⅛ teaspoon ground cloves
- ⅛ teaspoon ground allspice

Directions

- **Step 1**

Turn on a multi-functional pressure cooker (such as Instant Pot) and select Saute function. Melt butter. Add apple cider vinegar, brown sugar, and salt. Stir to combine. Mix in onion, grated apple, and red cabbage until well combined. Close and lock the lid. Select Steam function. Set timer for 3 minutes. Allow 10 to 15 minutes for pressure to build.

- **Step 2**

Release pressure carefully using the quick-release method according to manufacturer's instructions, about 5 minutes. Unlock and remove the lid. Mix in ground cloves and allspice.

Nutrition Facts

Per Serving:

187.6 calories; protein 3.5g 7% DV; carbohydrates 33.3g 11% DV; fat 6.2g 10% DV; cholesterol 15.3mg 5% DV; sodium 398mg 16% DV.

Instant Pot Vegan 15-Bean Soup

Prep: 10 mins Cook: 45 mins Additional: 15 mins Total: 1 hr 10 mins

Servings: 6

Ingredients

- 1 (20 ounce) package 15-bean soup mix (seasoning packet not used)
- 1 (14.5 ounce) can diced Italian-style tomatoes
- 8 cups vegetable broth
- 2 medium (blank)s carrots, diced
- 1 onion, diced
- 2 stalks celery, chopped
- 2 cloves garlic, minced
- 1 teaspoon sea salt
- 1 teaspoon smoked paprika
- ½ teaspoon ground black pepper

Directions

- **Step 1**

Combine rinsed beans, diced tomatoes, vegetable broth, carrots, onion, celery, garlic, salt, paprika, and black pepper in a multi-functional pressure cooker (such as Instant Pot). Close and lock the lid. Select high pressure according to manufacturer's instructions; set timer for 35 minutes. Allow 10 to 15 minutes for pressure to build

- **Step 2**

Release pressure using the natural-release method according to manufacturer's instructions, about 10 minutes. Complete releasing pressure carefully using the quick-release method according to manufacturer's instructions, about 5 minutes. Unlock and remove the lid.

Nutrition Facts

Per Serving:

389.6 calories; protein 23.6g 47% DV; carbohydrates 67g 22% DV; fat 2.2g 3% DV; cholesterolmg; sodium 1214.3mg 49% DV

Instant Pot Lentil Soup

Prep: 15 mins Cook: 30 mins Additional: 20 mins Total: 1 hr 5 mins

Servings: 6

Ingredients

- 3 tablespoons olive oil
- ½ onion, finely diced
- 1 carrot, peeled and diced
- 1 stalk celery, diced
- 2 cloves garlic, minced
- 2 teaspoons ground cumin
- ½ teaspoon ground coriander
- ½ teaspoon ground turmeric
- ½ teaspoon salt
- ½ teaspoon ground white pepper
- ¼ teaspoon fennel seeds
- ⅛ teaspoon chile powder
- 1 tablespoon tomato paste
- 4 cups vegetable broth
- 3 cups water
- 1 ¼ cups green lentils
- 1 small yellow squash, diced
- 1 cube vegetable bouillon
- 1 lemon, juiced
- 1 cup chopped kale, or to taste

Directions
- **Step 1**

Turn on a multi-functional pressure cooker (such as Instant Pot) and select Saute function. Warm olive oil for 3 minutes. Add onion, carrot, celery, and garlic. Cook until onion is soft and translucent, 4 to 5 minutes. Season with cumin, coriander, turmeric, salt, white pepper, fennel, and chile powder. Cook for 2 more minutes. Stir in tomato paste.
- **Step 2**

Pour in broth and water. Stir in lentils and squash. Crumble bouillon cube over the top and mix well, scraping the bottom of the pan to remove any browned bits. Cancel Saute Mode.
- **Step 3**

Close and lock the lid. Select high pressure according to manufacturer's instructions; set timer for 8 minutes. Allow 10 to 15 minutes for pressure to build.
- **Step 4**

Release pressure using the natural-release method according to manufacturer's instructions for 10 minutes. Open valve to vent remaining steam, about 5 minutes. Unlock and remove the lid.
- **Step 5**

Mix in lemon juice and toss kale leaves just on top of the soup. Replace lid and allow kale to steam for about 5 minutes. Remove lid and adjust seasonings, if desired, before serving.

Cook's Notes:
You can also use 1 large chicken bouillon cube instead of vegetable bouillon.
Use red lentils instead of green, if preferred.
Substitute lime juice for lemon juice if preferred.

Nutrition Facts

Per Serving:
254.4 calories; protein 12.4g 25% DV; carbohydrates 35.6g 12% DV; fat 8g 12% DV; cholesterolmg; sodium 547.4mg 22% DV.

Instant Pot No-Stress Buffalo Chicken Dip

Prep: 10 mins Cook: 20 mins Additional: 15 mins Total: 45 mins

Servings: 12

Ingredients

- 2 (8 ounce) frozen chicken breasts
- 1 cup chicken broth
- 8 ounces cream cheese
- ½ cup sriracha sauce
- ½ cup ranch dressing
- 1 tablespoon chile-garlic sauce
- 2 cups shredded Cheddar cheese
- 1 green onion, thinly sliced

Directions
- **Step 1**

Combine chicken breasts and broth in a multi-functional pressure cooker (such as Instant Pot). Close and lock the lid. Select high pressure according to manufacturer's instructions; set timer for 10 minutes. Allow 10 to 15 minutes for pressure to build.
- **Step 2**

Release pressure using the natural-release method according to manufacturer's instructions for 10 minutes. Release remaining pressure carefully using the quick-release method according to manufacturer's instructions, about 5 minutes. Unlock and remove the lid. Transfer chicken to a bowl and shred.
- **Step 3**

Select Saute function. Add cream cheese, sriracha, ranch dressing, and chile-garlic sauce. Return shredded chicken to the pot. Slowly add Cheddar cheese, constantly stirring until melted and all Ingredients are well combined. Select Keep Warm function until ready to serve. Garnish with green onions.

Cook's Notes:
You can cook thawed chicken breasts by setting the time for 15 minutes at high pressure and use a quick release.

Nutrition Facts
Per Serving:
242.8 calories; protein 14.2g 29% DV; carbohydrates 3.1g 1% DV; fat 19g 29% DV; cholesterol 65.3mg 22% DV; sodium 818.7mg 33% DV.

Instant Pot Puerto Rican Arroz con Pollo

Prep: 10 mins Cook: 40 mins Additional: 20 mins Total: 1 hr 10 mins

Servings: 8

Ingredients

- 2 tablespoons olive oil
- ½ cup salt pork, diced
- 2 pounds boneless skinless chicken breasts, chopped
- 2 (1.41 ounce) packages sazon seasoning with achiote
- 1 cup sofrito
- 1 (8 ounce) can tomato sauce
- ½ cup pimento-stuffed green olives
- 1 tablespoon capers
- 3 cups white rice, rinsed
- 1 (16 ounce) can gandules (green pigeon peas), undrained
- ¼ teaspoon salt, or to taste
- ⅛ teaspoon ground black pepper, to taste

Directions

- **Step 1**

Turn on a multi-functional pressure cooker (such as Instant Pot) and select Saute function. Heat olive oil. Add salt pork pieces and stir until edges start to brown, about 2 minutes. Add chicken and sazon seasoning. Cook, stirring occasionally, until chicken is white on all sides, about 5 minutes.

- **Step 2**

Add sofrito and cook, stirring occasionally, for 5 more minutes. Pour in tomato sauce, olives, and capers. Stir to combine and cook until bubbly and all flavors are incorporated, 1 to 2 minutes. Add rice and mix well. Turn off Saute function.

- **Step 3**

Drain liquid from the can of gandules into a large measuring cup. Add enough water to make 2 1/2 cups of liquid. Add gandules and liquid to the pot and stir well. Season with salt and pepper.

- **Step 4**

Close and lock the lid. Select high pressure according to manufacturer's instructions; set timer for 17 minutes. Allow 10 to 15 minutes for pressure to build.

- **Step 5**

Release pressure using the natural-release method according to manufacturer's instructions, about 15 minutes. Release remaining pressure carefully using the quick-release method, about 5 minutes. Unlock and remove the lid. Fluff rice with a fork and serve.

Cook's Notes:

You can use jarred sofrito sauce or freshly made with onion, garlic, bell pepper, cilantro, and oregano pureed in a food processor.
Bacon can be used instead of salt pork.

Nutrition Facts
Per Serving:
632 calories; protein 33.8g 68% DV; carbohydrates 66.1g 21% DV; fat 24.7g 38% DV; cholesterol 83.5mg 28% DV; sodium 2578.7mg 103% DV.

Instant Pot Keto Chicken and Kale Stew

Prep: 10 mins Cook: 30 mins Additional: 15 mins Total: 55 mins

Servings: 4

Ingredients

- 1 tablespoon butter
- ½ onion, chopped
- 2 eaches boneless chicken breasts, diced
- 1 (14.5 ounce) can diced tomatoes
- 3 cups chopped kale
- 1 cup chicken broth
- ½ teaspoon salt
- ½ teaspoon garlic powder
- ½ teaspoon oregano
- ¼ teaspoon ground black pepper

Directions
- **Step 1**

Turn on a multi-functional pressure cooker (such as Instant Pot) and select Saute function. Melt butter and cook onion until soft and tender, about 3 minutes. Add chicken; cook until golden and crispy, about 5 minutes. Place diced tomatoes, kale, chicken broth, salt, garlic powder, oregano, and black pepper in the pot. Close and lock the lid. Select high pressure according to manufacturer's instructions; set timer for 10 minutes. Allow 10 to 15 minutes for pressure to build.
- **Step 2**

Release pressure using the natural-release method according to manufacturer's instructions, about 10 minutes. Complete releasing pressure carefully using the quick-release method according to manufacturer's instructions, about 5 minutes. Unlock and remove the lid.

Nutrition Facts
Per Serving:
132.4 calories; protein 13.3g 27% DV; carbohydrates 8.9g 3% DV; fat 4.4g 7% DV; cholesterol 38.4mg 13% DV; sodium 795.8mg 32% DV.

Instant Pot Pickled Jalapeno Rings

Prep: 10 mins Cook: 10 mins Additional: 5 mins Total: 25 mins

Servings: 16

Ingredients

- 1 pound fresh jalapenos
- 1 cup white distilled vinegar
- ½ cup water
- 1 tablespoon minced garlic
- 1 tablespoon sugar
- 1 teaspoon sea salt

Directions
- **Step 1**

Slice jalapenos into thin rings using a mandoline.

- **Step 2**

Combine jalapeno rings, vinegar, water, garlic, sugar, and sea salt in a multi-functional pressure cooker (such as Instant Pot). Close and lock the lid. Select high pressure according to manufacturer's instructions; set timer for 0 minutes. Allow 10 minutes for pressure to build.
- **Step 3**

Release pressure carefully using the quick-release method according to manufacturer's instructions, about 5 minutes. Unlock and remove the lid.
- **Step 4**

Ladle jalapeno rings and cooking liquid between 2 pint-sized jars and immediately place in the refrigerator to cool.

Nutrition Facts
Per Serving:
12.6 calories; protein 0.4g 1% DV; carbohydrates 2.6g 1% DV; fat 0.2g; cholesterolmg; sodium 110.6mg 4% DV.

Instant Pot Chicken and Wild Rice Bowls

Prep: 15 mins Cook: 45 mins Additional: 20 mins Total: 1 hr 20 mins

Servings: 6

Ingredients

- 1 tablespoon olive oil
- 1 (8 ounce) package sliced fresh mushrooms
- ½ cup diced onion
- 3 cloves garlic, minced
- 2 cups low-sodium chicken broth
- 1 small firm apple, cored and chopped
- 1 ½ cups uncooked wild and brown rice blend (such as Lundberg Wild Blend)
- ½ cup sweetened dried cranberries (such as Craisins)
- 1 teaspoon ground thyme
- 1 pinch salt and ground black pepper to taste
- 1 ¼ pounds skinless, boneless chicken thighs
- 2 tablespoons chopped fresh parsley

Directions
- **Step 1**

Turn on a multi-functional pressure cooker (such as Instant Pot) and select Saute function. Heat olive oil in the pot until hot and add mushrooms and onion. Cook and stir for about 3 minutes. Stir in garlic and cook until fragrant, about 30 seconds. Turn the pressure cooker off.
- **Step 2**

Pour chicken broth into the pot and stir in apple, rice, cranberries, thyme, salt, and pepper. Place chicken thighs on top of the rice mixture, but do not stir. Close and lock the lid; set the pressure valve to Sealing. Select high pressure according to manufacturer's instructions; set timer for 30 minutes. Allow 10 to 15 minutes for pressure to build.
- **Step 3**

Release pressure using the natural-release method according to manufacturer's instructions for 15 minutes. Release remaining pressure carefully using the quick-release method. Unlock and remove the lid.
- **Step 4**

Transfer chicken thighs to a cutting board and cut or shred into bite-sized pieces. Return to the pot and stir. Garnish with parsley and serve in bowls.

Cook's Notes:
If there's too much liquid after cooking is complete, just turn to the Saute function and cook down for a few minutes. If you'd like a little more liquid, stir in some chicken broth. Just adapt to your preference.

Nutrition Facts
Per Serving:
384.7 calories; protein 24.3g 49% DV; carbohydrates 44.2g 14% DV; fat 12.8g 20% DV; cholesterol 60.2mg 20% DV; sodium 123.1mg 5% DV.

Instant Pot Guinness Corned Beef

Prep: 30 mins Cook: 1 hr 55 mins Additional: 10 mins Total: 2 hrs 35 mins

Servings: 12
Ingredients

- 2 cups water
- 1 (12 fluid ounce) can or bottle dark beer (such as Guinness)
- 4 cloves garlic, minced
- 1 (3 pound) corned beef brisket with spice packet
- 1 cup brown sugar
- 10 eaches baby red potatoes, quartered
- 4 large carrots, peeled and cut into matchstick pieces
- 1 onion, peeled and cut into bite-sized pieces
- ½ head cabbage, coarsely chopped

Directions
- **Step 1**

Combine water, beer, and garlic in a multi-functional pressure cooker (such as Instant Pot). Place trivet inside.
- **Step 2**

Rub all sides of brisket with brown sugar. Place on the trivet and sprinkle spice packet on top. Close and lock the lid.
- **Step 3**

Select high pressure according to manufacturer's instructions; set timer for 90 minutes. Allow 10 to 15 minutes for pressure to build.
- **Step 4**

Release pressure carefully using the quick-release method according to manufacturer's instructions, about 5 minutes. Unlock and remove the lid. Transfer brisket to a baking sheet.
- **Step 5**

Cover brisket with aluminum foil; let rest for 15 minutes.
- **Step 6**

Meanwhile, remove the trivet from the pot. Place potatoes, carrots, onion, and cabbage in the bottom of the pressure cooker. Close and lock the lid.
- **Step 7**

Select high pressure according to manufacturer's instructions; set timer for 5 minutes. Allow 10 to 15 minutes for pressure to build.
- **Step 8**

Release pressure carefully using the quick-release method according to manufacturer's instructions, about 5 minutes. Unlock and remove the lid. Serve vegetables with rested brisket.

Nutrition Facts
Per Serving:
260.3 calories; protein 10.9g 22% DV; carbohydrates 31.5g 10% DV; fat 9.6g 15% DV; cholesterol 48.7mg 16% DV; sodium 599mg 24% DV

Instant Pot Sweet and Spicy Chicken Thighs

Prep:5 mins Cook: 25 mins Additional: 5 minsTotal: 35 mins

Servings: 4

Ingredients

- ⅓ cup chicken broth
- ¼ cup soy sauce
- ¼ cup honey
- 4 cloves garlic, minced
- ½ teaspoon red pepper flakes
- 1 pinch freshly ground black pepper to taste
- 1 ½ pounds boneless, skinless chicken thighs
- 1 tablespoon water
- 2 teaspoons cornstarch

Directions
- **Step 1**

Whisk chicken broth, soy sauce, honey, garlic, red pepper flakes, and pepper together in a multi-functional pressure cooker (such as Instant Pot). Add chicken thighs and turn to coat with the sauce. Close and lock the lid. Select high pressure according to manufacturer's instructions; set timer for 8 minutes. Allow 10 to 15 minutes for pressure to build.
- **Step 2**

Release pressure carefully using the quick-release method according to manufacturer's instructions, about 5 minutes. Unlock and remove the lid. Remove chicken thighs and set aside, keeping them warm.
- **Step 3**

Select Saute function. Stir together water and cornstarch in a small bowl and add slurry to Instant Pot. Cook and stir until sauce has thickened and reduced, about 5 minutes. Return chicken thighs to the sauce and toss to coat.

Nutrition Facts
Per Serving:

367.4 calories; protein 30g 60% DV; carbohydrates 21.4g 7% DV; fat 17.8g 27% DV; cholesterol 106.5mg 36% DV; sodium 1096.5mg 44% DV.

Instant Pot Galbi (Korean-Style Short Ribs)

Prep: 20 mins Cook: 55 mins Additional: 1 hr 10 mins Total: 2 hrs 25 mins

Servings: 6

Ingredients

- 3 pounds beef short ribs
- 1 Asian pear - peeled, cored, and coarsely chopped
- 1 small onion, chopped
- 4 cloves garlic, chopped
- ½ tablespoon peeled and coarsely chopped fresh ginger
- 1 cup low-sodium soy sauce, divided
- ¼ cup rice wine
- ¼ cup water
- ¼ cup brown sugar
- 2 tablespoons sesame oil, divided
- ½ teaspoon ground black pepper
- 2 eaches carrots, peeled and cut in chunks
- 5 eaches radishes, peeled and cut into chunks
- ¼ cup white sugar
- ½ bunch green onions, chopped, or to taste
- 1 tablespoon sesame seeds, or to taste

Directions
- **Step 1**

Soak ribs in a large bowl of water for 1 hour.
- **Step 2**

Meanwhile, combine Asian pear, onion, garlic, and ginger in a blender or food processor; puree until smooth. Transfer mixture to a mixing bowl. Add 3/4 cup soy sauce, rice wine, water, brown sugar, 1 tablespoon sesame oil, and pepper and mix to create the sauce.
- **Step 3**

Drain ribs and dry them well. Trim off excess fat. Place ribs in a multi-functional pressure cooker (such as Instant Pot) and add carrots and radishes. Pour Asian pear sauce on top. Close and lock the lid. Select Meat function according to manufacturer's instructions; set timer for 35 minutes. Allow 10 to 15 minutes for pressure to build.
- **Step 5**

Release pressure using the natural-release method according to manufacturer's instructions, 10 to 40 minutes. Unlock and remove the lid. Transfer meat and vegetables to a plate and set aside.
- **Step 5**

Select the Saute function on your Instant Pot. Stir in remaining soy sauce, remaining sesame oil, and white sugar. Cook, stirring occasionally, until sugar has melted and sauce has thickened, about 10 minutes. Return ribs and vegetables to the pot to get nice and saucy.
- **Step 6**

Garnish ribs and vegetables with green onions and sesame seeds.

Nutrition Facts
Per Serving:
656.6 calories; protein 25.2g 50% DV; carbohydrates 30.6g 10% DV; fat 47.1g 73% DV; cholesterol 93.2mg 31% DV; sodium 1588.5mg 64% DV.

Instant Pot Red Beans and Rice with Sausage

Prep: 10 mins Cook: 1 hr Additional: 20 mins Total: 1 hr 30 mins

Servings: 12

Ingredients
- 1 tablespoon vegetable oil
- 14 ounces andouille sausage, sliced into rounds
- 1 medium onion, chopped
- 1 green bell pepper, chopped
- 3 stalks celery, chopped
- 1 clove garlic, minced
- 2 teaspoons Creole seasoning (such as Tony Chachere's)
- 1 teaspoon ground thyme
- 1 teaspoon oregano
- 1 pound dried red beans
- 4 cups chicken broth
- 1 tablespoon hot sauce (such as Louisiana)
- 1 bay leaf
- 4 cups hot cooked rice
- ¼ cup chopped fresh flat-leaf parsley
- 3 eaches green onions, chopped

Directions
- **Step 1**

Turn on a multi-functional pressure cooker (such as Instant Pot) and select Saute function. Add oil and let heat about 30 seconds. Add sausage and cook for 5 minutes. Transfer to a plate using a slotted spoon and set sausage aside.
- **Step 2**

Add onion, bell pepper, and celery to the Instant Pot and cook for 3 minutes. Add garlic, Creole seasoning, thyme, and oregano; cook 2 minutes more. Turn pot off.
- **Step 3**

Add beans, broth, hot sauce, and bay leaf to the Instant Pot with the vegetables. Close and lock the lid. Select high pressure and set the timer for 30 minutes. Allow 10 minutes for pressure to build.
- **Step 4**

Release pressure using the natural-release method according to manufacturer's instructions, 10 to 40 minutes. Unlock and remove the lid.
- **Step 5**

Remove bay leaf from the pot and discard. Add reserved cooked sausage. Select Saute function. Cook, stirring frequently to mash some of the beans and thicken the mixture, for about 10 minutes. Turn off pot and let stand for 10 minutes.
- **Step 6**

Serve beans over hot cooked rice garnished with parsley and green onions.

Nutrition Facts
Per Serving:

326.3 calories; protein 15.1g 30% DV; carbohydrates 41.2g 13% DV; fat 11.3g 17% DV; cholesterol 21mg 7% DV; sodium 815mg 33% DV.

Instant Pot Chicken Congee

Prep: 10 mins Cook: 50 mins Additional: 15 mins Total: 1 hr 15 mins

Servings: 6

Ingredients

- 1 cup uncooked short-grain white rice
- 1 tablespoon olive oil
- 14 ounces boneless, skinless chicken breast
- 6 cups chicken broth

Topping:
- 3 eaches spring onions, sliced
- 6 teaspoons black sesame seeds

- 1 (2 inch) piece grated fresh ginger
- 1 ear fresh corn, husked
- 1 pinch salt and ground black pepper to taste

- 6 teaspoons spicy chili crisp sauce

Directions
- **Step 1**

Rinse rice under cold running water until the water runs clear. Set aside.

- **Step 2**

Turn on a multi-functional pressure cooker (such as Instant Pot) and select Saute function. Heat oil and brown chicken on all sides, about 8 minutes, making sure each side is browned before flipping. Add a few tablespoons of chicken broth to the Instant Pot and scrape off any browned bits from the bottom with a wooden spatula. Turn off Saute function. Add drained rice, ginger, and remaining broth.

- **Step 3**

Cut the kernels from the corn cob and break cob into 3 pieces. Add corn kernels and cob pieces to the pot. Close and seal the lid. Select Porridge function and set timer for 30 minutes. Allow 10 to 15 minutes for pressure to build.

- **Step 4**

Release pressure using the natural-release method according to manufacturer's instructions, about 15 minutes. Open the lid and discard the corn cob pieces. Remove chicken breast. Shred chicken with two forks and return to the congee. Season with salt and pepper and mix well.

- **Step 5**

Divide congee amongst 6 bowls. Top each bowl with equal amounts of sliced spring onions, sesame seeds, and chili crisp.

Nutrition Facts
Per Serving:
299.4 calories; protein 18.3g 37% DV; carbohydrates 32.5g 11% DV; fat 9.7g 15% DV; cholesterol 43.7mg 15% DV; sodium 1272.2mg 51% DV.

Instant Pot Caldillo

Prep: 15 mins Cook: 1 hr 5 mins Additional: 10 mins Total: 1 hr 30 mins

Servings: 8

Ingredients

- 2 pounds cubed beef stew meat
- 1 onion, diced
- 4 cups beef broth
- 4 eaches russet potatoes, peeled and diced
- 1 (14.5 ounce) can fire-roasted diced tomatoes
- 1 (8 ounce) can chopped green chiles, drained (such as Hatch)
- 2 teaspoons Mexican oregano
- 2 teaspoons minced garlic
- 2 teaspoons cumin
- 1 teaspoon dried chipotle chile powder
- 1 teaspoon chili powder
- ½ teaspoon ground black pepper

Directions
- **Step 1**

Turn on a multi-functional pressure cooker (such as Instant Pot) and select Saute function. Heat olive oil and sear beef cubes until browned on all sides, 5 to 8 minutes. Remove browned beef from the pot and set aside. Add onion and cook until soft and translucent, about 5 minutes. Turn off Saute function.
- **Step 2**

Return beef to the pot with onions. Mix in beef broth, potatoes, diced tomatoes, green chiles, oregano, garlic, cumin, chipotle chile powder, chili powder, and pepper. Close and lock the lid. Select high pressure according to manufacturer's instructions; set timer for 45 minutes. Allow 10 to 15 minutes for pressure to build.
- **Step 3**

Release pressure using the natural-release method according to manufacturer's instructions, 10 to 40 minutes.

Nutrition Facts
Per Serving:
370 calories; protein 23.1g 46% DV; carbohydrates 25.4g 8% DV; fat 19.3g 30% DV; cholesterol 62.6mg 21% DV; sodium 919.6mg 37% DV.

Instant Pot Tomato Soup

Prep: 20 mins Cook: 30 mins Additional: 5 mins Total: 55 mins

Servings: 4

Ingredients

- 1 tablespoon olive oil
- 4 stalks celery, chopped
- 1 cup chopped carrot
- 1 small yellow onion, chopped
- 2 cloves garlic, chopped
- 4 cups vegetable broth
- 1 (14.5 ounce) can fire-roasted diced tomatoes
- 1 (14.5 ounce) can crushed San Marzano tomatoes
- 3 tablespoons tomato paste
- 2 teaspoons dried basil
- 1 pinch salt and ground black pepper to taste
- ¼ cup butter
- ¼ cup all-purpose flour
- 1 cup milk
- ½ cup grated Parmesan cheese
- 1 tablespoon raw cane sugar
- 1 teaspoon red pepper flakes

Directions

- **Step 1**

Turn on a multi-functional pressure cooker (such as Instant Pot) and select Saute function. Add olive oil, celery, carrot, onion, and garlic. Cook for 5 minutes, stirring occasionally.

- **Step 2**

Stir in vegetable broth, diced and crushed tomatoes, tomato paste, basil, salt, and pepper. Close and lock the lid. Select high pressure according to manufacturer's instructions; set timer for 6 minutes. Allow 10 to 15 minutes for pressure to build.

- **Step 3**

Meanwhile, melt butter in a small saucepan over low heat. Stir in flour until a smooth, thick paste forms, about 3 minutes.

- **Step 4**

Release pressure naturally for 2 minutes according to manufacturer's instructions. Release remaining pressure by opening the valve to vent.

- **Step 5**

Use an immersion blender to carefully puree the hot soup. Select Saute function again; set timer for 3 minutes. Add flour paste, stirring continuously. Add milk, Parmesan cheese, sugar, and red pepper flakes. Season with more salt and pepper if needed. Stir to combine until the timer ends.

Cook's Notes:

The cane sugar helps cut the acidity, but you can leave it out.
You can use a regular blender to puree the soup. The soup will be extremely hot, so work in batches and be careful when blending.

Nutrition Facts

Per Serving:
379.4 calories; protein 11.9g 24% DV; carbohydrates 39.8g 13% DV; fat 20.2g 31% DV; cholesterol 44.2mg 15% DV; sodium 1321.1mg 53% DV.

Instant Pot Chicken Marsala

Prep: 10 mins Cook: 15 mins Total: 25 mins

Servings: 6

Ingredients

- ¼ cup all-purpose flour
- ½ teaspoon salt, or to taste
- ¼ teaspoon freshly ground black pepper
- 1 ½ pounds skinless, boneless chicken breast halves
- ¼ cup oil
- 2 cups sliced fresh mushrooms
- ½ cup dry Marsala wine
- ¼ cup butter

Directions
- **Step 1**

Combine flour, salt, and pepper in a shallow dish. Dredge chicken breasts through flour mixture.
- **Step 2**

Turn on a multi-functional pressure cooker (such as Instant Pot), select Saute function, and allow pot to heat up. Add oil. Add chicken and cook until lightly browned, 3 about minutes. Turn chicken over and add mushrooms. Cook, stirring mushrooms occasionally, until other side of the chicken is lightly browned, about 3 more minutes. Pour Marsala wine around chicken. Close and lock the lid, and simmer until chicken is no longer pink in the center and the juices run clear, about 5 minutes.
- **Step 3**

Remove chicken from the pot and place on a serving platter. Add butter to the pot. Turn off heat and stir butter into sauce until fully blended. Pour sauce over chicken breasts and serve immediately.

Nutrition Facts
Per Serving:
322 calories; protein 23.7g 47% DV; carbohydrates 7.9g 3% DV; fat 19.2g 30% DV; cholesterol 78.9mg 26% DV; sodium 299.7mg 12% DV.

Instant Pot Lebanese Lentil Soup (Shorbat Adas)

Prep: 25 mins Cook: 25 mins Additional: 5 mins Total: 55 mins

Servings: 4

Ingredients

- 2 tablespoons extra-virgin olive oil
- 1 onion, finely chopped
- 1 Yukon Gold potato, peeled and diced
- 1 carrot, peeled and diced
- 1 tomato, diced
- 2 rib (blank)s celery ribs, diced
- 1 clove garlic, chopped, or more to taste
- 1 ½ teaspoons kosher salt
- ¾ teaspoon ground cumin
- ⅛ teaspoon ground cinnamon
- ⅛ teaspoon allspice

- 4 cups low-sodium vegetable broth
- 2 cups water
- 1 ½ cups red lentils
- 2 fruit, without seeds lemons
- 2 eaches pita bread, cut into squares
- 1 cooking spray
- 1 pinch salt

Directions
- **Step 1**

Preheat the oven to 400 degrees F (200 degrees C).
- **Step 2**

Turn on a multi-functional pressure cooker (such as Instant Pot) and select Saute function. Heat olive oil in the pot. Add onion, potato, carrot, tomato, celery, and garlic; cook and stir until starting to soften, 3 to 5 minutes. Sprinkle salt, cumin, cinnamon, and allspice over the vegetables and stir until fragrant.
- **Step 3**

Pour in stock, water, and lentils. Close and lock the lid. Select high pressure according to manufacturer's instructions; set timer for 10 minutes. Allow 10 to 15 minutes for pressure to build.
- **Step 4**

Meanwhile, spread pita squares on a lined baking sheet. Spray with cooking spray and season with salt.
- **Step 5**

Bake in the preheated oven until toasted, about 8 minutes.
- **Step 6**

Release pressure carefully using the quick-release method according to manufacturer's instructions, about 5 minutes. Unlock and remove the lid. Puree soup using an immersion blender. Stir in juice of 1 lemon.
- **Step 7**

Divide soup among bowls and scatter a handful of pita chips over each. Cut the second lemon into wedges and serve alongside.

Cook's Notes:
This soup tends to thicken as it sits. You can thin leftovers with some water when reheating.
Nutrition Facts
Per Serving:
456.2 calories; protein 23.2g 46% DV; carbohydrates 76.7g 25% DV; fat 8.9g 14% DV; cholesterolmg; sodium 1139.3mg 46% DV.

Easy Instant Pot Cranberry Sauce

Prep: 5 mins Cook: 20 mins Additional: 10 mins Total: 35 mins

Servings: 16

Ingredients

- 1 ½ pounds fresh cranberries
- 1 ¾ cups white sugar

- ¼ cup orange juice
- 2 teaspoons grated orange zest
- 1 pinch salt
- 1 cinnamon stick

Directions
- **Step 1**

Combine cranberries, sugar, orange juice, orange zest, and salt in a multi-functional pressure cooker (such as Instant Pot). Close and lock the lid. Select high pressure according to manufacturer's instructions; set timer for 5 minutes. Allow 10 to 15 minutes for pressure to build.
- **Step 2**

Release pressure using the natural-release method according to manufacturer's instructions, 10 to 40 minutes. Unlock and remove lid. Add cinnamon stick and select Saute function; cook until sauce thickens, 5 to 10 minutes. Remove and discard cinnamon stick.
- **Step 3**

Blend sauce with an immersion blender for a smoother consistency. Let cool; sauce will continue to thicken naturally.

Nutrition Facts
Per Serving:
106.5 calories; protein 0.2g; carbohydrates 27.6g 9% DV; fat 0.1g; cholesterolmg; sodium 10.6mg.

Instant Pot Chicken and Rice Stracciatella

Prep: 10 mins Cook: 20 mins Additional: 5 mins Total: 35 mins

Servings: 4

Ingredients
- 6 cups chicken broth
- 1 ½ cups diced rotisserie chicken meat
- ¼ cup long grain rice
- 3 large eggs eggs
- 3 tablespoons finely grated Parmigiano-Reggiano cheese
- 1 pinch freshly ground black pepper to taste
- 1 teaspoon chopped fresh parsley

Directions
- **Step 1**

Combine chicken broth, chicken, and rice in a multi-functional pressure cooker (such as Instant Pot). Close and lock the lid. Select high pressure according to manufacturer's instructions; set timer for 4 minutes. Allow 10 to 15 minutes for pressure to build.
- **Step 2**

Meanwhile, whisk eggs and Parmigiano-Reggiano cheese together in a small bowl. Season with black pepper. Set aside.
- **Step 3**

Release pressure carefully using the quick-release method according to manufacturer's instructions, about 5 minutes. Unlock and remove the lid. Change pressure cooker setting to Saute. Pour egg mixture into the broth in a slow steady stream while whisking. Cook for 1 minute. Serve immediately and garnish with parsley.

Nutrition Facts
Per Serving:
227.7 calories; protein 22g 44% DV; carbohydrates 11.7g 4% DV; fat 9.3g 14% DV; cholesterol 191.3mg 64% DV; sodium 1895.5mg 76% DV. F

Instant Pot Roasted Melting Sweet Potatoes

Prep: 5 mins Cook: 20 mins Additional: 5 mins Total: 30 mins

Servings: 2

Ingredients

- ½ cup butter
- 1 pound sweet potatoes, peeled and cut into 1-inch slices
- ¾ cup vegetable broth
- 1 teaspoon ground thyme
- 1 teaspoon salt
- ½ teaspoon ground black pepper

Directions
- **Step 1**

Turn on a multi-functional pressure cooker (such as Instant Pot) and select Saute function. Melt butter. Add sweet potato rounds in a single layer and cook until golden, about 4 minutes. Flip and cook for 4 minutes more. Pour vegetable broth over the sweet potatoes and sprinkle with thyme, salt, and pepper.
- **Step 2**

Close and lock lid. Select high pressure according to manufacturer's instructions; set timer for 2 minutes. Allow 10 to 15 minutes for pressure to build.
- **Step 3**

Release pressure carefully using the quick-release method according to manufacturer's instructions, about 5 minutes. Unlock and remove lid.

Nutrition Facts
Per Serving:
616.7 calories; protein 4.5g 9% DV; carbohydrates 48.4g 16% DV; fat 46.4g 71% DV; cholesterol 122mg 41% DV; sodium 1787.6mg 72% DV.

Instant Pot Tortellini Soup

Prep: 20 mins Cook: 20 mins Additional: 5 mins Total: 45 mins

Servings: 4

Ingredients

- 1 tablespoon olive oil
- 2 cups sliced carrots
- 2 rib (blank)s celery ribs with leaves, chopped
- 1 cup roughly chopped onion
- 1 large clove garlic, grated
- 4 cups beef broth
- 1 cup strained crushed tomatoes (such as Aurora)
- ½ teaspoon thyme
- 1 teaspoon dried parsley
- 1 pinch freshly ground black pepper to taste
- 13 ounces refrigerated small cheese tortellini
- 2 tablespoons finely grated Parmesan cheese, or more to taste

Directions
- **Step 1**

Turn on a multi-functional pressure cooker (such as Instant Pot), select Saute function, and adjust the heat to high. Pour oil into the pot and swirl to evenly coat the bottom. Add carrots, celery, and onion and cook, stirring consistently, about 4 minutes. Add garlic and cook 1 minute. Add tomato sauce, beef broth, parsley, and thyme; stir to combine. Close and lock the lid. Select high pressure according to manufacturer's instructions; set timer for 3 minutes. Allow 10 to 15 minutes for pressure to build.
- **Step 2**

Release pressure carefully using the quick-release method according to manufacturer's instructions, about 5 minutes. Unlock and remove the lid. Add tortellini and press down into the liquid, but do not stir.
- **Step 3**

Turn pot back on and choose Saute function. Simmer tortellini until tender and fully cooked, about 5 minutes; dense pasta will take longer. Spoon into bowls and top with freshly grated Parmesan cheese.

Nutrition Facts
Per Serving:
405.9 calories; protein 18.4g 37% DV; carbohydrates 57.3g 19% DV; fat 12.9g 20% DV; cholesterol 41.5mg 14% DV; sodium 1307.4mg 52% DV.

Instant Pot Barbacoa

Prep: 15 mins Cook: 1 hr 25 mins Additional: 25 mins Total: 2 hrs 5 mins

Servings: 8

Ingredients

- 3 eaches dried guajillo chile peppers
- 3 eaches dried pasilla chile peppers
- 1 (4 pound) beef chuck roast, cut into 2-inch pieces

- 1 pinch salt and ground black pepper to taste
- 1 onion, quartered
- ¼ cup apple cider vinegar
- 5 cloves garlic, minced
- 2 tablespoons lime juice
- 1 tablespoon ground cumin
- 1 tablespoon dried oregano
- 1 tablespoon agave nectar
- 1 teaspoon ground cinnamon

Directions
- **Step 1**

Place chile peppers in a large bowl and cover with hot water. Soak until soft, about 20 minutes. Drain.

- **Step 2**

Heat a large skillet over medium heat. Add chuck roast and season with salt and pepper. Cook meat until dark brown and crispy on all sides, 7 to 10 minutes.
- **Step 3**

While meat cooks, combine softened chile peppers, onion, vinegar, garlic, lime juice, cumin, oregano, agave nectar, and cinnamon in a blender. Process sauce until smooth.
- **Step 4**

Transfer browned meat and all juices to a multi-functional pressure cooker (such as Instant Pot). Stir in sauce from the blender. Close and lock the lid. Select high pressure according to manufacturer's instructions; set timer for 60 minutes. Allow 10 to 15 minutes for pressure to build.
- **Step 5**

Release pressure carefully using the quick-release method according to manufacturer's instructions, about 5 minutes. Unlock and remove the lid.

Nutrition Facts
Per Serving:
382.5 calories; protein 27.4g 55% DV; carbohydrates 8.2g 3% DV; fat 26.2g 40% DV; cholesterol 103.3mg 35% DV; sodium 88.9mg 4% DV.

Instant Pot Risotto

Prep: 5 mins Cook: 20 mins Additional: 5 mins Total: 30 mins

Servings: 3

Ingredients

- 1 cube chicken bouillon (such as Knorr)
- 2 cups hot water
- 2 tablespoons extra-virgin olive oil
- ¼ cup finely diced onion
- 1 clove garlic, minced
- 1 cup Arborio rice
- ¼ cup white wine
- 2 tablespoons butter
- ¼ cup grated Parmigiano-Reggiano cheese
- 2 teaspoons chopped fresh parsley

Directions

- **Step 1**

Dissolve the chicken bouillon cube in the hot water and set aside.
- **Step 2**

Turn on a multi-functional pressure cooker (such as Instant Pot) and select Saute function. Add olive oil to the pot. Add onion and cook for 1 minute. Add garlic and rice and stir until each grain of rice is coated with the oil mixture. Cook until rice is slightly toasted, about 2 minutes. Pour in white wine and simmer for about 30 seconds. Stir in chicken broth.
- **Step 3**

Turn off Saute function. Close and lock the lid. Select high pressure according to manufacturer's instructions; set timer for 6 minutes. Allow 5 to 10 minutes for pressure to build.
- **Step 4**

Release pressure carefully using the quick-release method according to manufacturer's instructions, about 5 minutes. Unlock and remove the lid. Add butter; stir until risotto is creamy, about 1 minute. Stir in Parmigiano-Reggiano cheese until melted and well combined. Serve sprinkled with parsley.

Nutrition Facts

Per Serving:
446.5 calories; protein 7.7g 15% DV; carbohydrates 57.2g 18% DV; fat 18.7g 29% DV; cholesterol 26.4mg 9% DV; sodium 547.4mg 22% DV.

Instant Pot Classic Hummus

Prep: 10 mins Cook: 45 mins Additional: 5 mins Total: 1 hr

Servings: 8

Ingredients

- 1 cup dry garbanzo beans
- 3 cups vegetable broth
- ⅓ cup lemon juice
- 3 tablespoons tahini
- 2 tablespoons olive oil
- 2 cloves garlic, chopped
- 1 teaspoon ground cumin
- ½ teaspoon salt

Directions
- **Step 1**

Combine garbanzo beans with vegetable broth in a multi-functional pressure cooker (such as Instant Pot). Close and lock the lid. Select high pressure according to manufacturer's instructions; set timer for 35 minutes. Allow 10 to 15 minutes for pressure to build.
- **Step 2**

Release pressure carefully using the quick-release method according to manufacturer's instructions, about 5 minutes. Unlock and remove lid.
- **Step 3**

Strain garbanzo beans, saving 2/3 cup liquid. Place garbanzo beans in the bowl of a food processor; add lemon juice, tahini, olive oil, and garlic. Blend until smooth and creamy, about 3 minutes. Scrape bowl and add reserved 2/3 cup liquid, cumin, and salt; blend for 1 minute more.

Nutrition Facts
Per Serving:
170.2 calories; protein 6.3g 13% DV; carbohydrates 19.5g 6% DV; fat 8.2g 13% DV; cholesterolmg; sodium 331mg 13% DV.

Instant Pot Cabbage and Beef Soup

Prep: 15 mins Cook: 40 mins Additional: 20 mins Total: 1 hr 15 mins

Servings: 6

Ingredients

- 1 tablespoon olive oil
- 1 pound ground beef
- 1 teaspoon dried oregano
- 1 teaspoon dried thyme
- 1 cup chopped carrot
- 1 cup chopped Yukon Gold potato
- ½ onion, chopped
- 2 cloves garlic, chopped
- 8 cups water
- 1 (14.5 ounce) can Italian-style stewed tomatoes, drained and diced
- ½ head cabbage, cored and coarsely chopped
- 8 teaspoons vegetable bouillon base (such as Better Than Bouillon)
- 1 teaspoon salt, or to taste
- ½ teaspoon ground black pepper, or to taste

Directions
- **Step 1**

Turn on a multi-functional pressure cooker (such as Instant Pot) and select Saute function for medium heat. When the display reads "Hot," add olive oil to coat the bottom of the pot. Add beef, oregano, and thyme; cook and stir until browned, breaking it apart as it cooks, 5 to 7 minutes. Add carrot, potato, onion, and garlic. Cook to soften, stirring frequently, about 5 minutes. Turn off Saute mode.
- **Step 2**

Stir water, tomatoes with their juices, cabbage, vegetable base, salt, and pepper into the pot. Stir briefly together.
- **Step 3**

Close and lock the lid. Select high pressure according to manufacturer's instructions; set timer for 20 minutes. Allow 10 to 15 minutes for pressure to build.
- **Step 4**

Release pressure using the natural-release method according to manufacturer's instructions for 15 minutes. Release remaining pressure carefully using the quick-release method according to manufacturer's instructions, about 5 minutes. Unlock and remove the lid; stir. Serve while hot.

Nutrition Facts
Per Serving:
237.1 calories; protein 15.5g 31% DV; carbohydrates 18.5g 6% DV; fat 11.6g 18% DV; cholesterol 47.3mg 16% DV; sodium 626.9mg 25% DV.

Instant Pot Khichdi

Prep: 10 mins Cook: 35 mins Additional: 50 mins Total: 1 hr 35 mins

Servings: 6

Ingredients

- 1 cup brown basmati rice
- ½ cup whole green mung beans
- ¼ cup split yellow dal
- 1 ½ teaspoons cumin seeds
- 1 ½ teaspoons brown mustard seeds
- 8 tablespoons ghee, divided
- 1 shallot, sliced
- 1 tablespoon minced fresh ginger root
- 1 tablespoon goda masala
- 1 teaspoon ground turmeric
- 1 teaspoon ground black pepper
- ½ teaspoon salt
- 6 cups water

Directions
- **Step 1**

Rinse rice and mung beans. Cover with water and soak for 15 minutes. Rinse split yellow dal and add to the rice and mung beans to soak for 15 minutes. Drain and set aside.
- **Step 2**

Turn on a multi-functional pressure cooker (such as Instant Pot) and select Saute function. Saute cumin and mustard seeds in 2 tablespoons ghee until fragrant, about 2 minutes. Add shallot and ginger and cook until shallot is tender and translucent, about 5 minutes. Add the drained rice and legumes; stir to combine. Turn off Saute function.
- **Step 3**

Stir in goda masala, turmeric, pepper, and salt. Add water; stir well. Close and lock the lid. Select high pressure and set timer for 18 minutes according to manufacturer's instructions. Allow 10 to 15 minutes for pressure to build.
- **Step 4**

Allow pressure to release naturally for 15 minutes. Manually release any remaining pressure, 5 to 10 minutes more. Stir khichdi and divide between 6 bowls. Top each with 1 tablespoon of remaining ghee.

Cook's Notes:
See my recipe for goda masala.

Nutrition Facts
Per Serving:

351.4 calories; protein 9.1g 18% DV; carbohydrates 40.2g 13% DV; fat 18.6g 29% DV; cholesterol 43.7mg 15% DV; sodium 206.2mg 8% DV.

Instant Pot Piccata Israeli Couscous

Prep: 10 mins Cook: 15 mins Additional: 5 mins Total: 30 mins

Servings: 4

Ingredients

- 1 tablespoon butter
- 1 teaspoon olive oil
- 2 tablespoons diced shallot
- 1 tablespoon lemon zest
- 1 clove garlic, minced
- 1 cup Israeli couscous
- 1 ½ cups low-sodium chicken broth
- 2 tablespoons fresh lemon juice
- 2 tablespoons capers
- 1 teaspoon caper brine
- 2 tablespoons chopped fresh parsley
- 1 tablespoon grated Parmesan cheese, or more to taste
- 4 wedge (blank)s lemon wedges

Directions
- **Step 1**

Turn on a multi-functional pressure cooker (such as an Instant Pot), and select Saute function. Heat butter and oil until butter is melted. Add shallot, lemon zest, and garlic; cook until garlic is translucent, 1 to 2 minutes. Add couscous and cook, stirring occasionally, until lightly browned and toasted, about 2 minutes. Turn off Saute function.
- **Step 2**

Pour in chicken broth and lemon juice. Close and lock the lid. Select high pressure according to manufacturer's instructions; set timer for 5 minutes. Allow 10 to 15 minutes for pressure to build.
- **Step 3**

Carefully release pressure using the quick-release method according to manufacturer's instructions, about 5 minutes. Unlock and remove the lid, and stir in the capers and caper brine.
- **Step 4**

Garnish with parsley and Parmesan cheese. Serve with lemon wedges.

Nutrition Facts
Per Serving:
60.7 calories; protein 2.3g 5% DV; carbohydrates 4.1g 1% DV; fat 4.7g 7% DV; cholesterol 10.2mg 3% DV; sodium 234.9mg 9% DV.

Instant Pot Pilau Rice

Prep: 10 mins Cook: 20 mins Additional: 10 mins Total: 40 mins

Servings: 6

Ingredients

- 1 tablespoon vegetable oil
- ½ teaspoon cumin seeds
- ¼ cup diced red onion
- ¾ tablespoon garam masala
- ½ teaspoon ground turmeric
- ½ teaspoon salt

- 1 ½ cups vegetable broth
- 1 cup uncooked basmati rice, rinsed and drained
- ½ cup frozen peas and carrots
- 1 bay leaf

Directions
- **Step 1**

Turn on a multi-functional pressure cooker (such as Instant Pot) and select Saute function. Heat oil in the pot. Add cumin seeds and stir until they just start to pop. Stir in onion and cook until they begin to soften, about 2 minutes. Season with garam masala, turmeric, and salt. Add vegetable broth, rice, frozen peas and carrots, and bay leaf; stir until well combined.
- **Step 2**

Close and lock the lid. Select high pressure according to manufacturer's instructions; set timer for 5 minutes. Allow 10 to 15 minutes for pressure to build.
- **Step 3**

Release pressure using the natural-release method according to manufacturer's instructions, 10 to 40 minutes. Manually release any remaining pressure. Unlock and remove the lid. Remove bay leaf. Taste rice and adjust seasoning if necessary before serving.

Nutrition Facts
Per Serving:
151.2 calories; protein 3.2g 6% DV; carbohydrates 28.5g 9% DV; fat 3.1g 5% DV; cholesterol1mg; sodium 321.3mg 13% DV.

Instant Pot Mexican Quinoa

Prep: 15 mins Cook: 15 mins Additional: 10 mins Total: 40 mins

Servings: 4

Ingredients

- 1 tablespoon olive oil
- 1 small onion, chopped
- 1 jalapeno pepper, minced, or to taste
- 3 cloves garlic, chopped

- 1 (15 ounce) can black beans, drained and rinsed
- 1 (14.5 ounce) can fire-roasted diced tomatoes

- ¾ cup corn kernels
- ¾ teaspoon salt, or to taste
- ½ teaspoon ground cumin
- ½ teaspoon smoked paprika
- ¼ teaspoon chili powder
- ⅛ teaspoon black pepper
- 1 cup dry quinoa
- 1 cup vegetable broth, or as needed
- 2 tablespoons chopped cilantro, or to taste
- 1 lime, juiced
- 1 avocado, diced

Directions
- **Step 1**

Turn on a multi-functional pressure cooker (such as Instant Pot) and select Saute function. Add oil, onion, jalapeno pepper, and garlic. Saute until onion is softened, about 2 minutes. Add black beans, tomatoes, and corn; mix well. Season with salt, cumin, paprika, chili powder, and black pepper. Add quinoa and toss until well combined. Pour in broth and mix.
- **Step 2**

Close and lock the lid; set valve to the sealing position. Select high pressure according to manufacturer's instructions; set timer for 1 minute. Allow 10 to 15 minutes for pressure to build.
- **Step 3**

Release pressure using the natural-release method according to manufacturer's instructions, 10 to 40 minutes.
Open the pot and fluff quinoa using a fork. Add cilantro and lime juice. Stir in avocado.

Nutrition Facts
Per Serving:
442.1 calories; protein 16g 32% DV; carbohydrates 66g 21% DV; fat 14.2g 22% DV; cholesterolmg; sodium 1245mg 50% DV.

Instant Pot Beef Stew with Frozen Meat

Prep: 25 mins Cook: 1 hr 5 mins Additional: 15 mins Total: 1 hr 45 mins

Servings: 8

Ingredients

- 2 tablespoons avocado oil
- 1 large onion, finely diced
- 3 cloves garlic, finely chopped
- ¼ cup dry red wine
- 2 cups beef broth
- 1 teaspoon dried thyme
- 1 teaspoon dried parsley
- 1 teaspoon dried oregano
- 1 bay leaf
- 1 teaspoon salt, or to taste
- ½ teaspoon freshly ground black pepper, or to taste
- 1 tablespoon tomato paste
- 2 (1 pound) packages cubed beef stew meat, frozen
- 6 medium carrots, sliced
- 5 large potatoes, peeled and cut into large cubes
- 3 stalks celery, sliced
- 2 tablespoons water
- 1 tablespoon cornstarch

Directions
- **Step 1**

Turn on a multi-functional pressure cooker (such as Instant Pot) and select Saute function. Pour in oil. Cook onions and garlic in the hot oil until soft and translucent, about 5 minutes. Pour in wine and continue sauteing until wine has reduced by half, 4 to 5 minutes.
- **Step 2**

Add beef broth, thyme, parsley, oregano, bay leaf, salt, and pepper; stir to combine. Mix in tomato paste. Place frozen meat into the pot and add carrots, potatoes, and celery. Close and lock the lid. Select Meat/Stew function and set timer for 45 minutes. Allow 10 to 15 minutes for pressure to build.
- **Step 3**

Release pressure using the natural-release method according to manufacturer's instructions, about 10 minutes. Carefully move the vent to release the remainder of the pressure, about 5 minutes. Unlock and remove the lid.
- **Step 4**

Mix water and cornstarch together in a small bowl and pour slowly into the pot. Press the Saute button and cook stew until slightly thickened, about 3 minutes.

Nutrition Facts
Per Serving:
586.3 calories; protein 36.3g 73% DV; carbohydrates 49.1g 16% DV; fat 26.4g 41% DV; cholesterol 98.6mg 33% DV; sodium 634.7mg 25% DV.

Instant Pot Venison Chili

Prep: 10 mins Cook: 40 mins Additional: 5 mins Total: 55 mins

Servings: 6

Ingredients

- 1 ½ pounds ground venison
- 1 medium onion, chopped
- 2 eaches jalapeno peppers, seeded and chopped
- 2 (15.5 ounce) cans chili beans, undrained
- 1 (28 ounce) can crushed tomatoes
- 1 (15.5 ounce) can kidney beans, drained
- 1 cup water
- 1 tablespoon chili powder
- 2 teaspoons ground cumin
- ½ teaspoon dried oregano
- ¼ teaspoon garlic powder
- ¼ teaspoon onion powder

Directions
- **Step 1**

Turn on a multi-functional pressure cooker (such as Instant Pot) and select Low Saute function. Add venison and cook for 5 minutes, breaking it up with a spoon as it cooks. Add onion and jalapeno peppers; cook and stir until softened, about 3 minutes. Cancel Saute mode.
- **Step 2**

Add chili beans, crushed tomatoes, kidney beans, water, chili powder, cumin, oregano, garlic powder, and onion powder to the pot. Close and lock the lid. Select high pressure

according to manufacturer's instructions; set timer for 20 minutes. Allow 10 to 15 minutes for pressure to build.
* **Step 3**

Release pressure carefully using the quick-release method according to manufacturer's instructions, about 5 minutes. Unlock and remove the lid.

Nutrition Facts
Per Serving:
367.5 calories; protein 37.8g 76% DV; carbohydrates 50.4g 16% DV; fat 4.7g 7% DV; cholesterol 86.2mg 29% DV; sodium 1037.6mg 42% DV.

Instant Pot Cream of Asparagus Soup

Prep: 10 mins Cook: 15 mins Additional: 20 mins Total: 45 mins

Servings: 4

Ingredients
* 1 tablespoon olive oil
* 4 slices bacon, diced
* ½ onion, diced
* 3 cloves garlic, minced
* 2 pounds asparagus, cut into 1 1/2-inch pieces
* 2 ½ cups chicken broth
* 1 teaspoon salt
* ½ teaspoon ground black pepper
* 1 cup heavy whipping crea

Directions
* **Step 1**

Turn on a multi-functional pressure cooker (such as Instant Pot), select Saute function, and add olive oil. Add bacon to warmed oil and saute for 2 minutes. Stir in onion and continue cooking until onion is soft and translucent, about 5 minutes. Add garlic and asparagus. Cook 1 to 2 minutes.
* **Step 2**

Pour chicken broth over asparagus mixture and bring to a boil. Turn Saute mode off and press the Manual mode. Close and lock the lid. Select High pressure according to manufacturer's instructions; set timer for 5 minutes. Allow 10 to 15 minutes for pressure to build.
* **Step 3**

Release pressure using the natural-release method according to manufacturer's instructions, 10 to 40 minutes. Unlock and remove the lid.
* **Step 4**

Puree asparagus mixture with an immersion blender until smooth. Mix in cream and select Saute function. Cook until soup is warmed through, but not boiling. Taste and season with salt and pepper.

Nutrition Facts
Per Serving:
355.9 calories; protein 10.8g 22% DV; carbohydrates 14.9g 5% DV; fat 29.8g 46% DV; cholesterol 95.2mg 32% DV; sodium 1545.4mg 62% DV.

Instant Pot Celery Soup

Prep: 20 mins Cook: 25 mins Additional: 15 mins Total: 1 hr

Servings: 4

Ingredients

- 2 tablespoons olive oil
- 2 pounds celery, sliced
- 1 large onion, sliced
- 3 cloves garlic, sliced
- ½ pound potatoes, peeled and chopped
- 4 cups vegetable broth
- ¼ teaspoon salt
- ⅛ teaspoon ground black pepper

Directions
- **Step 1**

Combine olive oil, celery, onion, and garlic in a multi-functional pressure cooker (such as Instant Pot). Select Saute function and cook, stirring occasionally, for 5 minutes. Add potatoes, broth, salt, and pepper and stir. Close and lock the lid and set the steamer valve to Sealing.
- **Step 2**

Select high pressure according to manufacturer's instructions; set timer for 10 minutes. Allow 10 to 15 minutes for pressure to build.
- **Step 3**

Release pressure using the natural-release method according to manufacturer's instructions, about 15 minutes. Unlock and remove the lid.
- **Step 4**

Use an electric hand mixer or blender to puree the soup until smooth.
Serve while warm or let cool and serve as a chilled soup on a hot day.

Nutrition Facts
Per Serving:
188.2 calories; protein 4.3g 9% DV; carbohydrates 25.9g 8% DV; fat 7.7g 12% DV; cholesterolmg; sodium 792.4mg 32% DV.

Instant Pot Sweet Baby Back Ribs

Prep: 10 mins Cook: 45 mins Additional: 20 mins Total: 1 hr 15 mins

Servings: 8

Ingredients

- 2 racks baby back pork ribs
- Dry Rub:

- ¼ cup dark brown sugar
- 2 tablespoons garlic salt (such as Lawry's)
- 2 tablespoons chili powder
- 1 teaspoon ground black pepper
- 1 teaspoon cayenne pepper, or to taste
- Cooking Liquid:
- 1 cup beef broth
- 12 fluid ounces root beer
- 2 tablespoons apple cider vinegar
- 1 teaspoon liquid smoke flavoring
- 1 cup barbecue sauce (such as Sweet Baby Ray's), or more to taste

Directions

- **Step 1**

Use a butter knife to cut into an edge of the rib racks. Use a paper towel to grab and lift off the silvery membranes.

- **Step 2**

Combine brown sugar, garlic salt, chili powder, black pepper, and cayenne pepper in bowl. Coat the ribs generously with the dry rub.

- **Step 3**

Place the trivet inside the Instant Pot. Pour in broth, root beer, vinegar, and liquid smoke. Place ribs on the trivet on their sides, with one inside the other. Close and lock the lid and make sure the vent is sealed. Select manual high pressure and set the timer for 30 minutes. Allow 10 to 15 minutes for pressure to build.

- **Step 4**

Release pressure using the natural-release method according to manufacturer's instructions for 15 minutes. Release remaining pressure carefully using the quick-release method according to manufacturer's instructions, about 5 minutes. Unlock and remove the lid.

- **Step 5**

Set an oven rack about 6 inches from the heat source and preheat the oven's broiler on the highest heat setting. Place a rack 6 inches from the heat source.

- **Step 6**

Transfer ribs to a broiling pan and generously coat with barbecue sauce.

- **Step 7**

Cook in the broiler until barbeque sauce is bubbly and caramelized, 5 to 7 minutes.

Nutrition Facts

Per Serving:
384.7 calories; protein 18.8g 38% DV; carbohydrates 24.8g 8% DV; fat 23.1g 36% DV; cholesterol 87.8mg 29% DV; sodium 1910.9mg 76% DV.

Instant Pot Orange Chicken

Prep: 15 mins Cook: 35 mins Additional: 20 mins Total: 1 hr 10 mins

Servings:8

Ingredients

- 3 pounds skinless, boneless chicken
- 2 tablespoons oil
- ¾ cup orange juice
- 1 (8 ounce) can tomato sauce
- ¼ cup white sugar
- ¼ cup blackstrap molasses

- ¼ cup soy sauce
- 4 cloves garlic, minced
- 1 orange, zested and juiced, divided
- 1 tablespoon grated fresh ginger
- 1 tablespoon rice wine
- 3 tablespoo ns cornstarch

Directions

- **Step 1**

Blot chicken with paper towels until completely dry. Cut into 1- to 2-inch chunks.

- **Step 2**

Turn on a multi-functional pressure cooker (such as Instant Pot®), select Saute function, and click to adjust to the highest heat. When the pot is hot, add oil and heat until shimmering. Add chicken and saute until it starts to get golden, stirring constantly so it doesn't stick to the bottom of the pot, for 2 to 3 minutes. Pour 3/4 cup orange juice into the pot and bring to a boil while scraping all the browned bits of food off the bottom of the pan with a wooden spoon.

- **Step 3**

Add tomato sauce, sugar, molasses, soy sauce, garlic, orange zest, ginger, and rice wine; gently stir until all Ingredients are combined and coated in sauce. Cancel Saute function.

- **Step 4**

Close and lock the lid, and make sure the vent is closed. Select high pressure according to manufacturer's instructions; set timer for 5 minutes. Allow 10 to 15 minutes for pressure to build.

- **Step 5**

Allow the Instant Pot® to remain on for 10 minutes with the Keep Warm function. Release pressure carefully using the quick-release method according to manufacturer's instructions, about 5 minutes. Unlock and remove the lid. Select Saute function and click to adjust to the lowest heat.

- **Step 6**

Combine 3 tablespoons freshly squeezed orange juice with cornstarch in a medium bowl; whisk until combined with no lumps. Add to the Instant Pot® and stir to combine. Cook, stirring gently, until sauce thickens, about 3 minutes. Simmer for 2 to 3 minutes more.

- **Step 7**

Cancel Saute function and let stand until sauce thickens further, 5 to 7 minutes. Serve.

Nutrition Facts
Per Serving:
296.2 calories; protein 34.3g 69% DV; carbohydrates 22.3g 7% DV; fat 7g 11% DV; cholesterol 87.9mg 29% DV; sodium 674.3mg 27% DV.

Instant Pot Creamy Vanilla Rice Pudding

Prep: 5 mins Cook: 30 mins Additional: 10 mins Total: 45 mins

Servings: 8

Ingredients

- 3 cups cooked short-grain rice
- 2 ¼ cups milk, divided
- ½ cup white sugar
- ¼ teaspoon salt
- 2 eaches egg yolks, whisked well
- ¼ cup heavy cream

- 1 teaspoon vanilla extract
- 1 pinch ground cinnamon, or as needed

Directions
- **Step 1**

Combine cooked rice, 2 cups milk, sugar, and salt in a multi-functional pressure cooker (such as Instant Pot®) and stir well. Close and lock the lid. Select porridge function according to manufacturer's instructions and seal the vent. Set timer for 20 minutes. Allow 10 to 15 minutes for pressure to build.
- **Step 2**

Release pressure using the natural-release method according to manufacturer's instructions, 10 to 40 minutes. Unlock and carefully remove the lid.
- **Step 3**

Whisk egg yolks together well in a bowl. Add a small amount of cooked porridge and whisk quickly into yolks. Pour mixture into the pot and stir to combine well with rice. Add heavy cream, remaining milk, and vanilla extract. Stir to combine completely.
- **Step 4**

Serve rice pudding in individual bowls garnished with cinnamon.

Nutrition Facts
Per Serving:
214 calories; protein 4.7g 10% DV; carbohydrates 36.3g 12% DV; fat 5.3g 8% DV; cholesterol 66.9mg 22% DV; sodium 105.7mg 4% DV.

Instant Pot Chocolate Cheesecake

Prep: 25 mins Cook: 1 hr 3 mins Additional: 7 hrs 20 mins Total: 8 hrs 48 mins

Servings: 10

Ingredients

- 2 (4.8 ounce) packages graham crackers, crushed
- 5 tablespoons butter
- 1 pinch kosher salt
- Filling:
- 1 (8 ounce) package cream cheese, softened
- 1 (8 ounce) package Neufchatel cheese, softened

- ¾ cup white sugar
- 2 large eggs eggs
- 2 teaspoons vanilla extract
- ¼ cup heavy whipping cream
- 1 (8 ounce) package semisweet chocolate chips
- 2 tablespoons all-purpose flour

Glaze:
- 1 (12 ounce) package frozen sweet cherries
- 2 tablespoons apricot jam
- 2 tablespoons white sugar

- 1 tablespoon water
- 1 tablespoon cornstarch

Directions
- **Step 1**

Wrap the bottom and sides of an 8-inch springform pan with aluminum foil.
* **Step 2**

Combine graham cracker crumbs, butter, and salt in a bowl; mix thoroughly. Pour into the prepared pan; press tightly onto the bottom and up the sides of the pan using the bottom of a measuring cup. Freeze crust until firm, 10 to 15 minutes.
* **Step 3**

Beat cream cheese, Neufchatel cheese, and 3/4 cup sugar in a bowl with an electric mixer until creamy, about 4 minutes. Beat in eggs one at a time; add vanilla. Beat in heavy cream.
* **Step 4**

Melt chocolate chips in a microwave-safe glass or ceramic bowl in 15-second intervals, stirring after each melting, 1 to 2 minutes. Beat melted chocolate into the cream cheese mixture. Fold in flour.
* **Step 5**

Pour chocolate cream cheese mixture over the chilled crust. Cover tightly with aluminum foil.
* **Step 6**

Pour 1 1/2 cup water into the pot of an electric pressure cooker (such as Instant Pot®). Place the steam rack in the pot; set springform pan on top. Close and lock the lid. Set timer for 45 minutes. Set to high pressure according to manufacturer's instructions, 10 to 15 minutes.
* **Step 7**

Release pressure naturally according to manufacturer's instructions, 10 to 12 minutes. Cool cheesecake to room temperature, about 1 hour.
* **Step 8**

Combine cherries, apricot jam, and 2 tablespoons sugar in a saucepan over medium heat. Simmer until cherries are heated through and release some of their juices, 5 to 7 minutes.
* **Step 9**

Mix water and cornstarch in a small bowl until smooth. Stir into the cherry mixture until thick and glossy, 2 to 3 minutes. Remove from heat; cool glaze to room temperature.
* **Step 10**

Pour glaze over cheesecake and refrigerate until firm, at least 6 hours or overnight. Remove the springform ring and transfer cheesecake to a serving platter.

Cook's Notes:
Substitute evaporated milk for the cream if desired.
I couldn't get the trivet to fit, so I used a small metal bowl upside down inside the pot as a "support" for the springform pan. Worked great!

Nutrition Facts
Per Serving:
567.8 calories; protein 9.4g 19% DV; carbohydrates 64.8g 21% DV; fat 32g 49% DV; cholesterol 102.3mg 34% DV; sodium 419.7mg 17% DV.

Instant Pot Curried Chicken Thighs

Prep: 10 mins Cook: 50 mins Additional: 15 mins Total: 1 hr 15 mins

Servings: 4

Ingredients

- 4 (6 ounce) chicken thighs
- 2 teaspoons mild yellow curry powder (such as Savory Spice®)
- 1 teaspoon honey powder (such as Savory Spice®)
- ¾ teaspoon salt
- ½ teaspoon ground black pepper
- 2 tablespoons olive oil
- 1 tablespoon butter
- 1 small onion, cut in half and thinly sliced
- 4 cloves garlic, minced
- 1 tablespoon minced fresh ginger root
- 1 (14.5 ounce) can diced tomatoes
- 1 tablespoon tomato powder
- ½ cup coconut milk
- 1 teaspoon ground cumin
- 1 tablespoon mild yellow curry powder (such as Savory Spice®)

Directions

- **Step 1**

Season chicken thighs with 2 teaspoons curry powder, honey powder, salt, and black pepper.

- **Step 2**

Turn on a multi-functional pressure cooker (such as Instant Pot®) and select Saute function. Heat oil and butter. Add chicken and cook until browned, 2 to 3 minutes per side. Transfer to a plate. Add onion; cook and stir until soft and translucent, about 5 minutes. Add garlic and ginger; cook until fragrant, about 2 minutes. Return chicken to Instant Pot®. Add tomatoes and tomato powder. Close and lock the lid.

- **Step 3**

Select high pressure according to manufacturer's instructions; set timer for 20 minutes. Allow 10 to 15 minutes for pressure to build.

- **Step 4**

Release pressure using the natural-release method according to manufacturer's instructions, for 10 minutes. Switch to the quick-release method according to manufacturer's instructions and release remaining pressure for about 5 minutes. Unlock and remove the lid.

- **Step 5**

Turn on Saute function. Add coconut milk, cumin, and remaining curry powder to the pot. Cook until sauce has thickened, about 5 minutes.

Cook's Notes:

I love using tomato powder as it has a robust taste, and while tomato paste may be used, I prefer tomato powder as I don't have to worry about leftover tomato paste. Honey powder is dehydrated honey, and while honey may be used I prefer honey powder as it is not sticky. Both may be found at the Savory spice shop, or your local grocer may carry them.

Nutrition Facts

Per Serving:
471.6 calories; protein 31g 62% DV; carbohydrates 11.2g 4% DV; fat 33.8g 52% DV; cholesterol 113.4mg 38% DV; sodium 721.3mg 29% DV.

Instant Pot Gyros

Prep: 5 mins Cook: 55 mins Additional: 5 mins Total: 1 hr 5 mins

Servings: 16

Ingredients

- 4 pounds pork butt, cut into 2-inch cubes
- 3 tablespoons Greek seasoning (such as Cavender's®)
- 1 teaspoon paprika
- 2 cloves garlic, minced
- 1 cup chicken broth
- 2 teaspoons olive oil

Directions
- **Step 1**

Turn on a multi-functional pressure cooker (such as Instant Pot®) and select the Saute function. Place cubed pork in the pot and cook until starting to brown, about 5 minutes. Turn pot off.
- **Step 2**

Add Greek seasoning, paprika, garlic, and chicken broth to the pot with the pork. Close and lock the lid. Select Manual and set timer for 35 minutes. Allow 10 minutes for pressure to build.
- **Step 3**

Release pressure carefully using the quick-release method according to manufacturer's instructions, about 5 minutes. Unlock and remove the lid.
- **Step 4**

Heat oil in a large skillet over medium-high heat. Transfer pork to the skillet using a slotted spoon and cook for 5 minutes or until most of the liquid has evaporated and pork has a nice crisp on it.

Nutrition Facts
Per Serving:
249.9 calories; protein 14.8g 30% DV; carbohydrates 1.2g; fat 20.7g 32% DV; cholesterol 65.2mg 22% DV; sodium 1654.1mg 66% DV.

Instant Pot Bang Bang Shrimp Pasta

Prep: 10 mins Cook: 25 mins Additional: 5 mins Total: 40 mins

Servings: 6

Ingredients
- 1 pound dry spaghetti
- 4 cups water
- 2 cloves garlic, minced
- 1 tablespoon olive oil
- 1 teaspoon salt
- 1 pound large shrimp, peeled and deveined
- ¾ cup mayonnaise
- ¾ cup Thai sweet red chili sauce
- ¼ cup lime juice
- 1 teaspoon chile-garlic sauce (such as Sriracha®)
- 2 eaches green onions, chopped

Directions
- **Step 1**

Break spaghetti noodles in half and place in a multi-functional pressure cooker (such as Instant Pot®). Add water, garlic, olive oil, and salt. Close and lock the lid. Select high pressure according to manufacturer's instructions; set timer for 6 minutes. Allow 10 to 15 minutes for pressure to build.
• **Step 2**
Release pressure carefully using the quick-release method according to manufacturer's instructions, about 5 minutes. Unlock and remove the lid.
• **Step 3**
Combine shrimp, mayonnaise, chili sauce, lime juice, and Sriracha® in a bowl; mix until well coated. Pour into the pot and select Saute function. Add chopped green onions and cook until shrimp are pink and green onions are tender, about 7 minutes.

Nutrition Facts
Per Serving:
612.2 calories; protein 22.6g 45% DV; carbohydrates 71.9g 23% DV; fat 26.1g 40% DV; cholesterol 125.5mg 42% DV; sodium 1061.4mg 43% DV.

Instant Pot Chicken Congee

Prep: 10 mins Cook: 50 mins Additional: 15 mins Total: 1 hr 15 mins

Servings: 6

Ingredients

- 1 cup uncooked short-grain white rice
- 1 tablespoon olive oil
- 14 ounces boneless, skinless chicken breast
- 6 cups chicken broth
- 1 (2 inch) piece grated fresh ginger
- 1 ear fresh corn, husked
- 1 pinch salt and ground black pepper to taste
- Topping:
- 3 eaches spring onions, sliced
- 6 teaspoons black sesame seeds
- 6 teaspoons spicy chili crisp sauce

Directions
• **Step 1**
Rinse rice under cold running water until the water runs clear. Set aside.
• **Step 2**
Turn on a multi-functional pressure cooker (such as Instant Pot®) and select Saute function. Heat oil and brown chicken on all sides, about 8 minutes, making sure each side is browned before flipping. Add a few tablespoons of chicken broth to the Instant Pot® and scrape off any browned bits from the bottom with a wooden spatula. Turn off Saute function. Add drained rice, ginger, and remaining broth.
• **Step 3**
Cut the kernels from the corn cob and break cob into 3 pieces. Add corn kernels and cob pieces to the pot. Close and seal the lid. Select Porridge function and set timer for 30 minutes. Allow 10 to 15 minutes for pressure to build.
• **Step 4**
Release pressure using the natural-release method according to manufacturer's instructions, about 15 minutes. Open the lid and discard the corn cob pieces. Remove

chicken breast. Shred chicken with two forks and return to the congee. Season with salt and pepper and mix well.
* **Step 5**
Divide congee amongst 6 bowls. Top each bowl with equal amounts of sliced spring onions, sesame seeds, and chili crisp.

Nutrition Facts
Per Serving:
299.4 calories; protein 18.3g 37% DV; carbohydrates 32.5g 11% DV; fat 9.7g 15% DV; cholesterol 43.7mg 15% DV; sodium 1272.2mg 51% DV.

Instant Pot Caldillo

Prep: 15 mins Cook: 1 hr 5 mins Additional: 10 mins Total: 1 hr 30 mins

Servings: 8

Ingredients

* 2 tablespoons olive oil
* 2 pounds cubed beef stew meat
* 1 onion, diced
* 4 cups beef broth
* 4 eaches russet potatoes, peeled and diced
* 1 (14.5 ounce) can fire-roasted diced tomatoes
* 1 (8 ounce) can chopped green chiles, drained (such as Hatch®)
* 2 teaspoons Mexican oregano
* 2 teaspoons minced garlic
* 2 teaspoons cumin
* 1 teaspoon dried chipotle chile powder
* 1 teaspoon chili powder
* ½ teaspoon ground black pepper

Directions
* **Step 1**
Turn on a multi-functional pressure cooker (such as Instant Pot®) and select Saute function. Heat olive oil and sear beef cubes until browned on all sides, 5 to 8 minutes. Remove browned beef from the pot and set aside. Add onion and cook until soft and translucent, about 5 minutes. Turn off Saute function.
* **Step 2**
Return beef to the pot with onions. Mix in beef broth, potatoes, diced tomatoes, green chiles, oregano, garlic, cumin, chipotle chile powder, chili powder, and pepper. Close and lock the lid. Select high pressure according to manufacturer's instructions; set timer for 45 minutes. Allow 10 to 15 minutes for pressure to build.
* **Step 3**
Release pressure using the natural-release method according to manufacturer's instructions, 10 to 40 minutes.

Nutrition Facts
Per Serving:
370 calories; protein 23.1g 46% DV; carbohydrates 25.4g 8% DV; fat 19.3g 30% DV; cholesterol 62.6mg 21% DV; sodium 919.6mg 37% DV.

Instant Pot Tomato Soup

Prep: 20 mins Cook: 30 mins Additional: 5 mins Total: 55 mins

Servings: 4

Ingredients

- 1 tablespoon olive oil
- 4 stalks celery, chopped
- 1 cup chopped carrot
- 1 small yellow onion, chopped
- 2 cloves garlic, chopped
- 4 cups vegetable broth
- 1 (14.5 ounce) can fire-roasted diced tomatoes
- 1 (14.5 ounce) can crushed San Marzano tomatoes
- 3 tablespoons tomato paste
- 2 teaspoons dried basil
- 1 pinch salt and ground black pepper to taste
- ¼ cup butter
- ¼ cup all-purpose flour
- 1 cup milk
- ½ cup grated Parmesan cheese
- 1 tablespoon raw cane sugar
- 1 teaspoon red pepper flakes

Directions
- **Step 1**

Turn on a multi-functional pressure cooker (such as Instant Pot®) and select Saute function. Add olive oil, celery, carrot, onion, and garlic. Cook for 5 minutes, stirring occasionally.
- **Step 2**

Stir in vegetable broth, diced and crushed tomatoes, tomato paste, basil, salt, and pepper. Close and lock the lid. Select high pressure according to manufacturer's instructions; set timer for 6 minutes. Allow 10 to 15 minutes for pressure to build.
- **Step 3**

Meanwhile, melt butter in a small saucepan over low heat. Stir in flour until a smooth, thick paste forms, about 3 minutes.

- **Step 4**

Release pressure naturally for 2 minutes according to manufacturer's instructions. Release remaining pressure by opening the valve to vent.
- **Step 5**

Use an immersion blender to carefully puree the hot soup. Select Saute function again; set timer for 3 minutes. Add flour paste, stirring continuously. Add milk, Parmesan cheese, sugar, and red pepper flakes. Season with more salt and pepper if needed. Stir to combine until the timer ends.

Cook's Notes:
The cane sugar helps cut the acidity, but you can leave it out.
You can use a regular blender to puree the soup. The soup will be extremely hot, so work in batches and be careful when blending.

Nutrition Facts
Per Serving:
379.4 calories; protein 11.9g 24% DV; carbohydrates 39.8g 13% DV; fat 20.2g 31% DV;
cholesterol 44.2mg 15% DV; sodium 1321.1mg 53% DV.

Instant Pot Chicken Marsala

Prep: 10 mins Cook: 15 mins Total: 25 mins

Servings: 6

Ingredients

- ¼ cup all-purpose flour
- ½ teaspoon salt, or to taste
- ¼ teaspoon freshly ground black pepper
- 1 ½ pounds skinless, boneless chicken breast halves
- ¼ cup oil
- 2 cups sliced fresh mushrooms
- ½ cup dry Marsala wine
- ¼ cup butter

Directions
- **Step 1**

Combine flour, salt, and pepper in a shallow dish. Dredge chicken breasts through flour mixture.
- **Step 2**

Turn on a multi-functional pressure cooker (such as Instant Pot®), select Saute function, and allow pot to heat up. Add oil. Add chicken and cook until lightly browned, 3 about minutes. Turn chicken over and add mushrooms. Cook, stirring mushrooms occasionally, until other side of the chicken is lightly browned, about 3 more minutes. Pour Marsala wine around chicken. Close and lock the lid, and simmer until chicken is no longer pink in the center and the juices run clear, about 5 minutes.
- **Step 3**

Remove chicken from the pot and place on a serving platter. Add butter to the pot. Turn off heat and stir butter into sauce until fully blended. Pour sauce over chicken breasts and serve immediately.

Nutrition Facts
Per Serving:
322 calories; protein 23.7g 47% DV; carbohydrates 7.9g 3% DV; fat 19.2g 30% DV;
cholesterol 78.9mg 26% DV; sodium 299.7mg 12% DV.

Instant Pot Lebanese Lentil Soup (Shorbat Adas)

Prep: 25 mins Cook: 25 mins Additional: 5 mins Total: 55 mins

Servings: 4

Ingredients

- 2 tablespoons extra-virgin olive oil
- 1 onion, finely chopped
- 1 Yukon Gold potato, peeled and diced
- 1 carrot, peeled and diced
- 1 tomato, diced
- 2 rib (blank)s celery ribs, diced
- 1 clove garlic, chopped, or more to taste
- 1 ½ teaspoons kosher salt
- ¾ teaspoon ground cumin
- ⅛ teaspoon ground cinnamon
- ⅛ teaspoon allspice
- 4 cups low-sodium vegetable broth
- 2 cups water
- 1 ½ cups red lentils
- 2 fruit, without seeds lemons
- 2 eaches pita bread, cut into squares
- 1 cooking spray
- 1 pinch salt

Directions
- **Step 1**

Preheat the oven to 400 degrees F (200 degrees C).
- **Step 2**

Turn on a multi-functional pressure cooker (such as Instant Pot®) and select Saute function. Heat olive oil in the pot. Add onion, potato, carrot, tomato, celery, and garlic; cook and stir until starting to soften, 3 to 5 minutes. Sprinkle salt, cumin, cinnamon, and allspice over the vegetables and stir until fragrant.
- **Step 3**

Pour in stock, water, and lentils. Close and lock the lid. Select high pressure according to manufacturer's instructions; set timer for 10 minutes. Allow 10 to 15 minutes for pressure to build.
- **Step 4**

Meanwhile, spread pita squares on a lined baking sheet. Spray with cooking spray and season with salt.
- **Step 5**

Bake in the preheated oven until toasted, about 8 minutes.
- **Step 6**

Release pressure carefully using the quick-release method according to manufacturer's instructions, about 5 minutes. Unlock and remove the lid. Puree soup using an immersion blender. Stir in juice of 1 lemon.
- **Step 7**

Divide soup among bowls and scatter a handful of pita chips over each. Cut the second lemon into wedges and serve alongside.

Cook's Note:
This soup tends to thicken as it sits. You can thin leftovers with some water when reheating.

Nutrition Facts
Per Serving:
456.2 calories; protein 23.2g 46% DV; carbohydrates 76.7g 25% DV; fat 8.9g 14% DV; cholesterolmg; sodium 1139.3mg 46% DV.

Easy Instant Pot Cranberry Sauce

Prep: 5 mins Cook: 20 mins Additional: 10 mins Total: 35 mins

Servings: 16

Ingredients

- 1 ½ pounds fresh cranberries
- 1 ¾ cups white sugar
- ¼ cup orange juice
- 2 teaspoons grated orange zest
- 1 pinch salt
- 1 cinnamon stick

Directions
- **Step 1**

Combine cranberries, sugar, orange juice, orange zest, and salt in a multi-functional pressure cooker (such as Instant Pot®). Close and lock the lid. Select high pressure according to manufacturer's instructions; set timer for 5 minutes. Allow 10 to 15 minutes for pressure to build.
- **Step 2**

Release pressure using the natural-release method according to manufacturer's instructions, 10 to 40 minutes. Unlock and remove lid. Add cinnamon stick and select Saute function; cook until sauce thickens, 5 to 10 minutes. Remove and discard cinnamon stick.
- **Step 3**

Blend sauce with an immersion blender for a smoother consistency. Let cool; sauce will continue to thicken naturally.

Nutrition Facts
Per Serving:
106.5 calories; protein 0.2g; carbohydrates 27.6g 9% DV; fat 0.1g; cholesterolmg; sodium 10.6mg.

Instant Pot Chicken and Rice Stracciatella

Prep: 10 mins Cook: 20 mins Additional: 5 mins Total: 35 mins

Servings: 4

Ingredients

- 6 cups chicken broth
- 1 ½ cups diced rotisserie chicken meat
- ¼ cup long grain rice
- 3 large eggs eggs
- 3 tablespoons finely grated Parmigiano-Reggiano cheese
- 1 pinch freshly ground black pepper to taste
- 1 teaspoon chopped fresh parsley

Directions

- **Step 1**

Combine chicken broth, chicken, and rice in a multi-functional pressure cooker (such as Instant Pot®). Close and lock the lid. Select high pressure according to manufacturer's instructions; set timer for 4 minutes. Allow 10 to 15 minutes for pressure to build.
- **Step 2**

Meanwhile, whisk eggs and Parmigiano-Reggiano cheese together in a small bowl. Season with black pepper. Set aside.
- **Step 3**

Release pressure carefully using the quick-release method according to manufacturer's instructions, about 5 minutes. Unlock and remove the lid. Change pressure cooker setting to Saute. Pour egg mixture into the broth in a slow steady stream while whisking. Cook for 1 minute. Serve immediately and garnish with parsley.

Nutrition Facts

Per Serving:
227.7 calories; protein 22g 44% DV; carbohydrates 11.7g 4% DV; fat 9.3g 14% DV; cholesterol 191.3mg 64% DV; sodium 1895.5mg 76% DV. F

Instant Pot Roasted Melting Sweet Potatoes

Prep: 5 mins Cook: 20 mins Additional: 5 mins Total: 30 mins

Servings: 2

Ingredients

- ½ cup butter
- 1 pound sweet potatoes, peeled and cut into 1-inch slices
- ¾ cup vegetable broth
- 1 teaspoon ground thyme
- 1 teaspoon salt
- ½ teaspoon ground black pepper

Directions
- **Step 1**

Turn on a multi-functional pressure cooker (such as Instant Pot®) and select Saute function. Melt butter. Add sweet potato rounds in a single layer and cook until golden, about 4 minutes. Flip and cook for 4 minutes more. Pour vegetable broth over the sweet potatoes and sprinkle with thyme, salt, and pepper.
- **Step 2**

Close and lock lid. Select high pressure according to manufacturer's instructions; set timer for 2 minutes. Allow 10 to 15 minutes for pressure to build.
- **Step 3**

Release pressure carefully using the quick-release method according to manufacturer's instructions, about 5 minutes. Unlock and remove lid.

Nutrition Facts

Per Serving:
616.7 calories; protein 4.5g 9% DV; carbohydrates 48.4g 16% DV; fat 46.4g 71% DV; cholesterol 122mg 41% DV; sodium 1787.6mg 72% DV.

Instant Pot Tortellini Soup

Prep: 20 mins Cook: 20 mins Additional: 5 mins Total: 45 mins

Servings: 4

Ingredients

- 1 tablespoon olive oil
- 2 cups sliced carrots
- 2 rib (blank)s celery ribs with leaves, chopped
- 1 cup roughly chopped onion
- 1 large clove garlic, grated
- 4 cups beef broth
- 1 cup strained crushed tomatoes (such as Aurora®)
- ½ teaspoon thyme
- 1 teaspoon dried parsley
- 1 pinch freshly ground black pepper to taste
- 13 ounces refrigerated small cheese tortellini
- 2 tablespoons finely grated Parmesan cheese, or more to taste

Directions
- **Step 1**

Turn on a multi-functional pressure cooker (such as Instant Pot®), select Saute function, and adjust the heat to high. Pour oil into the pot and swirl to evenly coat the bottom. Add carrots, celery, and onion and cook, stirring consistently, about 4 minutes. Add garlic and cook 1 minute. Add tomato sauce, beef broth, parsley, and thyme; stir to combine. Close and lock the lid. Select high pressure according to manufacturer's instructions; set timer for 3 minutes. Allow 10 to 15 minutes for pressure to build.
- **Step 2**

Release pressure carefully using the quick-release method according to manufacturer's instructions, about 5 minutes. Unlock and remove the lid. Add tortellini and press down into the liquid, but do not stir.
- **Step 3**

Turn pot back on and choose Saute function. Simmer tortellini until tender and fully cooked, about 5 minutes; dense pasta will take longer. Spoon into bowls and top with freshly grated Parmesan cheese.

Nutrition Facts
Per Serving:
405.9 calories; protein 18.4g 37% DV; carbohydrates 57.3g 19% DV; fat 12.9g 20% DV; cholesterol 41.5mg 14% DV; sodium 1307.4mg 52% DV.

Instant Pot Barbacoa

Prep: 15 mins Cook: 1 hr 25 mins Additional: 25 mins Total: 2 hrs 5 mins

Servings: 8

Ingredients

- 3 eaches dried guajillo chile peppers
- 3 eaches dried pasilla chile peppers

- 1 (4 pound) beef chuck roast, cut into 2-inch pieces
- 1 pinch salt and ground black pepper to taste
- 1 onion, quartered
- ¼ cup apple cider vinegar
- 5 cloves garlic, minced
- 2 tablespoons lime juice
- 1 tablespoon ground cumin
- 1 tablespoon dried oregano
- 1 tablespoon agave nectar
- 1 teaspoon ground cinnamon

Directions
- **Step 1**

Place chile peppers in a large bowl and cover with hot water. Soak until soft, about 20 minutes. Drain.
- **Step 2**

Heat a large skillet over medium heat. Add chuck roast and season with salt and pepper. Cook meat until dark brown and crispy on all sides, 7 to 10 minutes.
- **Step 3**

While meat cooks, combine softened chile peppers, onion, vinegar, garlic, lime juice, cumin, oregano, agave nectar, and cinnamon in a blender. Process sauce until smooth.
- **Step 4**

Transfer browned meat and all juices to a multi-functional pressure cooker (such as Instant Pot®). Stir in sauce from the blender. Close and lock the lid. Select high pressure according to manufacturer's instructions; set timer for 60 minutes. Allow 10 to 15 minutes for pressure to build.
- **Step 5**

Release pressure carefully using the quick-release method according to manufacturer's instructions, about 5 minutes. Unlock and remove the lid.

Nutrition Facts
Per Serving:
382.5 calories; protein 27.4g 55% DV; carbohydrates 8.2g 3% DV; fat 26.2g 40% DV; cholesterol 103.3mg 35% DV; sodium 88.9mg 4% DV.

Instant Pot Risotto

Prep: 5 mins Cook: 20 mins Additional: 5 mins Total: 30 mins

Servings: 3

Ingredients

- 1 cube chicken bouillon (such as Knorr®)
- 2 cups hot water
- 2 tablespoons extra-virgin olive oil
- ¼ cup finely diced onion
- 1 clove garlic, minced
- 1 cup Arborio rice
- ¼ cup white wine
- 2 tablespoons butter
- ¼ cup grated Parmigiano-Reggiano cheese
- 2 teaspoons chopped fresh parsley

Directions

- **Step 1**

Dissolve the chicken bouillon cube in the hot water and set aside.
- **Step 2**

Turn on a multi-functional pressure cooker (such as Instant Pot®) and select Saute function. Add olive oil to the pot. Add onion and cook for 1 minute. Add garlic and rice and stir until each grain of rice is coated with the oil mixture. Cook until rice is slightly toasted, about 2 minutes. Pour in white wine and simmer for about 30 seconds. Stir in chicken broth.
- **Step 3**

Turn off Saute function. Close and lock the lid. Select high pressure according to manufacturer's instructions; set timer for 6 minutes. Allow 5 to 10 minutes for pressure to build.
- **Step 4**

Release pressure carefully using the quick-release method according to manufacturer's instructions, about 5 minutes. Unlock and remove the lid. Add butter; stir until risotto is creamy, about 1 minute. Stir in Parmigiano-Reggiano cheese until melted and well combined. Serve sprinkled with parsley.

Nutrition Facts

Per Serving:

446.5 calories; protein 7.7g 15% DV; carbohydrates 57.2g 18% DV; fat 18.7g 29% DV; cholesterol 26.4mg 9% DV; sodium 547.4mg 22% DV.

Instant Pot Classic Hummus

Prep: 10 mins Cook: 45 mins Additional: 5 mins Total: 1 hr

Servings: 8

Ingredients

- 1 cup dry garbanzo beans
- 3 cups vegetable broth
- ⅓ cup lemon juice
- 3 tablespoons tahini
- 2 tablespoons olive oil
- 2 cloves garlic, chopped
- 1 teaspoon ground cumin
- ½ teaspoon salt

Directions
- **Step 1**

Combine garbanzo beans with vegetable broth in a multi-functional pressure cooker (such as Instant Pot®). Close and lock the lid. Select high pressure according to manufacturer's instructions; set timer for 35 minutes. Allow 10 to 15 minutes for pressure to build.
- **Step 2**

Release pressure carefully using the quick-release method according to manufacturer's instructions, about 5 minutes. Unlock and remove lid.
- **Step 3**

Strain garbanzo beans, saving 2/3 cup liquid. Place garbanzo beans in the bowl of a food processor; add lemon juice, tahini, olive oil, and garlic. Blend until smooth and creamy, about 3 minutes. Scrape bowl and add reserved 2/3 cup liquid, cumin, and salt; blend for 1 minute more.

Nutrition Facts
Per Serving:
170.2 calories; protein 6.3g 13% DV; carbohydrates 19.5g 6% DV; fat 8.2g 13% DV; cholesterolmg; sodium 331mg 13% DV.

Instant Pot Cabbage and Beef Soup

Prep: 15 mins Cook: 40 mins Additional: 20 mins Total: 1 hr 15 mins

Servings: 6

Ingredients

- 1 tablespoon olive oil
- 1 pound ground beef
- 1 teaspoon dried oregano
- 1 teaspoon dried thyme
- 1 cup chopped carrot
- 1 cup chopped Yukon Gold potato
- ½ onion, chopped
- 2 cloves garlic, chopped
- 8 cups water
- 1 (14.5 ounce) can Italian-style stewed tomatoes, drained and diced
- ½ head cabbage, cored and coarsely chopped
- 8 teaspoons vegetable bouillon base (such as Better Than Bouillon®)
- 1 teaspoon salt, or to taste
- ½ teaspoon ground black pepper, or to taste

Directions
- **Step 1**

Turn on a multi-functional pressure cooker (such as Instant Pot®) and select Saute function for medium heat. When the display reads "Hot," add olive oil to coat the bottom of the pot. Add beef, oregano, and thyme; cook and stir until browned, breaking it apart as it cooks, 5 to 7 minutes. Add carrot, potato, onion, and garlic. Cook to soften, stirring frequently, about 5 minutes. Turn off Saute mode.
- **Step 2**

Stir water, tomatoes with their juices, cabbage, vegetable base, salt, and pepper into the pot. Stir briefly together.
- **Step 3**

Close and lock the lid. Select high pressure according to manufacturer's instructions; set timer for 20 minutes. Allow 10 to 15 minutes for pressure to build.
- **Step 4**

Release pressure using the natural-release method according to manufacturer's instructions for 15 minutes. Release remaining pressure carefully using the quick-release method according to manufacturer's instructions, about 5 minutes. Unlock and remove the lid; stir. Serve while hot.

Nutrition Facts
Per Serving:
237.1 calories; protein 15.5g 31% DV; carbohydrates 18.5g 6% DV; fat 11.6g 18% DV; cholesterol 47.3mg 16% DV; sodium 626.9mg 25% DV.

Instant Pot Khichdi

Prep: 10 mins Cook: 35 mins Additional: 50 mins Total: 1 hr 35 mins

Servings: 6

Ingredients

- 1 cup brown basmati rice
- ½ cup whole green mung beans
- ¼ cup split yellow dal
- 1 ½ teaspoons cumin seeds
- 1 ½ teaspoons brown mustard seeds
- 8 tablespoons ghee, divided
- 1 shallot, sliced
- 1 tablespoon minced fresh ginger root
- 1 tablespoon goda masala
- 1 teaspoon ground turmeric
- 1 teaspoon ground black pepper
- ½ teaspoon salt
- 6 cups water

Directions
- **Step 1**

Rinse rice and mung beans. Cover with water and soak for 15 minutes. Rinse split yellow dal and add to the rice and mung beans to soak for 15 minutes. Drain and set aside.
- **Step 2**

Turn on a multi-functional pressure cooker (such as Instant Pot®) and select Saute function. Saute cumin and mustard seeds in 2 tablespoons ghee until fragrant, about 2 minutes. Add shallot and ginger and cook until shallot is tender and translucent, about 5 minutes. Add the drained rice and legumes; stir to combine. Turn off Saute function.
- **Step 3**

Stir in goda masala, turmeric, pepper, and salt. Add water; stir well. Close and lock the lid. Select high pressure and set timer for 18 minutes according to manufacturer's instructions. Allow 10 to 15 minutes for pressure to build.
- **Step 4**

Allow pressure to release naturally for 15 minutes. Manually release any remaining pressure, 5 to 10 minutes more. Stir khichdi and divide between 6 bowls. Top each with 1 tablespoon of remaining ghee.

Cook's Note:
See my recipe for goda masala.

Nutrition Facts
Per Serving:
351.4 calories; protein 9.1g 18% DV; carbohydrates 40.2g 13% DV; fat 18.6g 29% DV; cholesterol 43.7mg 15% DV; sodium 206.2mg 8% DV.

Instant Pot Piccata Israeli Couscous

Prep: 10 mins Cook: 15 mins Additional: 5 mins Total: 30 mins

Servings: 4

Ingredients

- 1 tablespoon butter
- 1 teaspoon olive oil
- 2 tablespoons diced shallot
- 1 tablespoon lemon zest
- 1 clove garlic, minced
- 1 cup Israeli couscous
- 1 ½ cups low-sodium chicken broth
- 2 tablespoons fresh lemon juice
- 2 tablespoons capers
- 1 teaspoon caper brine
- 2 tablespoons chopped fresh parsley
- 1 tablespoon grated Parmesan cheese, or more to taste
- 4 wedge (blank)s lemon wedges

Directions

- **Step 1**

Turn on a multi-functional pressure cooker (such as an Instant Pot®), and select Saute function. Heat butter and oil until butter is melted. Add shallot, lemon zest, and garlic; cook until garlic is translucent, 1 to 2 minutes. Add couscous and cook, stirring occasionally, until lightly browned and toasted, about 2 minutes. Turn off Saute function.

- **Step 2**

Pour in chicken broth and lemon juice. Close and lock the lid. Select high pressure according to manufacturer's instructions; set timer for 5 minutes. Allow 10 to 15 minutes for pressure to build.

- **Step 3**

Carefully release pressure using the quick-release method according to manufacturer's instructions, about 5 minutes. Unlock and remove the lid, and stir in the capers and caper brine.

- **Step 4**

Garnish with parsley and Parmesan cheese. Serve with lemon wedges.

Nutrition Facts

Per Serving:
60.7 calories; protein 2.3g 5% DV; carbohydrates 4.1g 1% DV; fat 4.7g 7% DV; cholesterol 10.2mg 3% DV; sodium 234.9mg 9% DV.

Instant Pot Pilau Rice

Prep: 10 mins Cook: 20 mins Additional: 10 mins Total: 40 mins

Servings: 6

Ingredients

- 1 tablespoon vegetable oil
- ½ teaspoon cumin seeds
- ¼ cup diced red onion
- ¾ tablespoon garam masala
- ½ teaspoon ground turmeric
- ½ teaspoon salt
- 1 ½ cups vegetable broth
- 1 cup uncooked basmati rice, rinsed and drained
- ½ cup frozen peas and carrots
- 1 bay leaf

Directions

- **Step 1**

Turn on a multi-functional pressure cooker (such as Instant Pot®) and select Saute function. Heat oil in the pot. Add cumin seeds and stir until they just start to pop. Stir in onion and cook until they begin to soften, about 2 minutes. Season with garam masala, turmeric, and salt. Add vegetable broth, rice, frozen peas and carrots, and bay leaf; stir until well combined.

- **Step 2**

Close and lock the lid. Select high pressure according to manufacturer's instructions; set timer for 5 minutes. Allow 10 to 15 minutes for pressure to build.

- **Step 3**

Release pressure using the natural-release method according to manufacturer's instructions, 10 to 40 minutes. Manually release any remaining pressure. Unlock and remove the lid. Remove bay leaf. Taste rice and adjust seasoning if necessary before serving.

Nutrition Facts

Per Serving:

151.2 calories; protein 3.2g 6% DV; carbohydrates 28.5g 9% DV; fat 3.1g 5% DV; cholesterolmg; sodium 321.3mg 13% DV.

Instant Pot Mexican Quinoa

Prep: 15 mins Cook: 15 mins Additional: 10 mins Total: 40 mins

Servings: 4

Ingredients

- 1 tablespoon olive oil
- 1 small onion, chopped
- 1 jalapeno pepper, minced, or to taste
- 3 cloves garlic, chopped
- 1 (15 ounce) can black beans, drained and rinsed
- 1 (14.5 ounce) can fire-roasted diced tomatoes
- ¾ cup corn kernels
- ¾ teaspoon salt, or to taste
- ½ teaspoon ground cumin
- ½ teaspoon smoked paprika
- ¼ teaspoon chili powder
- ⅛ teaspoon black pepper
- 1 cup dry quinoa
- 1 cup vegetable broth, or as needed
- 2 tablespoons chopped cilantro, or to taste
- 1 lime, juiced
- 1 avocado, diced

Directions

- **Step 1**

Turn on a multi-functional pressure cooker (such as Instant Pot®) and select Saute function. Add oil, onion, jalapeno pepper, and garlic. Saute until onion is softened, about 2 minutes. Add black beans, tomatoes, and corn; mix well. Season with salt, cumin, paprika, chili powder, and black pepper. Add quinoa and toss until well combined. Pour in broth and mix.

- **Step 2**

Close and lock the lid; set valve to the sealing position. Select high pressure according to manufacturer's instructions; set timer for 1 minute. Allow 10 to 15 minutes for pressure to build.

- **Step 3**

Release pressure using the natural-release method according to manufacturer's instructions, 10 to 40 minutes. Open the pot and fluff quinoa using a fork. Add cilantro and lime juice. Stir in avocado.

Nutrition Facts
Per Serving:
442.1 calories; protein 16g 32% DV; carbohydrates 66g 21% DV; fat 14.2g 22% DV; cholesterolmg; sodium 1245mg 50% DV.

Instant Pot Beef Stew with Frozen Meat

Prep: 25 mins Cook: 1 hr 5 mins Additional: 15 mins Total: 1 hr 45 mins

Servings: 8

Ingredients

- 2 tablespoons avocado oil
- 1 large onion, finely diced
- 3 cloves garlic, finely chopped
- ¼ cup dry red wine
- 2 cups beef broth
- 1 teaspoon dried thyme
- 1 teaspoon dried parsley
- 1 teaspoon dried oregano
- 1 bay leaf
- 1 teaspoon salt, or to taste
- ½ teaspoon freshly ground black pepper, or to taste
- 1 tablespoon tomato paste
- 2 (1 pound) packages cubed beef stew meat, frozen
- 6 medium carrots, sliced
- 5 large potatoes, peeled and cut into large cubes
- 3 stalks celery, sliced
- 2 tablespoons water
- 1 tablespoon cornstarch

Directions
- **Step 1**

Turn on a multi-functional pressure cooker (such as Instant Pot®) and select Saute function. Pour in oil. Cook onions and garlic in the hot oil until soft and translucent, about 5 minutes. Pour in wine and continue sauteing until wine has reduced by half, 4 to 5 minutes.
- **Step 2**

Add beef broth, thyme, parsley, oregano, bay leaf, salt, and pepper; stir to combine. Mix in tomato paste. Place frozen meat into the pot and add carrots, potatoes, and celery. Close and lock the lid. Select Meat/Stew function and set timer for 45 minutes. Allow 10 to 15 minutes for pressure to build.

- **Step 3**

Release pressure using the natural-release method according to manufacturer's instructions, about 10 minutes. Carefully move the vent to release the remainder of the pressure, about 5 minutes. Unlock and remove the lid.
- **Step 4**

Mix water and cornstarch together in a small bowl and pour slowly into the pot. Press the Saute button and cook stew until slightly thickened, about 3 minutes.

Instant Pot Venison Chili

Prep: 10 mins Cook: 40 mins Additional: 5 mins Total: 55 mins

Servings: 6

Ingredients

- 1 ½ pounds ground venison
- 1 medium onion, chopped
- 2 eaches jalapeno peppers, seeded and chopped
- 2 (15.5 ounce) cans chili beans, undrained
- 1 (28 ounce) can crushed tomatoes
- 1 (15.5 ounce) can kidney beans, drained
- 1 cup water
- 1 tablespoon chili powder
- 2 teaspoons ground cumin
- ½ teaspoon dried oregano
- ¼ teaspoon garlic powder
- ¼ teaspoon onion powder

Directions
- **Step 1**

Turn on a multi-functional pressure cooker (such as Instant Pot®) and select Low Saute function. Add venison and cook for 5 minutes, breaking it up with a spoon as it cooks. Add onion and jalapeno peppers; cook and stir until softened, about 3 minutes. Cancel Saute mode.
- **Step 2**

Add chili beans, crushed tomatoes, kidney beans, water, chili powder, cumin, oregano, garlic powder, and onion powder to the pot. Close and lock the lid. Select high pressure according to manufacturer's instructions; set timer for 20 minutes. Allow 10 to 15 minutes for pressure to build.
- **Step 3**

Release pressure carefully using the quick-release method according to manufacturer's instructions, about 5 minutes. Unlock and remove the lid.

Instant Pot Cream of Asparagus Soup

Prep: 10 mins Cook: 15 mins Additional: 20 mins Total: 45 mins

Servings: 4

Ingredients

- 1 tablespoon olive oil
- 4 slices bacon, diced
- ½ onion, diced
- 3 cloves garlic, minced
- 2 pounds asparagus, cut into 1 1/2-inch pieces
- 2 ½ cups chicken broth
- 1 teaspoon salt
- ½ teaspoon ground black pepper
- 1 cup heavy whipping cream

Directions
- **Step 1**

Turn on a multi-functional pressure cooker (such as Instant Pot®), select Saute function, and add olive oil. Add bacon to warmed oil and saute for 2 minutes. Stir in onion and continue cooking until onion is soft and translucent, about 5 minutes. Add garlic and asparagus. Cook 1 to 2 minutes.
- **Step 2**

Pour chicken broth over asparagus mixture and bring to a boil. Turn Saute mode off and press the Manual mode. Close and lock the lid. Select High pressure according to manufacturer's instructions; set timer for 5 minutes. Allow 10 to 15 minutes for pressure to build.
- **Step 3**

Release pressure using the natural-release method according to manufacturer's instructions, 10 to 40 minutes. Unlock and remove the lid.
- **Step 4**

Puree asparagus mixture with an immersion blender until smooth. Mix in cream and select Saute function. Cook until soup is warmed through, but not boiling. Taste and season with salt and pepper.

Nutrition Facts
Per Serving:
355.9 calories; protein 10.8g 22% DV; carbohydrates 14.9g 5% DV; fat 29.8g 46% DV; cholesterol 95.2mg 32% DV; sodium 1545.4mg 62% DV.

Instant Pot Celery Soup

Prep: 20 mins Cook: 25 mins Additional: 15 mins Total: 1 hr

Servings: 4

Ingredients

- 2 tablespoons olive oil
- 2 pounds celery, sliced
- 1 large onion, sliced
- 3 cloves garlic, sliced
- ½ pound potatoes, peeled and chopped
- 4 cups vegetable broth
- ¼ teaspoon salt
- ⅛ teaspoon ground black pepper

Directions
- **Step 1**

Combine olive oil, celery, onion, and garlic in a multi-functional pressure cooker (such as Instant Pot®). Select Saute function and cook, stirring occasionally, for 5 minutes. Add potatoes, broth, salt, and pepper and stir. Close and lock the lid and set the steamer valve to Sealing.
- **Step 2**

Select high pressure according to manufacturer's instructions; set timer for 10 minutes. Allow 10 to 15 minutes for pressure to build.
- **Step 3**

Release pressure using the natural-release method according to manufacturer's instructions, about 15 minutes. Unlock and remove the lid.
- **Step 4**

Use an electric hand mixer or blender to puree the soup until smooth. Serve while warm or let cool and serve as a chilled soup on a hot day.

Nutrition Facts
Per Serving:
188.2 calories; protein 4.3g 9% DV; carbohydrates 25.9g 8% DV; fat 7.7g 12% DV; cholesterolmg; sodium 792.4mg 32% DV.

Instant Pot Sweet Baby Back Ribs

Prep: 10 mins Cook: 45 mins Additional: 20 mins Total: 1 hr 15 mins

Servings: 8

Ingredients

- 2 racks baby back pork ribs
- Dry Rub:
- ¼ cup dark brown sugar
- 2 tablespoons garlic salt (such as Lawry's®)
- 2 tablespoons chili powder
- 1 teaspoon ground black pepper
- 1 teaspoon cayenne pepper, or to taste
- Cooking Liquid:
- 1 cup beef broth
- 12 fluid ounces root beer
- 2 tablespoons apple cider vinegar
- 1 teaspoon liquid smoke flavoring
- 1 cup barbecue sauce (such as Sweet Baby Ray's®), or more to taste

Directions
- **Step 1**

Use a butter knife to cut into an edge of the rib racks. Use a paper towel to grab and lift off the silvery membranes.
- **Step 2**

Combine brown sugar, garlic salt, chili powder, black pepper, and cayenne pepper in bowl. Coat the ribs generously with the dry rub.

- **Step 3**

Place the trivet inside the Instant Pot®. Pour in broth, root beer, vinegar, and liquid smoke. Place ribs on the trivet on their sides, with one inside the other. Close and lock the lid and make sure the vent is sealed. Select manual high pressure and set the timer for 30 minutes. Allow 10 to 15 minutes for pressure to build.

- **Step 4**

Release pressure using the natural-release method according to manufacturer's instructions for 15 minutes. Release remaining pressure carefully using the quick-release method according to manufacturer's instructions, about 5 minutes. Unlock and remove the lid.

- **Step 5**

Set an oven rack about 6 inches from the heat source and preheat the oven's broiler on the highest heat setting. Place a rack 6 inches from the heat source.

- **Step 6**

Transfer ribs to a broiling pan and generously coat with barbecue sauce.

- **Step 7**

Cook in the broiler until barbeque sauce is bubbly and caramelized, 5 to 7 minutes.

Nutrition Facts

Per Serving:
384.7 calories; protein 18.8g 38% DV; carbohydrates 24.8g 8% DV; fat 23.1g 36% DV; cholesterol 87.8mg 29% DV; sodium 1910.9mg 76% DV.

Instant Pot Orange Chicken

Prep: 15 mins Cook: 35 mins Additional: 20 mins Total: 1 hr 10 mins

Servings: 8

Ingredients

- 3 pounds skinless, boneless chicken
- 2 tablespoons oil
- ¾ cup orange juice
- 1 (8 ounce) can tomato sauce
- ¼ cup white sugar
- ¼ cup blackstrap molasses
- ¼ cup soy sauce
- 4 cloves garlic, minced
- 1 orange, zested and juiced, divided
- 1 tablespoon grated fresh ginger
- 1 tablespoon rice wine
- 3 tablespoons cornstarch

Directions

- **Step 1**

Blot chicken with paper towels until completely dry. Cut into 1- to 2-inch chunks.

- **Step 2**

Turn on a multi-functional pressure cooker (such as Instant Pot®), select Saute function, and click to adjust to the highest heat. When the pot is hot, add oil and heat until shimmering. Add chicken and saute until it starts to get golden, stirring constantly so it doesn't stick to the bottom of the pot, for 2 to 3 minutes. Pour 3/4 cup orange juice into the pot and bring to a boil while scraping all the browned bits of food off the bottom of the pan with a wooden spoon.

- **Step 3**

Add tomato sauce, sugar, molasses, soy sauce, garlic, orange zest, ginger, and rice wine; gently stir until all Ingredients are combined and coated in sauce. Cancel Saute function.

- **Step 4**

Close and lock the lid, and make sure the vent is closed. Select high pressure according to manufacturer's instructions; set timer for 5 minutes. Allow 10 to 15 minutes for pressure to build.
*   **Step 5**
Allow the Instant Pot® to remain on for 10 minutes with the Keep Warm function. Release pressure carefully using the quick-release method according to manufacturer's instructions, about 5 minutes. Unlock and remove the lid. Select Saute function and click to adjust to the lowest heat.
*   **Step 6**
Combine 3 tablespoons freshly squeezed orange juice with cornstarch in a medium bowl; whisk until combined with no lumps. Add to the Instant Pot® and stir to combine. Cook, stirring gently, until sauce thickens, about 3 minutes. Simmer for 2 to 3 minutes more.
*   **Step 7**
Cancel Saute function and let stand until sauce thickens further, 5 to 7 minutes. Serve.

Nutrition Facts
Per Serving:
296.2 calories; protein 34.3g 69% DV; carbohydrates 22.3g 7% DV; fat 7g 11% DV; cholesterol 87.9mg 29% DV; sodium 674.3mg 27% DV.

Instant Pot Creamy Vanilla Rice Pudding

Prep: 5 mins Cook: 30 mins Additional: 10 mins Total: 45 mins

Servings: 8

Ingredients

*   3 cups cooked short-grain rice
*   2 ¼ cups milk, divided
*   ½ cup white sugar
*   ¼ teaspoon salt
*   2 eaches egg yolks, whisked well
*   ¼ cup heavy cream
*   1 teaspoon vanilla extract
*   1 pinch ground cinnamon, or as needed

Directions
*   **Step 1**
Combine cooked rice, 2 cups milk, sugar, and salt in a multi-functional pressure cooker (such as Instant Pot®) and stir well. Close and lock the lid. Select porridge function according to manufacturer's instructions and seal the vent. Set timer for 20 minutes. Allow 10 to 15 minutes for pressure to build.
*   **Step 2**
Release pressure using the natural-release method according to manufacturer's instructions, 10 to 40 minutes. Unlock and carefully remove the lid.
*   **Step 3**
Whisk egg yolks together well in a bowl. Add a small amount of cooked porridge and whisk quickly into yolks. Pour mixture into the pot and stir to combine well with rice. Add heavy cream, remaining milk, and vanilla extract. Stir to combine completely.

*   **Step 4**
Serve rice pudding in individual bowls garnished with cinnamon.

Nutrition Facts
Per Serving:
214 calories; protein 4.7g 10% DV; carbohydrates 36.3g 12% DV; fat 5.3g 8% DV;
cholesterol 66.9mg 22% DV; sodium 105.7mg 4% DV.

Instant Pot Gyros

Prep: 5 mins Cook: 55 mins Additional:5 mins Total: 1 hr 5 mins

Servings: 16

Ingredients

- 4 pounds pork butt, cut into 2-inch cubes
- 3 tablespoons Greek seasoning (such as Cavender's®)
- 1 teaspoon paprika
- 2 cloves garlic, minced
- 1 cup chicken broth
- 2 teaspoons olive oil

Directions
- **Step 1**

Turn on a multi-functional pressure cooker (such as Instant Pot®) and select the Saute function. Place cubed pork in the pot and cook until starting to brown, about 5 minutes. Turn pot off.
- **Step 2**

Add Greek seasoning, paprika, garlic, and chicken broth to the pot with the pork. Close and lock the lid. Select Manual and set timer for 35 minutes. Allow 10 minutes for pressure to build.
- **Step 3**

Release pressure carefully using the quick-release method according to manufacturer's instructions, about 5 minutes. Unlock and remove the lid.
- **Step 4**

Heat oil in a large skillet over medium-high heat. Transfer pork to the skillet using a slotted spoon and cook for 5 minutes or until most of the liquid has evaporated and pork has a nice crisp on it.

Nutrition Facts
Per Serving:
249.9 calories; protein 14.8g 30% DV; carbohydrates 1.2g; fat 20.7g 32% DV;
cholesterol 65.2mg 22% DV; sodium 1654.1mg 66% DV.

Instant Pot Bang Bang Shrimp Pasta

Prep: 10 mins Cook: 25 mins Additional: 5 mins Total: 40 mins

Servings: 6

Ingredients

- 1 pound dry spaghetti
- 4 cups water
- 2 cloves garlic, minced
- 1 tablespoon olive oil
- 1 teaspoon salt
- 1 pound large shrimp, peeled and deveined
- ¾ cup mayonnaise
- ¾ cup Thai sweet red chili sauce
- ¼ cup lime juice
- 1 teaspoon chile-garlic sauce (such as Sriracha)
- 2 eaches green onions, chopped

Directions
- **Step 1**

Break spaghetti noodles in half and place in a multi-functional pressure cooker (such as Instant Pot). Add water, garlic, olive oil, and salt. Close and lock the lid. Select high pressure according to manufacturer's instructions; set timer for 6 minutes. Allow 10 to 15 minutes for pressure to build.
- **Step 2**

Release pressure carefully using the quick-release method according to manufacturer's instructions, about 5 minutes. Unlock and remove the lid.
- **Step 3**

Combine shrimp, mayonnaise, chili sauce, lime juice, and Sriracha in a bowl; mix until well coated. Pour into the pot and select Saute function. Add chopped green onions and cook until shrimp are pink and green onions are tender, about 7 minutes.

Nutrition Facts
Per Serving:
612.2 calories; protein 22.6g 45% DV; carbohydrates 71.9g 23% DV; fat 26.1g 40% DV; cholesterol 125.5mg 42% DV; sodium 1061.4mg 43% DV.

Instant Pot Chocolate Cheesecake

Prep: 25 mins Cook: 1 hr 3 mins Additional: 7 hrs 20 mins Total: 8 hrs 48 mins

Servings: 10

Ingredients
Crust:
- 2 (4.8 ounce) packages graham crackers, crushed
- 5 tablespoons butter
Filling:
- 1 (8 ounce) package cream cheese, softened
- 1 (8 ounce) package Neufchatel cheese, softened
- ¾ cup white sugar
- 2 large eggs eggs
Glaze:
- 1 (12 ounce) package frozen sweet cherries
- 2 tablespoons apricot jam
- 1 pinch kosher salt

- 2 teaspoons vanilla extract
- ¼ cup heavy whipping cream
- 1 (8 ounce) package semisweet chocolate chips
- 2 tablespoons all-purpose flour

- 2 tablespoons white sugar
- 1 tablespoon water
- 1 tablespoon cornstarch

Directions
- **Step 1**

Wrap the bottom and sides of an 8-inch springform pan with aluminum foil.
- **Step 2**

Combine graham cracker crumbs, butter, and salt in a bowl; mix thoroughly. Pour into the prepared pan; press tightly onto the bottom and up the sides of the pan using the bottom of a measuring cup. Freeze crust until firm, 10 to 15 minutes.
- **Step 3**

Beat cream cheese, Neufchatel cheese, and 3/4 cup sugar in a bowl with an electric mixer until creamy, about 4 minutes. Beat in eggs one at a time; add vanilla. Beat in heavy cream.
- **Step 4**

Melt chocolate chips in a microwave-safe glass or ceramic bowl in 15-second intervals, stirring after each melting, 1 to 2 minutes. Beat melted chocolate into the cream cheese mixture. Fold in flour.
- **Step 5**

Pour chocolate cream cheese mixture over the chilled crust. Cover tightly with aluminum foil.
- **Step 6**

Pour 1 1/2 cup water into the pot of an electric pressure cooker (such as Instant Pot). Place the steam rack in the pot; set springform pan on top. Close and lock the lid. Set timer for 45 minutes. Set to high pressure according to manufacturer's instructions, 10 to 15 minutes.
- **Step 7**

Release pressure naturally according to manufacturer's instructions, 10 to 12 minutes. Cool cheesecake to room temperature, about 1 hour.
- **Step 8**

Combine cherries, apricot jam, and 2 tablespoons sugar in a saucepan over medium heat. Simmer until cherries are heated through and release some of their juices, 5 to 7 minutes.
- **Step 9**

Mix water and cornstarch in a small bowl until smooth. Stir into the cherry mixture until thick and glossy, 2 to 3 minutes. Remove from heat; cool glaze to room temperature.
- **Step 10**

Pour glaze over cheesecake and refrigerate until firm, at least 6 hours or overnight. Remove the springform ring and transfer cheesecake to a serving platter.

Cook's Notes:

Substitute evaporated milk for the cream if desired.

I couldn't get the trivet to fit, so I used a small metal bowl upside down inside the pot as a "support" for the springform pan. Worked great!

Nutrition Facts

Per Serving:

567.8 calories; protein 9.4g 19% DV; carbohydrates 64.8g 21% DV; fat 32g 49% DV; cholesterol 102.3mg 34% DV; sodium 419.7mg 17% DV.

Instant Pot Curried Chicken Thighs

Prep: 10 mins Cook: 50 mins Additional: 15 mins Total: 1 hr 15 mins

Servings: 4

Ingredients

- 4 (6 ounce) chicken thighs
- 2 teaspoons mild yellow curry powder (such as Savory Spice)
- 1 teaspoon honey powder (such as Savory Spice)
- ¾ teaspoon salt
- ½ teaspoon ground black pepper
- 2 tablespoons olive oil
- 1 tablespoon butter
- 1 small onion, cut in half and thinly sliced
- 4 cloves garlic, minced
- 1 tablespoon minced fresh ginger root
- 1 (14.5 ounce) can diced tomatoes
- 1 tablespoon tomato powder
- ½ cup coconut milk
- 1 teaspoon ground cumin
- 1 tablespoon mild yellow curry powder (such as Savory Spice)

Directions

- **Step 1**

Season chicken thighs with 2 teaspoons curry powder, honey powder, salt, and black pepper.

- **Step 2**

Turn on a multi-functional pressure cooker (such as Instant Pot) and select Saute function. Heat oil and butter. Add chicken and cook until browned, 2 to 3 minutes per side. Transfer to a plate. Add onion; cook and stir until soft and translucent, about 5 minutes. Add garlic and ginger; cook until fragrant, about 2 minutes. Return chicken to Instant Pot. Add tomatoes and tomato powder. Close and lock the lid.

- **Step 3**

Select high pressure according to manufacturer's instructions; set timer for 20 minutes. Allow 10 to 15 minutes for pressure to build.

- **Step 4**

Release pressure using the natural-release method according to manufacturer's instructions, for 10 minutes. Switch to the quick-release method according to manufacturer's instructions and release remaining pressure for about 5 minutes. Unlock and remove the lid.

- **Step 5**

Turn on Saute function. Add coconut milk, cumin, and remaining curry powder to the pot. Cook until sauce has thickened, about 5 minutes.

Cook's Note:

I love using tomato powder as it has a robust taste, and while tomato paste may be used, I prefer tomato powder as I don't have to worry about leftover tomato paste. Honey powder is dehydrated honey, and while honey may be used I prefer honey powder as it is not sticky. Both may be found at the Savory spice shop, or your local grocer may carry them.

Nutrition Facts
Per Serving:
471.6 calories; protein 31g 62% DV; carbohydrates 11.2g 4% DV; fat 33.8g 52% DV; cholesterol 113.4mg 38% DV; sodium 721.3mg 29% DV.

Instant Pot Dark Chocolate Brownies

Prep: 15 mins Cook: 40 mins Additional: 20 mins Total: 1 hr 15 mins

Servings: 4

Ingredients

- 5 ounces dark chocolate (such as Lindt 78% Cocoa), chopped into small pieces
- 6 tablespoons unsalted butter
- 1 cup superfine sugar
- 2 tablespoons Greek yogurt
- 1 tablespoon vanilla extract
- 3 large eggs eggs
- ¾ cup all-purpose flour
- 1 tablespoon unsweetened cocoa powder
- 1 teaspoon baking soda
- ½ teaspoon salt

Directions
- **Step 1**

Heat chocolate and butter in a glass bowl placed inside a saucepan of simmering water. Stir frequently, scraping down the sides with a rubber spatula to avoid scorching, until chocolate is melted and glossy, about 5 minutes.
- **Step 2**

Let melted chocolate cool to room temperature, about 10 minutes. Add sugar; whisk thoroughly. Mix in yogurt and vanilla extract until combined. Beat in eggs 1 at a time using the whisk. Sift in flour, cocoa powder, baking soda, and salt; gently fold into the chocolate mixture until batter is thick and smooth. Do not overmix.
- **Step 3**

Butter a 6-inch round cake pan with 2-inch sides. Pour batter into the pan and seal top with a sheet of aluminum foil.
- **Step 4**

Set a trivet inside the pot of an electric pressure cooker (such as Instant Pot). Add 1 cup water. Make sure the steam release handle is in Sealing position according to manufacturers' instructions. Arrange long strips of aluminum foil crosswise under the cake pan; hold the ends to lower cake onto the trivet. Keep foil strips folded down to prevent contact with the lid.
- **Step 5**

Close and lock the lid. Select high pressure according to manufacturer's instructions; set timer for 25 minutes. Allow 10 to 15 minutes for pressure to build. Release pressure using the natural-release method according to manufacturer's instructions, about 10 minutes.
- **Step 6**

Check a toothpick inserted into the brownie comes out clean. Cook at high pressure for 3 minutes more if needed. Release pressure using the quick-release method, about 5 minutes. Let brownie cool before cutting.

Cook's Notes:
Sour cream can be substituted for the Greek yogurt, if desired.
If you like, you can add chopped walnuts/chocolate chunks at the end of Step 2.

Nutrition Facts
Per Serving:
693.9 calories; protein 9.9g 20% DV; carbohydrates 90.6g 29% DV; fat 33.5g 52% DV; cholesterol 188.5mg 63% DV; sodium 667.9mg 27% DV.

Instant Pot Curried Chicken Thighs

Prep: 10 mins Cook: 50 mins Additional: 15 mins Total: 1 hr 15 mins

Servings: 4

Ingredients

- 4 (6 ounce) chicken thighs
- 2 teaspoons mild yellow curry powder (such as Savory Spice)
- 1 teaspoon honey powder (such as Savory Spice)
- ¾ teaspoon salt
- ½ teaspoon ground black pepper
- 2 tablespoons olive oil
- 1 tablespoon butter
- 1 small onion, cut in half and thinly sliced
- 4 cloves garlic, minced
- 1 tablespoon minced fresh ginger root
- 1 (14.5 ounce) can diced tomatoes
- 1 tablespoon tomato powder
- ½ cup coconut milk
- 1 teaspoon ground cumin
- 1 tablespoon mild yellow curry powder (such as Savory Spice)

Directions
- **Step 1**

Season chicken thighs with 2 teaspoons curry powder, honey powder, salt, and black pepper.
- **Step 2**

Turn on a multi-functional pressure cooker (such as Instant Pot) and select Saute function. Heat oil and butter. Add chicken and cook until browned, 2 to 3 minutes per side. Transfer to a plate. Add onion; cook and stir until soft and translucent, about 5 minutes. Add garlic and ginger; cook until fragrant, about 2 minutes. Return chicken to Instant Pot. Add tomatoes and tomato powder. Close and lock the lid.
- **Step 3**

Select high pressure according to manufacturer's instructions; set timer for 20 minutes. Allow 10 to 15 minutes for pressure to build.
- **Step 4**

Release pressure using the natural-release method according to manufacturer's instructions, for 10 minutes. Switch to the quick-release method according to manufacturer's instructions and release remaining pressure for about 5 minutes. Unlock and remove the lid.
- **Step 5**

Turn on Saute function. Add coconut milk, cumin, and remaining curry powder to the pot. Cook until sauce has thickened, about 5 minutes.

Cook's Note:

I love using tomato powder as it has a robust taste, and while tomato paste may be used, I prefer tomato powder as I don't have to worry about leftover tomato paste. Honey powder is dehydrated honey, and while honey may be used I prefer honey powder as it is not sticky. Both may be found at the Savory spice shop, or your local grocer may carry them.

Nutrition Facts
Per Serving:

471.6 calories; protein 31g 62% DV; carbohydrates 11.2g 4% DV; fat 33.8g 52% DV; cholesterol 113.4mg 38% DV; sodium 721.3mg 29% DV.

Instant Pot Turkey Chili

Prep: 15 mins Cook: 35 mins Additional: 5 mins Total: 55 mins

Servings:8

Ingredients
Seasoning:
- 1 tablespoon chili powder
- 2 teaspoons smoked paprika
- 1 teaspoon salt
- 1 teaspoon oregano
- 1 teaspoon unsweetened cocoa powder

Chili:
- 1 tablespoon olive oil
- 1 pound ground turkey
- 1 onion, chopped
- 1 jalapeno pepper, seeded and minced
- 2 (14.5 ounce) cans fire-roasted diced tomatoes
- 1 (15.5 ounce) can dark red kidney beans, drained and rinsed

- ½ teaspoon cumin
- ¼ teaspoon ground cinnamon
- ¼ teaspoon ground coriander
- ¼ teaspoon black pepper

- 1 (15.5 ounce) can light red kidney beans, drained and rinsed
- 1 (15 ounce) can tomato sauce
- 1 chipotle pepper in adobo sauce, minced
- 2 tablespoons adobo sauce from chipotle peppers
- 1 pinch salt to taste

Directions
- **Step 1**

Combine chili powder, smoked paprika, salt, oregano, cocoa powder, cumin, cinnamon, coriander, and black pepper in a small bowl. Set seasoning mix aside.
- **Step 2**

Turn on a multi-functional pressure cooker (such as Instant Pot) and select Saute function. Heat olive oil over high heat and brown ground turkey until crumbly, 3 to 4 minutes. Add onion and jalapeno and cook an additional 2 to 3 minutes. Add tomatoes, kidney beans, tomato sauce, chipotle pepper, adobo sauce, and seasoning mix. Mix to combine, scraping up any browned bits off the bottom of the pot. Close and lock the lid.
- **Step 3**

Select high pressure according to manufacturer's instructions; set timer for 20 minutes. Allow 10 to 15 minutes for pressure to build.
- **Step 4**

Release pressure carefully using the quick-release method according to manufacturer's instructions, about 5 minutes. Unlock and remove the lid. Stir chili and adjust salt, if desired. Serve with your favorite toppings.

Cook's Notes:
Substitute ground beef or chicken if you prefer.
You can freeze leftover canned chipotle peppers in ice cube trays for future use.

Nutrition Facts
Per Serving:
246.5 calories; protein 19g 38% DV; carbohydrates 26.5g 9% DV; fat 7.5g 12% DV; cholesterol 45.1mg 15% DV; sodium 1085mg 43% DV

Instant Pot Sweet and Sour Pork

Prep: 20 mins Cook: 40 mins Additional: 10 mins Total: 1 hr 10 mins

Servings: 4

Ingredients
- 1 tablespoon vegetable oil
- 1 pound boneless pork loin, cut into 3/4-inch cubes
- 1 ¼ cups water, divided
- ½ cup ketchup
- ⅓ cup rice vinegar
- ⅓ cup pineapple juice
- 2 tablespoons brown sugar
- 2 tablespoons low-sodium soy sauce
- 2 teaspoons minced fresh ginger
- 1 teaspoon minced garlic aluminum foil
- 1 onion, vertically sliced
- 1 cup chopped fresh pineapple
- 1 red bell pepper, cut into large chunks
- 1 green bell pepper, cut into large chunks
- 2 tablespoons cornstarch
- 1 tablespoon toasted sesame seeds

Directions
- **Step 1**

Turn on a multi-functional pressure cooker (such as an Instant Pot) and select Saute function. Add oil and heat until hot. Add pork cubes, working in batches if necessary, and cook until browned on all sides, about 5 minutes. Return all the pork back to the pot and cancel Saute mode.
- **Step 2**

Whisk together 3/4 cup water, ketchup, rice vinegar, pineapple juice, brown sugar, soy sauce, ginger, and garlic in a small bowl. Pour over pork and stir to combine.
- **Step 3**

Close and lock the lid. Select high pressure according to manufacturer's instructions; set timer for 5 minutes. Allow 10 to 15 minutes for pressure to build.
- **Step 4**

Release pressure using the natural-release method according to manufacturer's instructions, about 5 minutes. Release remaining pressure using the quick-release method. Unlock the lid and remove. Transfer pork to a plate using a slotted spoon. Cover with foil to keep warm.
- **Step 5**

Select Saute mode and stir in onion, pineapple, and red and green bell peppers. Simmer until vegetables start to soften, 6 to 7 minutes.
- **Step 6**

Whisk together cornstarch and remaining 1/2 cup water in a small bowl until smooth. Pour slurry into the pot. Cook, stirring constantly, until sauce has thickened to your preferred consistency, about 2 minutes. Return cooked pork back to the pot and heat until just warmed through. Garnish with sesame seeds.

Cook's Notes:
Feel free to use whatever color bell peppers you like. Canned, drained pineapple chunks may be substituted for fresh.
Adjust thickness of sauce by either adding more water for a thinner sauce or whisking in cornstarch mixed with water to thicken it.

Nutrition Facts

Per Serving:
328.7 calories; protein 22.1g 44% DV; carbohydrates 36g 12% DV; fat 11.4g 18% DV; cholesterol 54.3mg 18% DV; sodium 648.8mg 26% DV

Instant Pot Green Chili Chicken and Rice

Prep: 20 mins Cook: 40 mins Additional: 5 mins Total: 1 hr 5 mins

Servings: 4

Ingredients
- 1 tablespoon olive oil
- 2 eaches boneless, skinless chicken breasts, cut into 1-inch pieces
- 1 tablespoon all-purpose flour
- 1 (7 ounce) can fire-roasted diced green chile peppers
- 1 (4 ounce) can diced jalapeno peppers
- 1 cup uncooked white rice
- ⅔ cup diced tomato
- ½ cup diced onion
- ½ cup diced Anaheim chile peppers
- ½ cup shredded Cheddar cheese
- 2 teaspoons salt, or more to taste
- 1 teaspoon seasoned salt (such as LAWRY'S)
- ½ teaspoon freshly ground black pepper, or more to taste
- 2 cups chicken stock

Directions
- **Step 1**

Turn on a multi-functional pressure cooker (such as Instant Pot) and select Saute function. Add olive oil and chicken. Sprinkle with flour and cook until browned on all sides, about 5 minutes. Turn off Saute function. Add green chile peppers, jalapenos, rice, tomato, onion, Anaheim chile, Cheddar cheese, salt, seasoned salt, and pepper; pour in chicken stock and mix to combine.
- **Step 2**

Close and lock the lid. Select high pressure according to manufacturer's instructions; set timer for 18 minutes. Allow 10 to 15 minutes for pressure to build.
- **Step 3**

Release pressure carefully using the quick-release method according to manufacturer's instructions, about 5 minutes. Unlock and remove the lid. Adjust seasoning with salt and pepper.

Cook's Notes:
If you are on a gluten-free diet, use cornstarch instead of flour.
For a healthier option, substitute the white rice with 1 1/2 cups precooked brown rice.
Nutrition Facts
Per Serving:
370 calories; protein 20.2g 41% DV; carbohydrates 48.3g 16% DV; fat 10.3g 16% DV; cholesterol 47.1mg 16% DV; sodium 3134.8mg 125% DV.

Instant Pot Crispy Chicken Carnitas

Prep: 25 mins Cook: 25 mins Additional: 10 mins Total: 1 hr

Servings: 10

Ingredients

- 1 tablespoon ground cumin
- ½ teaspoon chili powder
- ½ teaspoon dried oregano
- 1 pinch salt and ground black pepper to taste
- 3 tablespoons olive oil, divided
- 2 pounds skinless, boneless chicken breast halves
- 5 cloves garlic, pressed
- 1 yellow onion, quartered
- ¼ cup lime juice
- ¼ cup chicken broth
- ½ bunch cilantro
- 1 chipotle pepper in adobo sauce, or more to taste
- 1 orange, zested and juiced
- 1 bay leaf
- Chipotle Sauce:
- ½ cup mayonnaise
- 1 tablespoon milk
- 1 chipotle pepper in adobo sauce, or more to taste
- 1 pinch salt
- 1 pinch garlic powde

Directions

- **Step 1**

Combine cumin, chili powder, oregano, salt, and pepper in a bowl. Sprinkle over chicken breasts on both sides.

- **Step 2**

Turn on a multi-functional pressure cooker (such as Instant Pot) and select Saute function. Add 1 tablespoon olive oil and sear chicken breasts, 1 to 2 minutes per side, working in batches so chicken sears rather than steams. Transfer chicken to a plate.

- **Step 3**

Add garlic and onion to the hot cooker; cook and stir until browned evenly on all sides, about 2 minutes. Return chicken to the pressure cooker along with lime juice, chicken broth, cilantro, chipotle pepper with 1 tablespoon adobo sauce, orange zest and juice, and bay leaf. Close and lock the lid. Set timer for 8 to 10 minutes, depending on size of chicken breasts.

- **Step 4**

Meanwhile, combine mayonnaise, milk, chipotle pepper and 1 tablespoon adobo sauce, salt, and garlic powder to an electric blender. Blend chipotle sauce until smooth.

- **Step 5**

Release pressure from the cooker using the natural-release method according to manufacturer's instructions, 10 to 40 minutes. Unlock and remove the lid.

- **Step 6**

Set an oven rack about 6 inches from the heat source and preheat the oven's broiler.

- **Step 7**

Transfer chicken breasts to a clean surface and reserve cooking liquid. Shred chicken meat using 2 forks. Place in a large bowl and drizzle 1/4 cup cooking liquid over chicken; toss to coat. Drizzle 1 tablespoon oil over the surface of a baking sheet. Add chicken to the sheet and drizzle remaining 1 tablespoon oil on top. Stir to coat evenly.

- **Step 8**

Broil chicken in the preheated oven for 5 minutes. Toss chicken with 1 to 2 tablespoons reserved cooking liquid and rotate the pan for even broiling. Continue broiling until crispy, 5 to 7 minutes more. Serve with chipotle sauce.

Cook's Notes:

You can use chicken thighs instead of breasts, if you'd like.

Leftover chipotle peppers in adobo sauce can be kept in a zip-top bag in the freezer. Instead of releasing pressure naturally, you can also use the vent setting if available, allowing to vent completely before removing the lid.

Nutrition Facts
Per Serving:
235.8 calories; protein 19.6g 39% DV; carbohydrates 4.7g 2% DV; fat 15.3g 24% DV; cholesterol 56.1mg 19% DV; sodium 185.9mg 7% DV.

Instant Pot Loaded Baked Potato Soup

Prep: 10 mins Cook: 30 mins Additional: 20 mins Total: 1 hr

Servings: 6

Ingredients
- 1 yellow onion, diced
- 4 thick slices cherrywood-smoked bacon, cut into 1-inch pieces
- 1 tablespoon butter
- 2 ½ pounds Yukon Gold potatoes, peeled and chopped
- 1 cup water
- 1 ½ teaspoons garlic base (such as Better Than Bouillon Roasted Garlic Base)
- 1 ½ cups half-and-half
- ½ cup shredded Cheddar cheese
- ¼ cup sliced green onions
- 1 pinch ground black pepper to taste

Directions
- **Step 1**

Turn on a multi-functional pressure cooker (such as Instant Pot) and select Saute function. Add onion, bacon, and butter to the hot pot and saute until bacon is crispy, 5 to 8 minutes. Turn off Saute function and transfer contents to a small bowl.
- **Step 2**

Add potatoes, water, and garlic base to pot and close and lock the lid. Select high pressure according to manufacturer's instructions; set timer for 12 minutes. Allow 10 to 15 minutes for pressure to build.
- **Step 3**

Release pressure using the natural-release method according to manufacturer's instructions, about 15 minutes. Release remaining pressure carefully using the quick-release method, about 5 minutes. Unlock and remove the lid. Mash potatoes against the side of the pot, leaving some chunks if desired. Add onion-bacon mixture and half-and-half; stir to combine.
- **Step 4**

Ladle into soup bowls and top with green onions, Cheddar cheese, and black pepper.

Nutrition Facts
Per Serving:
341.6 calories; protein 11.6g 23% DV; carbohydrates 39.6g 13% DV; fat 15.9g 24% DV; cholesterol 46.5mg 16% DV; sodium 446.1mg 18% DV

Instant Pot Yankee Pot Roast

Prep: 20 mins Cook: 1 hr 20 mins Additional: 10 mins Total: 1 hr 50 mins

Servings: 14

Ingredients

- 1 (3 1/2) pound boneless beef chuck roast
- ¼ cup all-purpose flour
- 1 tablespoon kosher salt
- 1 ½ teaspoons freshly ground black pepper
- 3 tablespoons olive oil
- 1 large yellow onion, diced
- 3 cloves garlic, minced
- 1 ½ teaspoons minced fresh rosemary
- 1 cup beef stock, divided
- ¾ cup Merlot wine
- 2 tablespoons tomato paste
- 1 bay leaf
- aluminum foil
- 2 cups baby carrots
- 2 cups frozen pearl onions
- 3 stalks celery, cut into 2-inch pieces
- 3 sprigs fresh rosemary sprigs, for garnish

Directions
- **Step 1**

Pat chuck roast dry with a paper towel. Stir together flour, salt, and pepper in a small bowl. Sprinkle flour mixture all over the roast, pressing lightly to ensure it sticks to the meat.
- **Step 2**

Turn on a multi-functional pressure cooker (such as Instant Pot) and select Saute function. Add oil. Add roast to the hot oil and cook, without turning, until browned, about 3 minutes. Turn roast to brown each side, about 3 minutes per side. Transfer roast to a plate.
- **Step 3**

Add onion, garlic, and minced rosemary to the pot; cook, stirring often, until onion is translucent, about 6 minutes. Add beef stock, wine, and tomato paste and simmer while scraping the browned bits of food off the bottom of the pan with a wooden spoon. Return roast to the pot along with bay leaf.
- **Step 4**

Close and lock the lid, select Meat/Stew function, and set timer for 40 minutes.
- **Step 5**

Release pressure carefully using the quick-release method according to manufacturer's instructions, about 5 minutes. Unlock and remove the lid. Transfer roast to a plate and tent with aluminum foil for 15 minutes.

- **Step 6**

Add carrots, pearl onions, and celery to the pot. Close and lock the lid. Select high pressure according to manufacturer's instructions; set timer for 4 minutes. Allow 5 to 10 minutes for pressure to build.

- **Step 7**

Release pressure carefully using the quick-release method according to manufacturer's instructions, about 5 minutes. Unlock and remove the lid.

- **Step 8**

Slice roast against the grain, or use 2 forks to pull meat into chunks. Transfer roast, vegetables, and sauce to a serving platter. Discard bay leaf and garnish with rosemary sprigs
.

Nutrition Facts
Per Serving:
251.7 calories; protein 14.5g 29% DV; carbohydrates 10.1g 3% DV; fat 15.8g 24% DV; cholesterol 51.6mg 17% DV; sodium 496mg 20% DV.

Instant Pot Pinto Beans (No Soaking)

Prep: 15 mins Cook: 1 hr Additional: 10 mins Total: 1 hr 25 mins

Servings: 8

Ingredients

- 3 slices bacon
- 4 cups chicken broth
- 1 pound dried pinto beans, rinsed
- 1 ½ cups water
- ½ cup chopped onions, or to taste
- 2 peppers green chile peppers
- 1 ¼ teaspoons garlic powder
- 1 ¼ teaspoons kosher salt
- 1 teaspoon chili powder
- ½ teaspoon ground cumin
- ½ teaspoon paprika

Directions
- **Step 1**

Turn on a multi-functional pressure cooker (such as Instant Pot) and select Saute function. Add bacon and cook, 4 to 6 minutes, turning once. Add chicken broth, pinto beans, water, onions, chile peppers, garlic powder, salt, chili powder, cumin, and paprika. Close and lock the lid.
- **Step 2**

Select high pressure according to manufacturer's instructions; set timer for 45 minutes. Allow 10 to 15 minutes for pressure to build.

- **Step 3**

Release pressure using the natural-release method according to manufacturer's instructions, 10 to 40 minutes. Unlock and remove the lid. Remove bacon and chile peppers. Mash beans with a potato masher until they reach desired consistency.

Nutrition Facts
Per Serving:
236.2 calories; protein 14.5g 29% DV; carbohydrates 38.8g 13% DV; fat 2.6g 4% DV; cholesterol 6.7mg 2% DV; sodium 972.8mg 39% DV.

Instant Pot Vegan Cabbage Detox Soup

Prep: 15 mins Cook: 25 mins Additional: 10 mins Total: 50 mins

Servings: 6

Ingredients

- 3 cups coarsely chopped green cabbage
- 2 ½ cups vegetable broth
- 1 (14.5 ounce) can diced tomatoes
- 3 carrot, (7-1/2")s carrots, chopped
- 3 stalks celery, chopped
- 1 onion, chopped
- 2 cloves garlic
- 2 tablespoons apple cider vinegar
- 1 tablespoon lemon juice
- 2 teaspoons dried sage

Directions
- **Step 1**

Combine cabbage, vegetable broth, diced tomatoes, carrots, celery, onion, garlic, apple cider vinegar, lemon juice, and sage in a multi-functional pressure cooker (such as Instant Pot). Close and lock the lid. Select high pressure according to manufacturer's instructions; set timer for 15 minutes. Allow 10 to 15 minutes for pressure to build.
- **Step 2**

Release pressure using the natural-release method according to manufacturer's instructions, 10 to 40 minutes. Unlock and remove lid.

Nutrition Facts
Per Serving:
66.8 calories; protein 2.3g 5% DV; carbohydrates 13.4g 4% DV; fat 0.4g 1% DV; cholesterolmg; sodium 348mg 14% DV

Instant Pot Mexican Rice

Prep: 10 mins Cook: 20 mins Additional: 5 mins Total: 35 mins

Servings: 4

Ingredients

- 1 tablespoon avocado oil, or more as needed
- ½ medium onion, finely chopped
- 2 large cloves garlic, minced
- 1 cup long-grain rice
- 1 ½ cups low-sodium chicken stock
- ½ cup tomato sauce
- 1 teaspoon salt
- ¼ teaspoon ground cumin
- 1 pinch cayenne pepper

Directions
- **Step 1**

Turn on a multi-functional pressure cooker (such as Instant Pot); select Saute function and adjust to medium. Cover the bottom of the pot with avocado oil. Cook and stir onion until soft, 4 to 5 minutes. Add garlic and cook until fragrant, about 30 seconds.
• **Step 2**
Add rice to the pot and mix until coated with oil and lightly browned. Pour in chicken stock; stir any browned bits off the bottom of the pot. Mix in tomato sauce, salt, cumin, and cayenne pepper. Close and lock the lid. Seal the vent and select high pressure function. Set timer for 7 minutes; allow 10 to 15 minutes for pressure to build.
• **Step 3**
Release pressure carefully using the quick-release method according to manufacturer's instructions, about 5 minutes. Unlock and remove the lid. Stir rice before serving.

Nutrition Facts
Per Serving:
224.6 calories; protein 5.2g 11% DV; carbohydrates 41.1g 13% DV; fat 4.1g 6% DV; cholesterol 1.5mg 1% DV; sodium 787.7mg 32% DV

Instant Pot Best Beef Stew

Prep: 20 mins Cook: 55 mins Additional: 10 mins Total: 1 hr 25 mins

Servings: 4

Ingredient
- 1 tablespoon butter
- 1 pound beef chuck, cut into 1-inch cubes
- 4 medium (blank)s Yukon Gold potatoes, cubed
- 1 ½ cups mushrooms, halved
- 1 onion, cut into 6 wedges
- 2 eaches carrots, cut into 1/2-inch thick slices
- 2 cloves garlic, minced
- 3 cups beef broth
- 1 tablespoon Worcestershire sauce
- 1 tablespoon tomato paste
- 1 teaspoon salt
- ½ teaspoon ground black pepper
- ½ teaspoon dried rosemary

Directions
• **Step 1**
Turn on a multi-functional pressure cooker (such as Instant Pot) and select Saute function. Melt butter and cook beef chuck cubes in batches until browned on all sides, about 5 minutes per batch.
• **Step 2**
Return all beef chuck to the pot. Add potatoes, mushrooms, onion, carrots, and garlic; cover with beef broth. Stir in Worcestershire sauce, tomato paste, salt, pepper, and rosemary. Close and lock the lid. Select Meat/Stew function according to manufacturer's instructions; set timer for 35 minutes. Allow 10 to 15 minutes for pressure to build.
• **Step 3**
Release pressure using the natural-release method according to manufacturer's instructions, 10 to 40 minutes. Unlock and remove the lid.

Nutrition Facts

Per Serving:
351.7 calories; protein 20g 40% DV; carbohydrates 32.2g 10% DV; fat 16.4g 25% DV; cholesterol 59.1mg 20% DV; sodium 1320.5mg 53% DV.

Instant Pot Honey-Garlic Chicken

Prep :10 mins Cook: 25 mins Total: 35 mins

Servings: 8
Ingredients

- ⅓ cup honey
- ⅓ cup soy sauce
- 3 cloves garlic, minced
- 3 tablespoons ketchup
- 2 tablespoons sriracha sauce
- 2 pounds chicken breast, cut into 1-inch cubes
- ¼ cup cornstarch
- 2 tablespoons vegetable oil
- ¼ cup chicken broth
- 2 medium (4-1/8" long)s green onions, chopped
- 1 teaspoon sesame seeds, or as desired

Directions
- **Step 1**

Combine honey, soy sauce, garlic, ketchup, and sriracha sauce in a bowl; mix well and set aside.
- **Step 2**

Place chicken pieces in a large bowl, add cornstarch, and toss to combine.
- **Step 3**

Turn on a multi-functional pressure cooker (such as Instant Pot) and select the Saute function. Add oil until hot. Add 1/2 the chicken and cook for 3 minutes. Flip and cook 2 more minutes. Transfer chicken to a plate and repeat with remaining chicken. Pour chicken broth into the empty Instant Pot and cook for 2 minutes, scraping up the brown bits with a wooden spoon to deglaze the pot. Turn Instant Pot off. Return chicken to the pot and pour honey mixture on top. Stir to coat with sauce.
- **Step 4**

Close and lock the lid. Select high pressure according to manufacturer's instructions; set timer for 2 minutes. Allow 10 minutes for pressure to build.
- **Step 5**

Release pressure carefully using the quick-release method according to manufacturer's instructions, about 5 minutes. Unlock and remove the lid. Serve chicken sprinkled with green onions and sesame seeds.

Nutrition Facts
Per Serving:
304.5 calories; protein 19.9g 40% DV; carbohydrates 25.5g 8% DV; fat 13.7g 21% DV; cholesterol 64.8mg 22% DV; sodium 1069.8mg 43% DV.

Instant Pot Corned Beef

Prep: 5 mins Cook: 1 hr 40 mins Additional: 20 mins Total: 2 hrs 5 mins

Servings: 4

Ingredients
- 2 cups water
- 1 (12 fluid ounce) can or bottle beer
- 4 cloves garlic, minced
- 1 (3 pound) corned beef brisket with spice packet

Directions
- **Step 1**

Combine water, beer, and garlic in a multi-functional pressure cooker (such as Instant Pot). Place trivet inside. Place brisket on the trivet and sprinkle spice packet on top. Close and lock the lid. Select high pressure according to manufacturer's instructions; set timer for 90 minutes. Allow 10 to 15 minutes for pressure to build.
- **Step 2**

Release pressure carefully using the quick-release method according to manufacturer's instructions, about 5 minutes. Unlock and remove the lid. Transfer brisket to a baking sheet, cover with aluminum foil, and let rest for 15 minutes.

Nutrition Facts
Per Serving:
416.7 calories; protein 27.7g 55% DV; carbohydrates 4.9g 2% DV; fat 28.3g 44% DV; cholesterol 146mg 49% DV; sodium 1697.3mg 68% DV.

Instant Pot Ground Beef Stroganoff

Prep: 10 mins Cook: 20 mins Additional: 10 mins Total: 40 mins

Servings: 8

Ingredients

- 1 pound ground beef
- 16 ounces chopped fresh mushrooms
- 2 eaches onions, minced
- 4 cloves garlic, minced
- 4 cups water
- 2 (10.75 ounce) cans condensed cream of mushroom soup
- 1 (16 ounce) package egg noodles
- 2 tablespoons Worcestershire sauce
- 1 (1 ounce) package dry onion soup mix
- 1 cup sour cream

Directions
- **Step 1**

Turn on a multi-functional pressure cooker (such as Instant Pot) and select Saute function. Add ground beef, mushrooms, onions, and garlic. Cook and stir until beef is browned and crumbly and onions are soft, 5 to 7 minutes. Add water, soup, noodles, Worcestershire, and dry soup mix. Close and lock the lid.
- **Step 2**

Select high pressure according to manufacturer's instructions; set timer for 3 minutes. Allow 10 to 15 minutes for pressure to build.
- **Step 3**

Release pressure using the natural-release method according to manufacturer's instructions, 10 to 40 minutes. Unlock and remove the lid. Stir in sour cream.

Cook's Notes:
You can use ground turkey instead of beef, if preferred.

Nutrition Facts
Per Serving:
493.8 calories; protein 22.3g 45% DV; carbohydrates 56.9g 18% DV; fat 20.2g 31% DV; cholesterol 95.2mg 32% DV; sodium 911.2mg 36% DV

Instant Pot Mushroom Risotto

Prep: 15 mins Cook: 30 mins Additional: 5 mins Total: 50 mins

Servings: 4

Ingredients

- ¼ cup unsalted butter
- ¼ cup olive oil
- 3 cups diced mushrooms
- 1 cup chopped onion
- 1 sprig rosemary
- 1 ½ cups Arborio rice
- ¾ cup white wine
- 1 quart chicken stock
- 1 pinch salt and ground black pepper to taste
  ½ cup grated Parmesan cheese

Directions
- **Step 1**

Select the Saute function on an electric pressure cooker (such as Instant Pot). Add butter and olive oil; stir until butter melts, about 2 minutes. Add mushrooms; cook, stirring occasionally, until slightly softened, about 3 minutes. Stir in onion; cook for 2 minutes. Add rosemary sprig; cook for 1 minute.
- **Step 2**

Stir rice into the pot until each grain is coated with butter-olive oil mixture, about 2 minutes. Pour in wine; simmer for 3 minutes. Pour in chicken stock, stirring to scrape the sides of the pot. Simmer for 1 minute.
- **Step 3**

Close and lock the lid. Turn the venting knob to sealing. Select high pressure according to manufacturer's instructions; set timer for 6 minutes. Allow 10 to 15 minutes for pressure to build.
- **Step 4**

Tap venting knob a few times with a wooden spoon or spatula. Stand back; turn knob to point at Vent. Remove lid when pressure is released, about 5 minutes.
- **Step 5**

Stir risotto until creamy, about 1 minute. Discard rosemary sprig. Season with salt and pepper. Stir in Parmesan cheese until melted and combined.

Cook's Notes:

Substitute vegetable stock for the chicken stock if preferred.
The Instant Pot(R) will take about 15 minutes to come to full pressure, then the timer wil
begin counting down, so you can walk away and come back when it beeps.
The magazine version of this recipe uses 1 quart low-sodium vegetable broth and 3/4 cup
Parmesan cheese.

Nutrition Facts
Per Serving:
644.9 calories; protein 12.4g 25% DV; carbohydrates 76.6g 25% DV; fat 28.7g 44% DV;
cholesterol 40mg 13% DV; sodium 881.4mg 35% DV.

Instant Pot Salisbury Steak with Onion and Mushroom Gravy

Prep: 10 mins Cook: 45 mins Additional: 1 hr 40 mins Total: 2 hrs 35 mins

Servings:4

Ingredients

- ¼ cup fresh bread crumbs
- ¼ cup finely diced onion
- 1 egg
- 1 teaspoon dried parsley
- 1 teaspoon Worcestershire sauce
- 1 clove garlic, minced, or more to taste
- 1 pound ground beef
- ½ pound lean ground pork
- 2 tablespoons avocado oil
- 1 large onion, thinly sliced
- 1 (8 ounce) package sliced cremini mushrooms
- ¼ cup dry red wine
- 2 cups beef broth
- 1 tablespoon tomato paste
- 1 teaspoon salt
- ½ teaspoon ground black pepper
- 4 tablespoons beef broth
- 2 tablespoons cornstarch

Directions
- **Step 1**

Combine bread crumbs, onion, egg, parsley, Worcestershire sauce, and garlic in a large
bowl. Stir well and add beef and pork. Mix gently and form 8 equal portions. Place
patties on a plate, cover with plastic wrap, and refrigerate 1 hour. Remove from the
refrigerator 30 minutes before cooking.
- **Step 2**

Turn on a multi-functional pressure cooker (such as Instant Pot) and select Saute
function. Add oil. Add patties in batches to avoid overcrowding the pot. Saute 2 minutes
per side. Transfer cooked patties to a plate. Add onions to the pot and cook until brown,
about 2 minutes. Add mushrooms and cook 2 minutes more.
- **Step 3**

Pour wine into the pot and stir, scraping up all the brown bits from the bottom. Add
broth, tomato paste, salt, and pepper; stir well. Return cooked patties and any
accumulated liquid to the pot and turn to coat.
- **Step 4**

Close and lock the lid. Select high pressure according to manufacturer's instructions; set timer for 15 minutes. Allow 10 to 15 minutes for pressure to build.
- **Step 5**

Release pressure using the natural-release method according to manufacturer's instructions, 10 to 40 minutes. Unlock and remove the lid.
- **Step 6**

Combine 4 tablespoons broth and cornstarch in a bowl and stir until dissolved. Add mixture to the pot slowly, stirring constantly. Select Saute function; cook until thickened, about 5 minutes.

Cook's Notes:
Refrigerating the patties before cooking them is optional, but it does help the flavor. The gravy will be fairly thin. Add an additional 1 tablespoon corn starch and 2 tablespoons broth for a thicker gravy

Nutrition Facts
Per Serving:
523.8 calories; protein 35.4g 71% DV; carbohydrates 13.4g 4% DV; fat 34.5g 53% DV; cholesterol 152.8mg 51% DV; sodium 1227.1mg 49% DV.

Instant Pot Chicken and Gravy

Prep: 15 mins Cook: 25 mins Additional: 15 mins Total: 55 mins

Servings: 2

Ingredients
- ¾ teaspoon salt
- ¾ teaspoon paprika
- ½ teaspoon thyme
- ¼ teaspoon ground black pepper
- ¼ teaspoon garlic powder
- ⅛ teaspoon sage
- 2 (10 ounce) boneless, skinless chicken breasts
- 1 tablespoon olive oil
- 1 cup chicken stock
- aluminum foil
- 2 tablespoons cold water
- 2 tablespoons cornstarch
- 1 pinch salt and ground black pepper to taste

Directions

- **Step 1**

Combine salt, paprika, thyme, pepper, garlic powder, and sage in a small bowl.
- **Step 2**

Pound thicker end of chicken breasts to about 1-inch thickness. Sprinkle with seasonings and rub on both sides.
- **Step 3**

Turn on a multi-functional pressure cooker (such as Instant Pot) and select Saute function and high heat. Heat olive oil and cook chicken breasts until browned, 2 to 3 minutes per side. Transfer chicken to a plate. Add chicken stock to the pot, scraping up any browned bits off the bottom. Turn off the pot. Place a trivet inside the pot and lay chicken breasts

on top. Close and lock the lid. Select high pressure according to manufacturer's instructions; set timer for 5 minutes. Allow 10 to 15 minutes for pressure to build.
* **Step 4**

Release pressure using the natural-release method according to manufacturer's instructions, for 10 minutes. Switch to the quick-release method according to manufacturer's instructions to release remaining pressure, about 5 minutes. Unlock and remove the lid. Remove chicken to a clean plate and cover with foil to keep warm.
* **Step 5**

Combine water and cornstarch in a small bowl and stir to dissolve. Switch pot to Saute function and medium heat. Slowly whisk in enough of the cornstarch mixture to thicken the gravy to your desired consistency. Season with salt and pepper. Remove from heat and serve gravy over chicken breasts.

Cook's Notes:
For smaller breasts, naturally-release pressure for 8 minutes instead of 10.

Nutrition Facts
Per Serving:
418.3 calories; protein 59.8g 120% DV; carbohydrates 9.1g 3% DV; fat 14g 22% DV; cholesterol 164.5mg 55% DV; sodium 1674mg 67% DV.

Instant Pot Salsa Chicken

Prep: 5 mins Cook: 15 mins Additional: 20 mins Total: 40 mins

Servings: 2
Ingredients

* 1 pound frozen skinless, boneless chicken breast halves
* 1 (1 ounce) packet taco seasoning mix
* ½ cup salsa
* ½ cup low-sodium chicken broth

Directions
* **Step 1**

Place chicken breasts in an electric pressure cooker (such as Instant Pot). Sprinkle all sides with taco seasoning. Pour salsa and chicken broth on top.
* **Step 2**

Place lid on the pot and lock in place. Select the Poultry setting and set the timer for 15 minutes. Allow pressure to release naturally after the cooking time has ended, about 20 minutes. An instant-read thermometer inserted into the center of the chicken should read at least 165 degrees F (74 degrees C). Shred the cooked chicken.
Cook's Notes:
You can use water in place of chicken broth if desired.
If you thaw the chicken breasts, shorten the cooking time to 8 to 10 minutes.
Both quick-release and natural-release work for this recipe.

Nutrition Facts
Per Serving:

300.1 calories; protein 45.9g 92% DV; carbohydrates 13.9g 5% DV; fat 4.8g 7% DV; cholesterol 118mg 39% DV; sodium 1545.5mg 62% DV.

Instant Pot Lasagna

Prep: 15 mins Cook: 35 mins Additional: 10 mins Total: 1 hr

Servings: 4

Ingredients
- 2 teaspoons olive oil
- 1 pound ground beef
- 1 teaspoon salt
- 1 (6 ounce) package no-boil lasagna noodles, broken into large pieces
- 1 ½ cups marinara sauce, or to taste
- 2 cups fresh spinach
- 1 (8 ounce) package shredded mozzarella cheese
- 1 (8 ounce) package soft goat cheese

Directions
- **Step 1**

Turn on a multi-cooker (such as Instant Pot) and the select Saute function. Heat olive oil; add ground beef and salt. Cook, breaking it into clumps with a spatula, until thoroughly browned, about 6 minutes. Transfer beef to a bowl. Wash the pot and return it to the machine.

- **Step 2**

Pour 1 1/2 cup water into the pot. Set the metal trivet inside.
- **Step 3**

Arrange lasagna pieces over the bottom of a 6-inch springform pan. Ladle 1/3 the tomato sauce on top; add 1/3 of the cooked beef and 1/3 of the fresh spinach. Dollop 1/2 the mozzarella cheese on top. Repeat layers using 1/2 the goat cheese. Repeat once more, finishing with remaining mozzarella and goat cheese on top.
- **Step 4**

Tent the top of the lasagna loosely with aluminum foil. Lower it gently onto the trivet. Close and lock the lid. Select high pressure according to manufacturer's instructions; set timer for 20 minutes. Allow 10 to 15 minutes for pressure to build. Release pressure using the natural-release method according to manufacturer's instructions, 10 to 40 minutes. Unlock and remove lid.
- **Step 5**

Set oven rack about 6 inches from the heat source and preheat the oven's broiler.
- **Step 6**

Transfer the springform pan carefully to a baking sheet. Broil until cheese on top is lightly browned and bubbling, about 5 minutes.

Cook's Notes:
You can use regular lasagna noodles instead of the no-boil type if desired.

Nutrition Facts
Per Serving:
755.9 calories; protein 50.9g 102% DV; carbohydrates 46.1g 15% DV; fat 40.5g 62% DV; cholesterol 134.7mg 45% DV; sodium 1600.4mg 64% DV.

Instant Pot Coconut Curry Chicken

Prep: 15 mins Cook: 35 mins Additional: 15 mins Total: 1 hr 5 mins

Servings: 4

Ingredients
- 1 tablespoon coconut oil
- 1 medium onion, chopped
- 3 tablespoons curry powder, or to taste, divided
- 2 cloves garlic, chopped
- 1 (14.5 ounce) can diced tomatoes, drained
- 1 (8 ounce) can tomato sauce
- ½ cup chicken broth
- 2 tablespoons white sugar
- 2 pounds chicken breasts
- 1 pinch salt to taste
- 1 pinch ground black pepper to taste
- 1 (14 ounce) can coconut milk

Directions
- **Step 1**

Turn on a multi-functional pressure cooker (such as Instant Pot) and select Saute function. Add coconut oil; when hot, add onion and cook for 1 minute. Add 2 tablespoons curry powder and garlic. Mix well and cook for 2 minutes. Turn off Saute function. Stir in diced tomatoes, tomato sauce, chicken broth, and sugar.
- **Step 2**

Poke holes into each chicken breast using a fork. Sprinkle with salt, pepper, and remaining curry powder. Add seasoned chicken to the pot. Close and lock the lid. Select high pressure according to manufacturer's instructions; set timer for 10 minutes. Allow 10 to 15 minutes for pressure to build.
- **Step 3**

Release pressure using the natural-release method according to manufacturer's instructions for 10 minutes. Release remaining pressure carefully using the quick-release method according to manufacturer's instructions, about 5 minutes. Unlock and remove the lid.
- **Step 4**

Remove chicken; use 2 forks to shred the meat and return it to the pot. Turn on Saute function; cook and stir until liquid is lightly boiling, 2 to 3 minutes.
- **Step 5**

Turn pressure cooker to Keep Warm. Add coconut milk and stir well; cook for 10 minutes more to allow flavors to come together.

Nutrition Facts
Per Serving:
563.3 calories; protein 51.9g 104% DV; carbohydrates 21.5g 7% DV; fat 30.6g 47% DV; cholesterol 130mg 43% DV; sodium 766.2mg 31% DV.

Instant Pot Pork Chops and Gravy

Prep: 5 mins Cook: 55 mins Additional: 10 mins Total: 1 hr 10 mins

Servings: 5
Ingredients

- 1 tablespoon avocado oil, or more as needed
- 5 eaches bone-in pork chops, trimmed of fat
- ¼ teaspoon ground black pepper
- 1 large clove garlic, finely chopped
- ¼ cup dry white wine
- 1 (10.75 ounce) can condensed cream of mushroom soup
- 1 ¼ cups water
- ¼ cup water
- 2 tablespoons all-purpose flour
- 1 teaspoon low-sodium soy sauce (such as Bragg)

Directions
- **Step 1**

Heat oil in the pot of an electric pressure cooker (such as Instant Pot) set on the Saute function.
- **Step 2**

Season pork chops with black pepper. Cook 2 to 3 chops in the hot oil, flipping halfway, until browned, 7 to 8 minutes. Move to a plate; sear the remaining chops and place on a plate.
- **Step 3**

Add garlic to the pot and cook until just fragrant, about 30 seconds. Deglaze the bottom of the pot with wine, scraping up any browned bits. Simmer until sauce is reduced by half, 5 to 7 minutes.
- **Step 4**

Stir mushroom soup and 1 1/4 cup water into the pot with the sauce. Simmer until smooth, about 3 minutes. Add the seared pork chops and turn to coat. Close and lock the lid. Select high pressure according to manufacturer's instructions; set timer for 18 minutes. Allow 10 to 15 minutes for pressure to build.
- **Step 5**

Release pressure using the natural-release method according to manufacturer's instructions, about 10 minutes. Remove chops from the pot.
- **Step 6**

Mix 1/4 cup water and flour together; add slurry to the pot. Select Saute function and cook until gravy is thickened, about 3 minutes. Add soy sauce and stir well. Return chops to the pot and turn to coat.

Cook's Notes:
Substitute thick boneless pork chops for the bone-in chops, if desired.
The gravy will not be thick; use more slurry if that's the consistency that you're looking for

Nutrition Facts
Per Serving:
284.3 calories; protein 26.9g 54% DV; carbohydrates 7.3g 2% DV; fat 14.7g 23% DV; cholesterol 65.2mg 22% DV; sodium 488.2mg 20% DV.

Instant Pot Meatloaf

Prep: 20 mins Cook: 40 mins Additional: 5 mins Total: 1 hr 5 mins

Servings: 8

Ingredients
- 2 pounds ground beef
- 1 cup dry bread crumbs
- ½ cup diced onion
- ½ apple - peeled, cored, and diced
- 2 teaspoons garlic powder
- ½ teaspoon salt
- ½ teaspoon ground black pepper
- Topping:
- ⅓ cup ketchup
- 2 tablespoons prepared yellow mustard
- 2 tablespoons brown sugar

Directions
- **Step 1**

Combine beef, bread crumbs, onion, apple, garlic powder, salt, and pepper in a large bowl until evenly blended.
- **Step 2**

Shape the beef mixture into a loaf and place on a large piece of aluminum foil. Fold the foil up and around the edges of the meatloaf, creating a makeshift loaf pan.
- **Step 3**

Pour 1/2 cup water into a multi-functional pressure cooker (such as Instant Pot) and place the steam rack inside with the handles up. Place the meatloaf on top of the rack. Close and lock the lid; seal the vent. Select high pressure according to manufacturer's instructions; set timer for 25 minutes. Allow 10 to 15 minutes for pressure to build.
- **Step 4**

Set an oven rack about 6 inches from the heat source and preheat the oven's broiler.
- **Step 5**

Release cooker pressure carefully using the quick-release method according to manufacturer's instructions, about 5 minutes. Unlock and remove the lid. Transfer meatloaf, still on the rack, to a baking sheet. Broil meatloaf in the oven until browned, about 5 minutes.
- **Step 6**

Combine ketchup, mustard, and brown sugar in a small bowl. Brush over meatloaf and broil again until caramelized, 1 to 2 minutes.

Nutrition Facts
Per Serving:
294.9 calories; protein 21.5g 43% DV; carbohydrates 18.5g 6% DV; fat 14.6g 23% DV; cholesterol 71mg 24% DV; sodium 466.3mg 19% DV.

Instant Pot Quick and Easy Spaghetti Sauce

Prep: 10 mins Cook: 45 mins Additional: 10 mins Total: 1 hr 5 mins

Servings: 6

Ingredients

- 2 tablespoons olive oil
- 2 eaches yellow onions, chopped
- 2 cloves garlic, minced
- 1 carrot, chopped
- 1 celery stalk, chopped
- 3 pounds plum tomatoes
- 1 teaspoon dried oregano
- 1 teaspoon Italian seasoning
- 1 teaspoon sea salt
- 1 teaspoon dried basil
- ½ teaspoon ground black pepper

Directions
- **Step 1**

Turn on a multi-functional pressure cooker (such as Instant Pot) and select Saute function. Heat olive oil and stir in onions and garlic; cook until soft and translucent, about 5 minutes. Add carrot, celery, and tomatoes; cook until tender, about 4 minutes. Season with oregano, Italian seasoning, salt, basil, and pepper. Close and lock the lid. Select high pressure according to manufacturer's instructions; set timer for 25 minutes. Allow 10 to 15 minutes for pressure to build.
- **Step 2**

Release pressure using the natural-release method according to manufacturer's instructions, 10 to 40 minutes. Unlock and remove the lid. Blend with an immersion blender to desired consistency.

Nutrition Facts
Per Serving:
124.9 calories; protein 3.4g 7% DV; carbohydrates 18.8g 6% DV; fat 5.2g 8% DV; cholesterolmg; sodium 351.5mg 14% DV.

Instant Pot Simple Steamed Crab Legs

Prep: 5 mins Cook: 15 mins Additional: 5 mins Total: 25 mins

Servings: 4

Ingredients

- 1 ½ cups water
- 2 pounds frozen king crab legs
- 2 tablespoons juice of one lemon
- ⅓ cup butter, melted

Directions
- **Step 1**

Place a trivet in the multi-functional pressure cooker (such as Instant Pot) and add water. Place crab legs on top of the trivet; you may need to let them thaw for a few minutes so they will fit.

- **Step 2**

Close and lock the lid. Select high pressure according to manufacturer's instructions; set timer for 3 minutes. Allow 10 minutes for pressure to build.
- **Step 3**

Release pressure carefully using the quick-release method according to manufacturer's instructions, about 5 minutes. Unlock and remove the lid. Using tongs, transfer crab legs to a serving dish. Squeeze lemon juice on top and serve with melted butter.

Nutrition Facts
Per Serving:
199.4 calories; protein 12.7g 26% DV; carbohydrates 1.2g; fat 16g 25% DV; cholesterol 83.4mg 28% DV; sodium 324.3mg 13% DV.

Instant Pot Pot Roast with Potatoes and Carrots

Prep: 15 mins Cook: 1 hr 20 mins Additional: 5 mins Total: 1 hr 40 mins

Servings: 8

Ingredients

- 4 tablespoons olive oil, divided
- 3 pounds beef chuck roast
- 2 cups beef broth
- 1 pound baby potatoes
- 1 ½ cups baby carrots
- 1 medium onion, quartered
- 1 packet dry onion soup mix
- ¼ cup water
- 2 ½ tablespoons cornstarch
- 1 ½ teaspoons garlic salt
- 1 teaspoon Dash freshly ground black pepper

Directions
- **Step 1**

Turn on a multi-functional pressure cooker (such as Instant Pot) and select Saute function. Pour in 2 tablespoons oil. Add roast to hot oil and cook until browned all over, 4 to 5 minutes per side. Add broth.
- **Step 2**

Combine remaining oil, potatoes, carrots, onion, and soup mix in a resealable plastic bag. Seal and shake to coat evenly. Pour mixture into the pressure cooker and spread out evenly.
- **Step 3**

Close and lock the lid. Select high pressure according to manufacturer's instructions; set timer for 60 minutes. Allow 10 to 15 minutes for pressure to build.
- **Step 4**

Release pressure carefully using the quick-release method according to manufacturer's instructions, about 5 minutes. Unlock and remove the lid.
- **Step 5**

Remove roast from pot and place on a serving platter, leaving drippings in the pot.
- **Step 6**

Select Saute function and bring drippings to a boil. Combine water and cornstarch in a bowl and add to drippings. Cook, stirring frequently, until slightly thickened, 2 to 3 minutes. Season gravy with garlic salt and pepper.
- **Step 7**

Slice roast and serve with vegetables and gravy.

Nutrition Facts
Per Serving:
323.2 calories; protein 25.7g 51% DV; carbohydrates 19g 6% DV; fat 15.6g 24% DV; cholesterol 78.8mg 26% DV; sodium 1005.4mg 40% DV.

Instant Pot Pasta with Italian Sausage

Prep: 30 mins Cook: 25 mins Additional: 10 mins Total: 1 hr 5 mins

Servings: 4

Ingredients
- 1 ½ tablespoons olive oil
- 1 cup sliced onion
- 1 cup sliced bell peppers, any color
- 1 (12 ounce) package Italian-style chicken sausage links, or more to taste, casings removed
- 2 cloves garlic, minced
- 1 (26 ounce) jar marinara sauce
- 3 cups water
- 3 cups chopped fresh spinach, or more to taste
- 10 ounces penne pasta
- 1 tablespoon chopped fresh basil
- 1 tablespoon Italian seasoning
- 1 cup shredded Italian cheese blend

Directions
- **Step 1**

Turn on a multi-functional pressure cooker (such as Instant Pot) and select Saute function. Add oil and allow to heat. Add onion and peppers to hot oil; cook until they begin to get tender, 3 to 4 minutes. Add sausages and cook, breaking them up with a wooden spoon, until lightly browned, 4 to 5 minutes. Add garlic and saute for 1 to 2 minutes. Add marinara sauce, water, spinach, pasta, basil, and Italian seasoning; mix to combine. Cancel Saute function.
- **Step 2**

Close and lock the lid. Select high pressure according to manufacturer's instructions; set timer for 5 minutes. Allow 10 to 15 minutes for pressure to build.
- **Step 3**

Release pressure using the natural-release method according to manufacturer's instructions, 5 minutes. Then release pressure carefully using the quick-release method according to manufacturer's instructions, about 5 minutes. Unlock and remove the lid. Stir in 1/2 cup shredded Italian cheese until combined. Serve with remaining cheese sprinkled on top.

Nutrition Facts

Per Serving:
785.7 calories; protein 32.2g 65% DV; carbohydrates 86g 28% DV; fat 35.7g 55% DV; cholesterol 59.2mg 20% DV; sodium 1737.7mg 70% DV.

Instant Pot Haluski with Kielbasa

Prep: 15 mins Cook: 25 mins Additional: 5 mins Total: 45 mins

Servings: 8
Ingredients

- 2 tablespoons butter
- 1 small yellow onion, diced
- 1 medium head cabbage, shredded
- 1 pound kielbasa sausage, sliced

- 2 cups chicken broth
- 1 (12 ounce) bag egg noodles
- 1 pinch salt and ground black pepper to taste

Directions
- **Step 1**

Turn on a multi-functional pressure cooker (such as Instant Pot) and select Saute function. Add butter and onion. Cook and stir until lightly browned, 1 to 2 minutes. Add cabbage and kielbasa; cook and stir until cabbage has wilted down, about 10 minutes. Add chicken broth and egg noodles; mix well.
- **Step 2**

Close and lock the lid. Select High pressure according to manufacturer's instructions; set timer for 3 minutes. Allow 10 to 15 minutes for pressure to build.
- **Step 3**

Release pressure carefully using the quick-release method according to manufacturer's instructions, about 5 minutes. Unlock and remove the lid. Season with salt and pepper. Serve immediately.

Nutrition Facts
Per Serving:
400.5 calories; protein 14.8g 30% DV; carbohydrates 39.6g 13% DV; fat 20.5g 32% DV; cholesterol 82.3mg 27% DV; sodium 873.5mg 35% DV.

Instant Pot Pot Roast

Prep: 20 mins Cook: 1 hr 30 minsAdditional: 15 mins Total: 2 hrs 5 mins

Servings: 12
Ingredients

- 1 teaspoon salt
- 1 teaspoon dried marjoram
- 1 teaspoon dried rosemary
- 1 teaspoon garlic powder
- 1 teaspoon onion powder
- ½ teaspoon ground black pepper
- ½ teaspoon paprika
- 1 tablespoon vegetable oil
- 1 (3 pound) beef chuck roast, or more to taste
- 1 pound baby red potatoes
- 4 large carrots, chopped into large chunks
- 1 large yellow onion, sliced
- 4 cups beef broth
- 2 tablespoons Worcestershire sauce

Directions
- **Step 1**

Turn on a multi-functional pressure cooker (such as Instant Pot) and select Saute function.
- **Step 2**

Combine salt, marjoram, rosemary, garlic powder, onion powder, black pepper, and paprika in a small bowl. Rub mixture all over roast to coat all sides
- **Step 3**

Drizzle oil into the preheated pot. Wait 30 seconds, then place roast into the pot; do not move the meat, allowing it to sear for 3 or 4 minutes. Turn the roast and sear again, 3 to 4 minutes. Repeat until all sides are browned, about 15 minutes total.
- **Step 4**

Add potatoes, carrots, and onion to the pot. Pour in broth and Worcestershire sauce. Close and lock the lid; set vent to sealing. Select high pressure according to manufacturer's instructions; set timer for 60 minutes for a 3-pound roast or 80 minutes for a 5-pound roast. Allow 10 to 15 minutes for pressure to build.
- **Step 5**

Release pressure using the natural-release method according to manufacturer's instructions for 10 minutes. Release remaining pressure carefully using the quick-release method according to manufacturer's instructions, about 5 minutes. Unlock and remove the lid.
- **Step 6**

Transfer roast, potatoes, carrots, and onions to a platter for serving.

Cook's Notes:

If you use baby carrots, set your pressure cooking time to 10 minutes shorter than the recipe states and leave the carrots out of the pot. Once the pressure cooking time is finished, add the baby carrots to the pot and set the pot to pressure cook for 10 more minutes.

Nutrition Facts

Per Serving:
232.9 calories; protein 15.3g 31% DV; carbohydrates 10.6g 3% DV; fat 14.2g 22% DV; cholesterol 51.7mg 17% DV; sodium 536mg 21% DV.

Instant Pot Popcorn

Prep: 5 mins Cook: 10 mins Total: 15 mins

Servings: 4

Ingredients

- 2 tablespoons coconut oil
- ½ cup unpopped popcorn
- 1 pinch salt to taste

Directions
- **Step 1**

Turn on a multi-functional pressure cooker (such as Instant Pot) and select High Saute function. When the display indicates the pot is hot, spoon coconut oil into the pot and let it melt.
- **Step 2**

Add popcorn and stir with a rubber spatula until kernels are coated. Wait 30 seconds and stir again; kernels should be making a sizzling sound at this point. Cover pot with the glass lid on and cook for 5 minutes. Cancel Saute mode and let sit until kernels have completely stopped popping, about 1 minute.
- **Step 3**

Transfer popcorn to a large bowl and sprinkle with salt.

Cook's Notes:

Plan on more unpopped kernels than you would cooking it on the stove due to not being able to shake the Instant Pot(R) around on the heat source like you would a pot on the stove burner. While there is more waste, popcorn is cheap and having no oil splatter is worth it to me.

Nutrition Facts
Per Serving:
151.4 calories; protein 3g 6% DV; carbohydrates 18.5g 6% DV; fat 8g 12% DV; cholesterolmg; sodium 39.5mg 2% DV

Instant Pot Roasted Brussels Sprouts

Prep: 5 mins Cook: 16 mins Additional: 5 mins Total: 26 mins

Servings: 4

Ingredients

- 2 tablespoons olive oil
- 1 onion, chopped
- 1 pound whole Brussels sprouts
- 1 teaspoon salt
- ½ teaspoon ground black pepper
- ½ cup vegetable broth

Directions
- **Step 1**

Turn on a multi-functional pressure cooker (such as Instant Pot) and select Saute function. Heat olive oil and cook onion until translucent, about 2 minutes. Add Brussels sprouts and cook for 1 minute more. Sprinkle with salt and pepper; pour vegetable broth over Brussels sprouts. Close and lock the lid. Select high pressure according to

manufacturer's instructions; set timer for 3 minutes. Allow 10 to 15 minutes for pressure to build.
• **Step 2**
Release pressure carefully using the quick-release method according to manufacturer's instructions, about 5 minutes. Unlock and remove lid.

Nutrition Facts
Per Serving:
135.6 calories; protein 4.6g 9% DV; carbohydrates 16.3g 5% DV; fat 7.2g 11% DV; cholesterolmg; sodium 669.8mg 27% DV.

Instant Pot Red Thai Curry Chicken

Prep: 10 mins Cook: 15 mins Additional: 10 mins Total: 35 mins

Servings: 5

Ingredients

- 1 tablespoon cooking oil
- 2 tablespoons red curry paste, or more to taste
- 1 ½ pounds thin chicken breasts, cut into 1-inch strips
- 1 (14 ounce) can unsweetened light coconut milk
- 1 tablespoon fish sauce, or more to taste
- 1 tablespoon palm sugar
- 1 cup sliced yellow onion
- 1 cup sliced red bell pepper
- 1 cup sliced yellow bell pepper
- 1 cup sliced orange bell pepper

Directions
• **Step 1**
Turn on a multi-functional pressure cooker (such as Instant Pot) and select Saute function. Add oil and red curry paste to the hot pot; saute for 30 seconds. Add chicken and mix well with curry paste. Pour in coconut milk. Close and lock the lid. Select high pressure according to manufacturer's instructions; set timer for 2 minutes. Allow 10 to 15 minutes for pressure to build.
• **Step 2**
Release pressure using the natural-release method according to manufacturer's instructions, 10 to 40 minutes.
• **Step 3**
Unlock and remove the lid. Stir in fish sauce and palm sugar. Stir in onion and bell peppers until well combined. Select Saute function. Bring curry to a gentle boil and simmer for only 2 to 3 minutes to keep vegetables crunchy.

Cook's Notes:
If you prefer a thicker curry, add only half a can of coconut milk.
If you are using thicker chicken breasts, increase cook time to 4 minutes.
Add more red curry paste for a spicier curry.

Nutrition Facts
Per Serving:

382.5 calories; protein 24.5g 49% DV; carbohydrates 20.4g 7% DV; fat 22g 34% DV; cholesterol 77.5mg 26% DV; sodium 597mg 24% DV.

Instant Pot Bacon-Ranch Chicken Thighs

Prep: 5 mins Cook: 40 mins Additional: 5 mins Total: 50 mins

Servings: 6

Ingredients

- 4 slices bacon, cut into 1-inch pieces
- 1 ½ pounds boneless, skinless chicken thighs
- 1 pinch salt and freshly ground black pepper to taste
- 1 cup chicken broth
- 1 (8 ounce) package cream cheese, cut into pieces
- 1 tablespoon dry ranch dressing mix
- 2 cups frozen chopped spinach, thawed and drained

Directions
- **Step 1**

Turn on a multi-functional pressure cooker (such as Instant Pot) and select Saute function. Add bacon once pot is hot and cook to desired crispiness, about 5 minutes. Remove bacon and drain on paper towel lined plate. Add chicken thighs to pot and season with salt and pepper. Cook in bacon grease until each side is browned, about 2 minutes per side. Remove from pot and set aside.
- **Step 2**

Pour in chicken broth and deglaze pot, scraping up all the browned bits. Stir in cream cheese and dry ranch dressing mix; cook until cream cheese has melted, about 3 minutes. Cancel Saute mode.
- **Step 3**

Return bacon to pot and stir to combine. Add chicken thighs and turn until they are covered with cream cheese sauce. Close and lock the lid. Select high pressure according to manufacturer's instructions; set timer for 12 minutes. Allow 10 to 15 minutes for pressure to build.
- **Step 4**

Release pressure carefully using the quick-release method according to manufacturer's instructions, about 5 minutes. Unlock and remove the lid. Remove chicken and keep warm.
- **Step 5**

Select Saute function. Add drained spinach to pot and cook until warmed. Return chicken and turn until well covered with sauce and cook for 1 minute until warmed through.
Nutrition Facts

Per Serving:
358.5 calories; protein 24.3g 49% DV; carbohydrates 4g 1% DV; fat 27.3g 42% DV; cholesterol 112.5mg 38% DV; sodium 632.1mg 25% DV.

Instant Pot Beef-Stuffed Peppers

Prep: 15 mins Cook: 35 mins Additional: 5 mins Total: 55 mins

Servings: 4

Ingredients

- 1 tablespoon olive oil
- 1 pound lean ground beef
- 1 medium onion, diced
- 1 ½ cups water
- 1 (6 ounce) can tomato paste
- 1 (1.25 ounce) package taco seasoning mix
- 4 medium (blank)s green bell peppers, tops and seeds removed

Directions
- **Step 1**

Add olive oil to the inner liner of a multi-functional electric pressure cooker (such as Instant Pot) and select Saute function. Add beef and onion to the hot oil and cook until beef is browned and no longer pink, about 5 minutes. Remove from pot and drain.
- **Step 2**

Return beef and onion to the pot, still on Saute mode. Stir in water, tomato paste, and taco seasoning. Bring mixture to a simmer and cook until thickened, 8 to 10 minutes. Fill bell peppers with the mixture.
- **Step 3**

Pour 1 cup of water into the inner liner; set trivet inside and place stuffed bell peppers on top. Close and lock the lid. Select high pressure according to manufacturer's instructions; set timer for 8 minutes. Allow 10 to 15 minutes for pressure to build.
- **Step 5**

Release pressure carefully using the quick-release method according to manufacturer's instructions, about 5 minutes. Unlock and remove the lid.

Cook's Notes:
Use any color bell peppers you prefer.

Nutrition Facts
Per Serving:
353.7 calories; protein 22.9g 46% DV; carbohydrates 22.1g 7% DV; fat 19.3g 30% DV; cholesterol 68.5mg 23% DV; sodium 1052.7mg 42% DV.

Instant Pot Charro (Refried Beans)

Prep: 20 mins Cook: 55 mins Additional: 10 mins Total: 1 hr 25 mins

Servings: 8

Ingredients

- 4 cups water
- 2 cups dry pinto beans, rinsed
- 1 large onion, chopped
- ½ cup salsa
- ½ cup roughly chopped cilantro, or to taste
- 1 jalapeno pepper, minced
- 4 cloves garlic, minced

- 2 teaspoons tomato-flavored bouillon
- 2 teaspoons vegetable bouillon
- ½ teaspoon chili powder
- ½ teaspoon ground paprika
- ½ teaspoon ground cumin
- ½ teaspoon ground black pepper

Directions
- **Step 1**

Combine water, pinto beans, onion, salsa, cilantro, jalapeno pepper, garlic, tomato bouillon, vegetable bouillon, chili powder, paprika, cumin, and black pepper in an electric pressure cooker (such as Instant Pot). Close and lock the lid. Select Bean/Chili function; set timer for 45 minutes. Cooker will reach high pressure in 10 to 15 minutes.
- **Step 2**

Release pressure using the natural-release method according to manufacturer's instructions, 10 to 40 minutes. Unlock and remove lid.

Cook's Notes:
Substitute chicken bouillon for the tomato bouillon if desired.

Nutrition Facts
Per Serving:
184.1 calories; protein 11g 22% DV; carbohydrates 33.9g 11% DV; fat 0.7g 1% DV; cholesterolmg; sodium 113.5mg 5% DV.

Instant Pot Coconut Cream Chicken Noodle Soup

Prep: 20 mins Cook: 25 mins Total: 45 mins

Servings: 4

Ingredients

- 1 tablespoon canola oil
- 1 yellow onion, chopped
- 2 cloves garlic, chopped
- 4 large carrots, peeled and chopped
- 2 cups chopped spinach
- 2 eaches chicken breasts

- 2 cups elbow macaroni
- 28 fluid ounces chicken stock
- 1 (14 ounce) can coconut cream
- 1 tablespoon sriracha hot sauce
- 1 tablespoon paprika
- 1 pinch salt to taste

Directions
- **Step 1**

Pour oil into the pot and add onion and garlic; turn to the "Saute" setting. Cook, stirring occasionally, until onion is tender, about 10 minutes.
* **Step 2**

Mix carrots and spinach into onion mixture; stir well. Lay chicken on top; add macaroni. Pour chicken stock and coconut cream over macaroni; add sriracha sauce, paprika, and salt.
* **Step 3**

Close lid and cook using the "Manual" setting on high until chicken is no longer pink in the center, about 15 minutes. An instant-read thermometer inserted into the center should read at least 165 degrees F (74 degrees C). Release pressure through manual release.

Nutrition Facts
Per Serving:
672.7 calories; protein 23.7g 48% DV; carbohydrates 58.5g 19% DV; fat 40.9g 63% DV; cholesterol 29.9mg 10% DV; sodium 892mg 36% DV.

Instant Pot Creamy Mushroom Soup

Prep: 15 mins Cook: 25 mins Additional: 10 mins Total: 50 mins

Servings: 6

Ingredients

* 2 tablespoons butter
* 1 small onion, finely chopped
* 2 cloves garlic, minced
* 1 ½ pounds fresh mushrooms, sliced
* 4 cups chicken broth
* ½ cup sherry
* 1 ½ teaspoons dried thyme
* 1 teaspoon Worcestershire sauce
* 1 teaspoon salt, or more to taste
* ½ teaspoon ground black pepper, or more to taste
* 4 tablespoons all-purpose flour
* 1 cup heavy cream

Directions
* **Step 1**

Turn on a multi-functional pressure cooker (such as Instant Pot) and select Saute function. Heat butter until melted. Saute onion for 2 to 3 minutes. Add garlic and cook for 1 to 2 minutes more. Add mushrooms and saute for 2 to 3 minutes more.
* **Step 2**

Stir chicken broth, sherry, thyme, Worcestershire sauce, salt, and pepper into the pot. Close and lock the lid. Select Manual function; set timer for 5 minutes. Allow 10 to 15 minutes for pressure to build.
* **Step 3**

Release pressure using the natural-release method according to manufacturer's instructions, about 10 minutes. Release remaining pressure carefully using the quick-release method. Unlock and remove the lid.
* **Step 4**

Select Saute function again to bring the soup to a light simmer. Whisk flour into heavy cream. Slowly add cream mixture to the simmering soup, whisking constantly until thickened, 2 to 3 minutes. Turn pressure cooker off. Season soup with additional salt and pepper if desired.

Cook's Notes:
Use vegetable broth instead of chicken broth to make it vegetarian.

Nutrition Facts
Per Serving:
254.1 calories; protein 6g 12% DV; carbohydrates 14.7g 5% DV; fat 19.4g 30% DV; cholesterol 68.6mg 23% DV; sodium 1341.2mg 54% DV.